Traditions of Spiritual

D1167496

Traditions of Spiritual Guidance

collected from *The Way*
and edited by Lavinia Byrne IBVM

THE LITURGICAL PRESS
Collegeville, Minnesota

Published in the United States of America by
The Liturgical Press
St John's Abbey, Collegeville, Minnesota 56321

Published in Great Britain by
Geoffrey Chapman, an imprint of Cassell Publishers Limited

These articles were originally published in *The Way*
Heythrop College, 11–13 Cavendish Square, London W1M 0AN, England

First published in collected form 1990

British Library Cataloguing in Publication Data
Traditions of spiritual guidance.
1. Religious life. Spiritual directors, history
I. Byrne, Lavinia   II. The Way
291.4

ISBN 0–8146–2005–1

Typeset by Fakenham Photosetting Ltd, Fakenham, Norfolk
Printed and bound in Great Britain by
Biddles Ltd, Guildford and King's Lynn

Contents

Introduction

Lavinia Byrne IBVM

This book has a two-fold purpose. It consists of a collection of articles on spiritual guidance which are assembled here together for the first time. Each of them has already been published in *The Way*, the international review of contemporary Christian spirituality. In order to make them more generally available and accessible they are presented here in one volume.

In commissioning the articles in the first place the editors had another purpose in mind. So great is the current wave of interest in the ministry of spiritual direction that it is tempting to see it uniquely as a late twentieth-century phenomenon. Equally, Ignatius of Loyola's influence has been so considerable, given the accessibility of his *Spiritual Exercises*, that other names and practices are less well-known. Such an ahistorical view risks cutting off present-day practice from its honourable roots. The 'Traditions of Spiritual Guidance' articles which have been run in *The Way* as a regular feature since 1984 have attempted to put good quality writing on the tradition before our wide international readership. In this way, we hoped, the insights of the desert fathers, of monasticism and the Celtic tradition—to name but a few—could take their place alongside those of our own days.

It soon became obvious, however, that this kind of balance and redress would be incomplete without reference to the practice of guidance in other faiths. That is why we included in *The Way*—and now in this volume—material on spiritual masters in Hinduism, Zen and Islam. Dialogue between East and West is a feature of our times as is ecumenical understanding among Christians of differing denominations. Spirituality has provided a rich common ground for shared reflection; training courses for spiritual directors proliferate. Where this reflection and training are underpinned by an understanding of the tradition, they stand a chance both of contributing to the ministry of those involved and of promoting respect and understanding when genuine differences emerge.

Spiritual direction is both an art and a science. The artist learns by constant dogged practice in exercising skills which are already there. The scientist learns by examining the evidence and turning it this way and that until it configurates in new ways. The spiritual director learns by practising the gift and skills of discernment which she or he has been perceived as having. This perceiving or recognition by those who seek out the individual in question—at first for a chat or a quick word and then maybe for help and advice—seems to be the hallmark of a true call to the ministry.

But if spiritual direction is a science as well as an art, the call alone is not enough, nor are the exercise and everyday practice of this ministry. The science in this case is theology and theology is learnt like any science, by attending to the evidence.

The evidence or matter of study presented in this collection is fairly specific. Each of the articles is concerned with the spiritual theology and practice of individual directors or groups of directors from the tradition. They are arranged in chronological order for clarity's sake, not because the book pretends to make a complete survey of the field. Indeed were this the case the reader would rightly note that there is nothing here from the seventeenth-century Anglican tradition nor from the nineteenth century.

The authors represent many differing Christian backgrounds; a Benedictine writes about guidance (or the absence of it) in the monastic tradition; a Jesuit about the contribution of Ignatius of Loyola, and Carmelites about the Carmelite tradition and Teresa of Avila. But equally an Anglican priest writes about the Carthusians and an Anglican lay woman about Fray Luis de León. The material from the world's other great faiths is examined by Jesuits. The common thread running through each of these articles is an interest and concern that the wisdom of the past should not be forgotten in our enthusiasm for the present. What emerges when we look at this wisdom in some detail is an interesting variety in the ways in which spiritual direction has been understood and practised down the ages.

Those who read the book will come from a variety of different starting points as well. It is not compiled exclusively for people who give or are training to give spiritual direction. Nor is it intended only for those who receive guidance. Anyone who is interested in the way in which individuals or groups have grown towards God down the ages will find something to reflect upon here. This is not to make exaggerated claims for spiritual direction. Indeed direction is only one method which has proved helpful to people and can claim to be no more than that. Yet the very fact that it emerged as early as it did in Christianity and that it has its place in Hinduism, Zen and Islam makes it a field of study in its own right. If this collection encourages the reader to begin to investigate this field it will have served its purpose.

My thanks go to my colleagues David Lonsdale sj and Philip Sheldrake sj and to Mary Critchley, our editorial assistant.

PART I

The Christian Tradition

Spiritual Direction in the Desert Fathers

Benedicta Ward SLG

Do not be afraid to hear about virtue and do not be a
stranger to the term. For it is not distant from us nor
does it stand external to us, but its realization lies within
us and the task is easy if only we will it. Now the
Greeks leave home and traverse the sea in order to gain
an education but there is no need for us to go abroad on
account of the Kingdom of Heaven nor to cross the sea
for virtue. For the Lord has told us before, 'The
Kingdom of God is within you'. The only thing
goodness needs, then, is that which is within the human
mind.[1]

'Its realization lies within us': this conviction that the kingdom
of God is to be discovered within the human heart lies at the
centre of the spiritual teaching of the desert. The fourth century in Egypt saw the invention of Christian monasticism and
it produced some of the finest texts ever written about conversion of the heart, that is to say, of the whole person, within the
tradition of the gospel. The whole life of the monks was a
training, not a search for 'illumination', but a training, an
ascesis, both for and in the life of the kingdom of God. The
perspective of things has subtly changed in the clear air of the
desert, the 'huge quiet' of Nitria, Scetis and the Cells. They
said:

There is no labour greater than that of prayer to God.
For every time a man wants to pray, his enemies the
demons want to prevent him, for they know that it is
only by turning him from prayer that they can hinder

3

his journey. . . . Prayer is warfare to the last breath.
(Agathon 9 in *Sayings*)

And when Abba Sisoes was dying, even though his face 'shone like the sun', he said, 'I do not think I have even made a beginning yet' (Sisoes 14 in *Sayings*).

In this lifetime of conversions, the monks found that they needed the assistance of others, not only in the practical matters of life in the desert, though that was of great import-ance to them, but in the inner ways of the heart. It would be an anachronism to talk about 'spiritual direction' among the desert fathers; they were very clear that the process of turning towards God was a matter of the spirit and the body together, and that this was given in direction only by Christ. Any help they asked or received from one another was with this in mind: 'we ought to live as having to give account to God for our way of life every day' (*Systematic Series* 4). They are like the dogs who hunt hares, the one who has seen the hare:

> pursues it until he catches it, without being concerned
> with anything else . . . so it is with him who seeks
> Christ as master: ever mindful of the cross, he cares for
> none of the scandals that occur, till he reaches the
> Crucified. (*Systematic Series* 71)

Their 'training' is a process of turning from the bonds and limitations of the self into the freedom of the sons of God, and any words spoken between them are for this end, the attain-ment of that stillness in which the Spirit of God alone guides the monk. For this reason they are very sparing with their words, and one should not be misled by the fact that the records of the desert come to us primarily in the form of conversations. They stand together on the page and we have the illusion that they were said one after another in a busy kind of dialogue, but in fact they are sentences remembered over many years and finally grouped together from several periods and areas. Some are so changed that their context and much of their meaning is lost. It is these fragmentary words which lead into the atmosphere of the desert more than the literary con-structions created later by John Cassian in his *Institutes* and *Conferences*. More truly of the desert than those elegant reminiscences is, for instance, the story of Abba Macarius and the two young strangers who came to him for guidance: he showed them where to live and left them alone for three years before he inquired any further about them; or of Abba Sisoes who decided that his own part of the desert was becoming crowded and went to live on the mountain of Antony; there, he said to a brother, he lived peacefully for 'a little time', and when the brother asked how long this 'little time' of total silence and solitude was, he replied 'seventy-two years' (Sisoes 28 in *Sayings*).

Against this background of the 'ages of quiet without end', the timelessness and silence of the desert, is it possible to say anything about their assistance of each other in their lives of conversion? It would be wrong to look for a coherent programme of spiritual direction in such texts but it is possible to see something of their expectations and experiences through some of the *Sayings*. It is important to remember when looking at these texts, however, that they are in no sense a treatise on a theme, but fragments of stories glimpsed through many layers of transmission; sometimes they seem contradictory, sometimes inconclusive, and they should not be given a coherence they do not have. However, some practical ways of learning *metanoia* seem to emerge from the texts, and seem, moreover, to be virtually the same for both the hermits and the cenobites. I will therefore suggest certain 'sayings' as revealing the basic understanding of training in the monastic life in the desert. It is also perhaps worth recalling before I do so the conviction of the desert fathers that the life of salvation is for all, and is not the exclusive preserve of monks, a theme sometimes forgotten among themselves, but which was always there and is best expressed perhaps in the words of a later writer:

> God is for all those who chose him, life for all, salvation
> for all, faithful, unfaithful; just, unjust; religious,
> irreligious; passionate, passionless; monks, seculars;
> healthy, sick; young, advanced in age; even as the
> outpouring of the light and the sight of the sun, and the
> winds of heaven, so and not otherwise; for there is no
> respect of persons with God.[2]

While still living in the palace, Abba Arsenius prayed to God in these words, 'Lord, lead me in the way of salvation', and a voice came saying to him, 'Arsenius, flee from men and you will be saved'. Having withdrawn to the solitary life he made the same prayer again and he heard a voice saying to him, 'Arsenius, flee, be silent, pray always, for these are the sources of sinlessness'. (Arsenius 1 and 2 in *Sayings*)

These sayings, attributed to Arsenius, one of the most famous of the fathers of Scetis at the beginning of the fourth century, contain several things that are of the essence of the spirituality of the desert. There is the desire for one thing only, salvation; there is the immediate practical action of doing, not only thinking; there is the command to flee, to go away from what is familiar; then the idea of silence, solitude, aloneness, which is the desert; and the ideal of constant prayer for the whole of life. But there is also the 'voice', the direction which comes from God at the very beginning of this conversion and this is the first and perhaps the most vital of the ways of spiritual understanding in this tradition. There are many accounts of the way in which the monks decided to undertake their lives of asceticism, and always there is in some form this 'voice', this command from God. In the case of Arsenius, it is a direct answer to him when he prays. In the case of others, it is mediated through one or other of the many ways in which a Christian can expect to hear the will of God. For instance, Antony the Great, the father of hermits, heard the gospel read in church, 'if you will be perfect, go, sell all that you have and give to the poor and come and follow me and you will have treasure in heaven'. This time a word from the scriptures pierced his heart. It was followed by the same reaction as with Arsenius: 'Antony immediately left the church and gave to the townsfolk the property he had . . . then he devoted all his time to the ascetic living' and after a while, he went deeper and deeper into the desert (*Life of Antony*, 2, 3 and 8). A practical action, and then flight, exile, a going away from the familiar world of the village, as Arsenius had fled from the palace of the Emperor. For Pachomius, the father of cenobites, it was the charity of Christians that moved him, and caused him to leave his life as a soldier and go away into the solitude of the desert. For Apollo, a rough Coptic peasant, it was horror at his own sin that caused him to flee, followed by a further piercing of his heart when he came near to Scetis and heard the monks repeating a psalm: 'So he passed all his time in prayer, saying "I as man have sinned, do thou as God forgive"' (Apollo 2 in *Sayings*).

This pattern of being moved by the action of God first, of leaving the familiar place, going away and giving oneself over to the action of God in silence and solitude is the gateway in the desert to prayer and conversion of heart. What follows until death is the hard work of becoming the new man in Christ: 'one of the Fathers asked Abba John the Dwarf, "What is a monk?" And he said, "He is toil. The monk toils at all he does. That is what a monk is"' (John the Dwarf 36 in *Sayings*). This 'toil', this 'hard work' lasted a lifetime. And the direction had to be constantly followed and kept clear. In this task, the monk had three assets: one was the cell; the second was the scriptures and the third was an old man, a father, as a point of reference in all he did.

The *Sayings* are full of references to the cell of the monk as the place which in itself directed the monk's life. The flight into the desert leads to a place of stability: 'Just as a tree cannot bring forth fruit if it is always being transplanted, so the monk who is always going from one place to another is not able to bring forth virtue' (*Systematic Series* 72). The first action of the newcomer to the desert was either to build a cell for himself, a simple one-roomed hut, or to join an established monk in his cell. The idea of staying in the cell is stressed again and again. 'Go, sit in your cell, and give your body in pledge to the walls of your cell, and do not come out of it' (*Systematic Series* 73). 'A brother came to Scetis to visit Abba Moses and asked him for a word. The old man said to him, "Go, sit in your cell and your cell will teach you everything"' (Moses 6 in *Sayings*). Why is it that they saw this stability in the cell as vital in their training? It was because they could learn there and there only that God exists, because if God is not here and now in this moment and in this place, he is nowhere. To remain in the cell was to stay at the centre of human suffering and discover that God is there, that at the centre there is life and not death, salvation not damnation, light and not darkness. They said, 'the cell of a monk is the furnace of Babylon, but it also is where the three children found the Son of God; it is like the pillar of cloud, and it is where God spoke to Moses' (*Systematic Series* 74). The cell was the place of hard work: Abba Sarapion once visited a celebrated recluse who lived always in one small room and he asked her, 'Why are you sitting here?' And she replied, 'I am not sitting. I am on a journey.'

The first teacher of the monk was God; the second was his cell. Within the cell, the monk had one sure guide and often it was the same guide that began his conversion—the scriptures. The language of the writings of the desert was so formed by the meditation of the scriptures that it is almost impossible to say where quotation ends and comments begin. The thought of the monks was shaped by constant reading and learning by heart of the text of the Bible, and in particular by the constant repetition of the psalms in the cell. Later generations used also the constant prayer of the name of Jesus, and while this particular form of words ('Lord Jesus Christ Son of the Living God have mercy upon me a sinner') is not found in the *Apophthegmata*, the idea of continual prayer by using a set form of words in the psalms was central to it. The combination of attention to God, the stability of the cell and the meditation of the scriptures is found in a saying of Abba Antony:

> Always have God before your eyes; whatever you do,
> do it according to the testimony of the holy scriptures;
> in whatever place you live, do not easily leave it. Keep
> these three precepts and you will be saved. (Antony 3 in
> *Sayings*)

Epiphanius of Cyprus urged the reading of the scriptures for the monk, 'Reading the scriptures is a great safeguard against sin. . . . Ignorance of the scriptures is a precipice and a deep abyss' (Epiphanius 9 and 11 in *Sayings*). But for more simple Coptic monks the scriptures were more than this. They were the bread of heaven on which they fed as often as they could and as literally as possible. The breaking of the bread of the scriptures was to them the bread of life, and there are stories of monks going for many days without food because they were fed by this bread of heaven. Abba Patermuthius, a robber, went after his conversion into the desert for three years, having learnt only the first psalm; he spent his time there 'praying and weeping, and wild plants were sufficient for his food'; when he returned to the church, he said that God had given him the power to recite all the scriptures by heart. The fathers were astonished at 'this high degree of ascesis' and baptized him as a Christian (*Lives*, ch. X). The meditation of the scriptures, the main guide to the monk, is here presented as a sacrament; not as an intellectual study but as a free gift of God and, moreover, as the bread of life in the wilderness, even for one not yet baptized.

This consideration of the scriptures as sacrament leads to the next channel by which the monk learned the lessons of the desert, that is, the words of a father. The most frequent request of one monk to another was 'speak a word to me', and by this request the monk was not asking for either information or instruction. He was asking, as with the scriptures, for a sacrament. The 'word' was not to be discussed or analysed or disputed in any way; at times, it was not even understood; but it was to be memorized and absorbed into life, as a sure way towards God. Pachomius even said that if someone asked for a 'word' and you could think of nothing to say, you should tell him a parable of some sort and God would still use it for his salvation. Again and again, there are stories of monks who would go to live with an old man, and find that he would never give them instructions or orders; they could imitate him if they wished; and if he spoke, the words were for them to use, not debate. A brother asked a monk what he should do because he always forgot whatever was said to him and the old man used the image of a jug which is frequently filled with oil and then emptied out: 'So it is with the soul; for even if it retains nothing of what it has been told, yet it is . . . purified' (*Systematic Series* 91). It was not the words of the father that mattered in themselves. Nor were his personality and treatment of the disciple central, a point made very clearly in a story of Abba Ammoes:

At first Abba Ammoes said to Abba Isaiah (his disciple), 'What do you think of me?' And he said to him, 'You are an angel, father'. Later on he said to him,

'And now, what do you think of me?' He replied, 'You are like Satan. Even when you say a good word to me, it is like steel.' (Ammoes 2 in *Sayings*)

The father of a monk in the desert was not a guru nor was he a master; he was a father and several things followed from this. The abba did not give 'spiritual direction'; if asked, he would give 'a word' which would become a sacrament to the hearer. The action of God was paramount and the only point of such 'words' was to free the disciple to be led by the Spirit of God, just as the abba himself would. In the desert there could only be one father to a disciple and even when he died, he was still the father of his sons. There was no need to change fathers, or to find a new one if one died. It was a lasting and permanent relationship. In such a relationship, tradition was passed on by life as well as by word; those who had already been a certain way into the experience of the monastic life must be able to become this channel of grace to others. But the aim was always for the abba to disappear. The real guide was the Holy Spirit, who would be given to those who learned to receive him. Moreover, in this relationship, it was almost always the disciple who asked for a word, not the abba who offered one. The lesson to be learnt, and the *Sayings* are full of stories of puzzled newcomers who found it incomprehensible not to be instructed, was that each one had to learn to receive the gift of God himself; and it was precisely in learning this that the disciple began to pray. There was no set of instructions, no pattern, for the monk; just some simple external ways of living, the word of the scriptures and, if requested, the sacrament of the words of a fellow monk.

It was and remains a hard way, and in order to use it properly, the disciple needed to see it as a crucifixion with Christ, wound against wound, so that the life of the Spirit might be truly given.

A brother asked an old man, 'How can I be saved?' The latter took off his habit, girded his loins, and raised his hands to heaven, saying, 'So should the monk be: denuded of all things in this world and crucified. In the contest, the athlete fights with his fists; in his thoughts, the monk stands, his arms stretched out in the form of a cross towards heaven, calling on God. The athlete stands naked when fighting in a contest; the monk stands naked and stripped of all things, anointed with oil and taught by his master how to fight. So God leads us to victory.' (*Systematic Series* 11)

The necessary abdication of the selfish centre of a man, which John of Lycopolis saw as a serpent deeply coiled round the heart of men, so deeply embedded that it was impossible to remove it for oneself, demanded the full attention, daily and in minute detail, of the monk for his whole life. The literature of the desert is not about visions and spiritual experiences; it is about the long process of the breaking of hearts. The monks defined themselves as sinners, as penitents, as those who needed and would always need mercy.

There are, in this tradition, many things that resulted from this approach. One of them was that suppleness of the spirit which breaks through the stiff lines of determination and self-righteousness, and makes the soul supple and pliable to receive, as they would say, the impress of the Spirit as upon wax. One of the ways of discovering if this process was continuing lay in the acceptance of the abba by the disciple as the one who discerned reality, against the evidence of the senses; as the one who knew what should be done, against the limited understanding of family obligations; as one who knew what was possible, against the dictates of common sense. The well-known story of the disciple who was commanded to plant a dry stick and water it should be seen in this context; it is told in several versions, in some of which the story has gained picturesque imagery, with the dry stick flowering; but in its more primitive form it was simply an illustration of how supple and obedient the disciple had become to do such a thing. The words, the actions, the opinions, did not matter in themselves; what concerned the monk was his ability to listen and obey. So, when an old man said to his disciple, 'Look, there is a buffalo', the disciple looked and said, 'Yes, abba' even when his eyes told him that it was a wild boar (Mark 2 in *Sayings*).

This life of discovery of the power of the cross in a human

life, lived practically and realistically, without notions and theories, produced three 'signs'. First, there was the sign of tears; it was said of Abba Arsenius that he wept so much that 'he had a hollow in his chest channelled out by the tears that fell from his eyes all his life' (Arsenius 41 in *Sayings*); and the young monk Theodore, the favourite disciple of Abba Pachomius, wept so much that his eyesight was endangered. Tears signified the baptism of repentance rather than superficial emotional disturbance in this tradition and were often associated with meditation on the passion of Christ. One old man asked another, 'Tell me where you were . . .' and he said, 'My thoughts were with St Mary the Mother of God as she wept by the cross of the Saviour. I would that I could always weep like that' (Poemen 144 in *Sayings*). These tears were valued, not ignored or explored; in this theme of weeping and allowing others to weep there is a vital element in the 'spiritual direction' in the desert. It is this: the monk undertook a life of ascetic prayer and it was held that this was what he most desired; so that when he wept or groaned or had to fight against temptations, in fact, whenever he suffered profoundly and continually, he was allowed to do so, indeed, he was encouraged by others, and especially by his abba, to stay at this point of pain in order to enter into the only true healing which is God. When Moses the Black, one of the most attractive of the monks of Scetis, was tempted to fornication, he came to Abba Isidore and told him he could not bear the temptation. Isidore urged him to return to his cell and continue the battle, but he said, 'Abba, I cannot'; Isidore then showed him the 'multitudes of angels shining with glory' who were fighting within the monks against the demons, and with this assurance, but with no alleviation of the suffering to be endured, he returned to his cell (Moses 1 in *Sayings*). The women of the desert seem to have been as clear about this as the men: 'It was said of Amma Sarah that for thirteen years she waged war against the demon of fornication. She never prayed that the warfare should cease but she said, "O God give me strength for the fight"' (Sarah 1 in *Sayings*).

This concentration upon the value of suffering in the light of the cross of Christ leads to the second sign which was seen as a mark of authenticity in the lives of the monks: charity. In

12

so far as the monk truly found himself 'crucified with Christ', so far did he receive the Holy Spirit, and display in his life the gifts of the Spirit of God. The charity of the monks, their warmth, their unaffected welcome of each other and of strangers, their practical care of one another were as famous as their asceticism; the other side of their pain was their joy. This was not the kind of pleasure which is an alternative to and an escape from suffering nor is it an exploitation of others, but a realization of that 'Christ between us' that gives deep and true relationship. It is the life of the kingdom, of the Second Adam, of man restored to paradise, and though at no moment did they forget that this was only so through the cross at the centre of their lives, the result was not gloom but radiance. The most striking result of this spirituality is closely connected with the reserve of the elder fathers about giving orders or rebukes to the newcomers: they did not judge one another in any way. It was said of Abba Macarius that he 'became as it is written a god upon earth, because just as God protects the world, so Abba Macarius would cover the faults that he saw as if he did not see them, and those which he heard as though he did not hear them' (Macarius 32 in *Sayings*).

This freedom to live increasingly in the power of the Spirit points to the third sign of desert spirituality: there is a concern for unceasing prayer in this tradition, not as a support to works but as the life of the monk, and this is often expressed in terms of 'the prayer of fire'. The end and aim of the monk was to become so open to the action of God that his life would fill each moment of the day and night. Prayer was not a duty or obligation but a burning desire. The older monks never 'taught' prayer; they prayed and the newcomers could find in their prayer a way for them to follow. Abba Joseph said to Abba Lot, 'You cannot become a monk unless you become like a consuming fire', and when Abba Lot asked what more he could do beyond his moderate attention to prayer each day, 'the old man stood up and stretched his hands towards heaven, his fingers became like ten lamps of fire and he said to him, "If you will, you can become all flame"' (Joseph Panephysis 6 and 7 in *Sayings*).

The search for God in the deserts of Egypt in the fourth century came to an end with the devastation of Egypt in 407, though there is at present a revival of this way of life in the monasteries of the Wadi al'Natrun, which is in some sense a continuation as well as a revival. What remains to us are the written records of their lives. Certain documents of the early generations, a few letters and some brief sayings of the fathers provide a clue to the lives they lived; the accounts of their actions and their conversations with visitors also survive, in the *Institutes* and *Conferences* of John Cassian, the *History of the monks of Egypt*, and the *Lausiac history*. The theology of the monastic life of Egypt was first analysed by Evagrius Ponticus and John Cassian. In Palestine and in Syria, other men experimented with monastic life and left other records, most notable of which are the *Letters of Barsanulfus and John*. But it is in the sayings of the fathers, the collections of their words, that the spirit of the desert can best be found. They themselves began to commit their words to writing and many of them regretted that this had already become necessary even in Scetis and Nitria; the first fathers, they said, lived practical and realistic lives, the second generation seemed to them to rely upon that distorting mirror, the wriitten word, more and more. Abba Poemen asked Abba Macarius, weeping, for a word, but he said, 'What you are looking for has disappeared among monks' (Macarius 25 in *Sayings*). Perhaps the essential message of the desert lies precisely there: it is not in reading or discussing or even in writing articles that the life of the soul is to be discovered; nor is it in the advice of anyone else however experienced; it lies in the simplicity of Antony the Great who, hearing the gospel read, went and did what he had heard said, and so came at the end of his life to such a point of discovery of the kingdom of God within himself that he could say, 'I no longer fear God; I love him' (Antony 32 in *Sayings*).

Notes

[1] St Athanasius: *Life of Antony*, trans. Robert C. Gregg (London, 1980), section 20. This will be referred to as *Life of Antony*. References in the text are to this and the following books:
Sayings of the Desert Fathers, trans. Benedicta Ward (London, 1975)—to be referred to as *Sayings*. *Wisdom of the Desert Fathers*, ed. Benedicta Ward (Systematic Series; Oxford: SLG Press, 1979)—to be quoted as *Systematic Series*.
Lives of the Desert Fathers, trans. Norman Russell (London: Mowbray,

1980), which is a translation of the *History of the monks of Egypt*. This will be referred to as *Lives*. The numbers refer to numbered sections in these works and not to pages.

[2] Climacus, John: *The ladder of divine ascent*.

(vol. 24, no. 1, January 1984)

Spiritual Direction in the Benedictine Tradition

Jean Leclercq OSB

The request to write this article has given me the opportunity to make a fresh survey of the field. Documentary material ought to be extensive because we are talking here about a tradition which reaches from the sixth century to our own days. As it happens, in reality such material is limited because spiritual guidance has not been a favourite theme of Benedictine spiritual literature. No extended historical study has ever been conducted on this material; any research that has been done has provided a few surprises.

In presenting the results of such research, this long past must first be briefly described. Then will it be possible to see if any particular themes stand out and what they are.

The source

A first point which may surprise us comes from the contrast between the importance attributed to spiritual guidance given by one person to another in monasticism before the middle of the sixth century and the lack of attention it receives in the Benedictine tradition, beginning with the text upon which this is founded: the *Rule of St Benedict*. Towards the end of this document, in chapter 73, in a passage where he uses the vocabulary and the notion of 'guidance' on the path that leads to God, St Benedict refers his reader to sacred scripture and to the tradition preserved in the writings of the ancient monks:

> But for anyone hastening on towards the perfection of monastic life, there are the teachings of the holy

Fathers, the observance of which will lead him to the
very heights of perfection. What page, what passage of
the inspired books of the Old and the New Testaments
is not the truest of guides for human life? What book of
the holy catholic Fathers does not resoundingly
summon us along the true way to reach the Creator?
Then, besides the *Conferences* of the Fathers, their
Institutes and their *Lives*, there is also the rule of our
holy father Basil. For observant and obedient monks,
all these are nothing less than tools for the cultivation of
virtues.

Earlier in the text, in a few rather brief passages, St Benedict
speaks of the relations the monk must have with one or two
other people concerning his progress to God, but he does not
treat these in as much detail as previous authors had done
before him. They are presented as though personal guidance
had lost something of the importance it enjoyed in the lives of
those who lived alone, now that the way of God is pursued in
the common life. At all times this offers examples to be
followed, just as conventual prayer and its readings assure
constant teaching. The collective guidance of the community
is further guaranteed by the doctrinal exhortations to be given
by the abbot, who must 'direct souls' (*animas regere*). He is
responsible for everyone and in this sense he is their father,
their *abba*, according to a title which, in the New Testament,
Jesus gave to his Father and which St Benedict applies to
Christ and to the abbot who 'holds his place' (*agere vices*). He
exercises this duty by handing on a 'teaching', the 'truth', also
by 'warnings, precepts and orders'. He must 'propose' and
'demonstrate' God's way to his 'sons' and to his 'disciples'
and, in order to do this, adapt himself to each monk's character. He has a role in discerning and restraining, illustrated by
the admirable chapter on The observance of Lent (chapter 49):
in this penitential season, each monk will have 'something
above the assigned measure to offer God of his own will with
the joy of the Holy Spirit', but he must make this known
(*suggerat*) to the abbot who approves it.

In two places, St Benedict speaks of opening one's conscience. Firstly, in chapter 7: 'The fifth step of humility is that a

man does not conceal from his abbot any sinful thoughts entering his heart, or any wrongs committed in secret, but rather confesses them humbly'. Then, in chapter 46, with regard to those who 'commit a fault while at any work': if this is a public offence, it must be manifested to the abbot and the community.

> When the cause of the sin lies hidden in his conscience,
> he is to reveal it only to the abbot or to one of the
> spiritual elders, who know how to heal their own
> wounds as well as those of others, without exposing
> them or making them public.

From this last reference—but only from here—it appears that this kind of admission offers the opportunity for receiving private counsel and exhortation. Clearly everyone understood that this was not the same thing as sacramental confession.

Finally, in chapter 58, with regard to what we would nowadays call first formation, a sober text discusses the qualities required of the person in charge, his role and of the light which knowledge of the Rule will shed on this.

> A senior chosen for his skill in winning souls should be
> appointed to look after them with careful attention. The
> concern must be whether the novice truly seeks God
> and whether he shows eagerness for the work of God,
> for obedience and for trials. The novice should be
> clearly told all the hardships and difficulties that will
> lead him to God.

The Rule is then read three times to each novice.

Medieval interpretations

These few, very beautiful, texts began to be analysed in the two first commentaries on the Rule: in the ninth century, that of a certain Hildemar and that of Smaragdus, Abbot of the monastery of Saint-Mihiel, in Lotharingia. The first was known under different names from northern Gaul to south Italy. This range indicates its influence. St Benedict's thoughts on manifestation of conscience are usefully clarified: 'Why does he say that sinful thoughts are to be admitted and not good ones?' For two reasons, Hildemar replies: firstly because 'almost all' the monks' thoughts are good; secondly because what they are thinking about when they are contemplating is difficult to describe. But why does St Benedict speak of 'all sinful thoughts'? Surely it is impossible to enumerate all of them? Not at all, because St Benedict has said elsewhere that what he means are those sinful thoughts which are entertained, that is to say, those which are accepted; where no consent is given, they are not accepted. It is not a matter of 'all those thoughts which come and go'—nowadays we would talk about fancies which run through our heads—but those which 'set up home in our hearts and stay there', which presupposes that we have consented to them. Hildemar refers to a contemporary controversy about what should be admitted to the abbot and what should be admitted to a 'spiritual brother'. He does not resolve the question and each monk remains free to choose his own confidant.[1]

Smaragdus is even less definite. In his *The crown of the monks* as in his *Commentary on the Rule*, he is content to confirm St Benedict's sayings in the light of Old Testament texts and those Cassiodorus gave on the need to consult God, oneself and others.

> He who is filled with compunction by the Lord and
> sent by him to the monastery desiring to live there
> according to the desires of his heart, which he believes
> to be good, will say to himself: 'Question your abbot
> and spiritual brothers about your intention, because it is
> written: Do nothing without asking advice. And if
> these men judge that your desire is good, if they
> consent to it, then fulfill it, because it is no longer your
> own desire but held in common by those who are in
> agreement with you. If they do not agree that it is
> good, you must realise that your desire is only a private
> one and that if you wish to be saved, you must flee
> from it as if from a serpent.'

In this text, as in St Benedict's on Lent, we can admire the harmony established between personal inspiration and initiative and the fact that these are submitted to the abbot and members of the community, who are to act as 'spiritual brothers': the expression 'spiritual father' is not used in the Rule.[2]

From the tenth century we have a Rule for nuns. St Benedict's text is abridged and adapted for their use. What Benedict wrote about 'thoughts' is applied to 'sins': these must be 'confessed to another person' whose identity is not specified; St James is quoted where he writes: 'Confess your sins to another and pray for one another that you may be saved'.[3] Elsewhere we read that 'all should manifest their faults to the abbess; every Sunday they should be reconciled among themselves on account of their negligences and ask pardon one of another'.[4] As to Lent, each one must submit to the abbess, who is called 'spiritual mother', whatever she wishes to offer to God.[5] In the chapter which treats of the admission of novices, St Benedict's few words on formation are suppressed; but we are told that the abbess must warn the newcomer that she will be expected to 'keep the Rule carefully and with humility', as if the Rule alone were enough to bring people to God. And in the admission ceremony each time the abbess is mentioned so too are 'all the sisters'[6]—a fresh indication of the communal character attributed to spiritual guidance.

In the tenth and eleventh centuries a thorough-going renewal of monasticism aided the reform of the whole Church and the promotion of Christian values throughout society. Spiritual guidance was not one of the means which made a particularly useful contribution to this movement. In any case, it left few traces in contemporary writing. In the *Lives* of one or two saints we can find allusions to it. Thus of St Mayeul, who was Abbot of Cluny from 965 to 993, we read that by his sermons,

> as spiritual father, he encouraged those of his sons who
> were tempted to discouragement. He led others
> imperceptibly to taste and see that the Lord is good by
> means of careful reading . . . By his example he filled
> his sons with joy.[7]

Preaching and good example: in each case the guidance is given to the whole community. Conventual life of its very

nature, is a school of formation. The fact that one was conformed to the 'customs' which fashioned all attitudes, whether
exterior or interior, was taken for granted. Hence the importance, in each period of history, of the custom books, which are
sometimes called 'constitutions'. These describe the behaviour to be adopted, but never speak of any oral teaching to be
given by one person to another; obviously this happened, but
no prescriptions were laid down about it.

For instance, in the *Constitutions* Lanfranc wrote for Canterbury, there is only a description of the first discernment of
vocation in the case of newcomers:

> When anyone turns from the world to the monastic life
> . . . the abbot or prior or some other spiritual brother
> chosen for the purpose shall speak with him, and if he
> sees that the newcomer's desire is from God, the matter
> shall be made known to the brethren in chapter . . .[8]

Of the novicemaster, no more is said than: 'This master shall
be such a one as may by the example of his life and by the
words of his teaching give him good advice for his soul and
teach him our way of life'.[9] What is clear however, is that he
should not receive any confession of sins.

> As for the faults committed in the world, or occurring
> in the monastic life, he shall make frequent confession
> to the abbot, prior and spiritual brethren appointed for
> this purpose. . . .[10]
>
> They shall make their confessions to the abbot or
> prior or those whom the abbot has especially appointed
> in chapter. While one is confessing, the next shall sit on
> the footplace; their master meanwhile shall sit nearby
> outside the chapter-house.[11]

The only work from this period which treats of the formation
of adolescents, the *De ordine vitae*, written towards 1050 by
John, Abbot of Fruttuaria in Piedmont, has one paragraph—
only one but it happens to be beautiful—on the value for
young people of not being 'without a guide' (*sine duce*): they
need older men to instruct them, to lead them, both by their
example and by their 'friendship'. But nothing is said about
the way this 'teaching'[12] should be given. If monastic authors

at this time practised spiritual direction in writing, this was given above all in letters addressed to bishops and to lay people—especially to great ladies: St Peter Damien (†1072), Jean de Fecamp (†1078) and above all St Anselm of Canterbury (†1109) made noteworthy contributions to this genre. To Ida, countess of Boulogne, Anselm wrote: 'I am quite certain that you still have me in your heart as your spiritual father . . .'.[13] But advice given in such letters remains very general. The public character of every letter at that time, dictated as they were to secretaries and read by several people, meant that any possibility of raising personal problems was out of the question.

In the twelfth century, the biographer of Peter the Venerable makes what he sees as an exceptional claim for him:

> He exhorted his subjects to purity and to cleanse themselves by means of confession. In this art, he showed himself to be an exceptional father and the gentleness of his own devotion outshone that of others. In accordance with the gift he held in God's Church, he taught of the benefits of confession as sanctifying the soul like a baptism of salvation. He had the grace of being drawn to love people who made their confessions to him, of embracing them and comforting them as a good counsellor. This explains why, and this did not happen with other superiors, everyone genuinely wished lovingly to make their confessions to him, because he knew, without the need for revelations, how to care for and heal his own wounds and those of other people, by using the medicine of his word and his consolation.[14]

In texts such as these which date from before the thirteenth century, at no time is the claim made that this is sacramental confession. Bernard of Aygluier's *Commentary on the Rule* (he was Abbot of Cassino from 1263 to 1282) does perhaps refer to confession. He makes a distinction between the confession of thoughts, 'which require advice rather than authority', and the confession of sins which demands, 'both advice and authority and which, consequently, must only be made to the abbot . . . . Because mortal sin offends the divine majesty, but also the

Church and so calls for a confession made in the presence of God's vicar and of a minister of the Church.'[15] It is not said here that the abbot is a priest and acts as such. But gradually we can detect a movement away from traditional monastic confession to sacramental confession made only to a priest.

Nowadays, the famous *Imitation of Christ* is attributed to Gersenio di Cavaglia, the Benedictine abbot of Verceil from 1220 to 1240. This admirable text which is so full of spiritual advice does not lay out any methodical system of guidance. The confession it speaks of is made to God.[16] No chapter recommends the manifestation of conscience, nor sacramental confession, nor the benefits to be gained by taking advice. From start to finish the book describes the spiritual conversation of one individual with God.

The golden age of direction

With the Catholic Reformation of the second half of the sixteenth century and above all from the seventeenth century onwards, what was beginning to be called 'spiritual direction' achieved a certain prominence. One or two Benedictine authors used this kind of language. But the reality it described hardly featured in their writings. Cisneros of Montserrat († 1510) refers to it briefly, while sacramental confession gets full treatment and is recommended even as a daily exercise.[17] In the three-volume *Works* of Louis de Blois († 1566), only this short extract can be found: 'Nevertheless enjoy asking a man who fears God and is enlightened to help you know the will of God, especially when this is difficult'.[18] Abbot Haeften († 1648) of Afligherm, whose *Disquisitiones monasticae* constitute a '*summa*' of the monastic tradition, is even less explicit. He gives no treatment of direction. He speaks a little of the confession required by St Benedict, in order to show that this is not sacramental. He quotes this decree from a Council held at Aix-la-Chapelle in the ninth century: 'Let the abbot, as spiritual father, give an example to his spiritual sons by walking before them (*praeeundo*) and giving them religious instruction'.[19] This adds nothing to what the middle ages had already handed on. Fine pages are consecrated to the model of novice-master given us in the person of Christ as he appears in the gospels, especially that of Luke. What are treated here are the virtues the novicemaster should have rather than the forma-tion he should give. His role is to discern vocations, to test them as much as to give any teaching, and nothing is said about any such teaching.[20]

Out of the great fund of seventeenth-century spiritual writ-ing, we will only look at two sources here, both of which are particularly representative. Dom Augustine Baker († 1641) in his *Holy Wisdom*, which is still a classical masterpiece, has a chapter with a promising title: *Of an external director*.[21] By and large, however, this consists of a series of restrictions, as 'it is too general a humour in directors nowadays to make them seem necessary unto their disciples'. The director's role is limited both as to its object ('contemplative prayer, attending to divine inspirations etc.'); to its length ('teach the soul how to dispose herself . . . to stand in no more need of consulting her exterior director'); to the qualities he needs—deep spiritual experience rather than knowledge; as to his activities ('there will be little need for the soul to have recourse to her director. Neither ought he to examine her about her external exercises . . .'). His role should not be confused either with that of a '*confessarius*, that is only to hear the faults confessed, to give absolution, and there an end'. A good director is extremely rare; such a person can be lay, a man or a woman, and 'his necessity is not to last always'. 'Scarce any directors can be more improper (for those who tend to contemplation) than are religious guides of active spirits. . . . In a well-governed monastery of women . . . it is very expedient that instruction . . . should rather come from superiors within.' In many cases, 'God will be the faithful counsellor'.[22] In a previous chapter, on the Divine Spirit as 'internal guide', Baker had stated: 'God alone is our only master and director'.[23]

Likewise, the Maurist Dom Claude Martin († 1696) warns against the indiscreet director who wants, 'as happens all too often, to reduce everyone to his own way of praying'.[24] Obviously one would be negligent were one 'not to listen as willingly as usual to the spiritual father's advice, and not to ask for it as usual, and only to be guided by the lights of one's own spirit'.[25] But once this danger of self-sufficiency has been avoided it nevertheless remains true that 'God is our primary director; it is up to him to guide our steps and to put us on the way in which he knows that we must walk in order to please him more'.[26]

In our own time

From the first half of this century, several great abbots remain famous on account of their spiritual teaching. First, Dom Columba Marmion, the Irishman who became Abbot of Maredsous in Belgium, where he died in 1923. In his work on *Christ the ideal of the monk*, he says nothing about direction. He claimed that he was not a 'great partisan of a large amount of direction'. Nevertheless his biographer and admirer, R. Thibaut, was able to present him as an 'eminent spiritual director', above all on account of his vast correspondence, even while insisting that 'no director was less like a tyrant or an oracle'. Above all else Marmion recommended 'great fidelity to movements of the Holy Spirit'.[27]

Paul Delatte, the Abbot of Solesmes († 1937), spoke more often in his numerous writings of the attitude of the directee who should 'open his soul simply',[28] rather than of the director. He made known his lack of interest in any method which, in monastic life, would enhance the paternal and filial relationships between the abbot and his monks, or fraternal ones between the members of a community. One of the texts which P. Delatte liked above all others was Paul's in Romans 8:14: 'Those who are led by the Spirit are children of God'.[29]

Finally, John Chapman, Abbot of Downside († 1936), could claim: 'I have been my own director, and that is very hard'.[30] So he did not refuse to direct others as his *Spiritual letters* testify, though with two reservations. First of all, he said: 'I am not inclined to assume the role of a professional "director" to anyone'.[31] As well, he thought of direction as leading to the moment when it would no longer be necessary. 'A good director must be a nurse, no more. He should confine himself to the task of teaching his penitent how to walk alone and unaided.'[32] John Chapman's advice inclined to send people towards a contemplative and characteristically simple form of prayer. He willingly quoted St Ignatius, St Francis de Sales and particularly St John of the Cross and in this was very revealing; the Benedictine tradition has always been able to draw from the full spectrum of experts on prayer.

Limits and relevance of a tradition

During the last fifteen centuries, countless Benedictine monks and nuns have been guided by others from their immediate circle in words which have remained unrecorded in the texts. To go through the series of testimonies that did get written down has seemed to be the only way of seeing how they understood their task. The result of this inquiry could cause a certain disappointment which, in all honesty, has to be accepted. In comparison with what has been taught by other spiritual writers, especially since the sixteenth century, and the material published so profusely nowadays, representatives of the Benedictine tradition have left neither copious or precise teaching, nor a detailed method. Whatever has been edited from certain of these authors tells us a great deal about what their commentators thought. Each tradition cannot illustrate all the charisms in equal measure; one is hard put to it to find evidence of a homogeneous teaching handed down through the ages in the Benedictine tradition. A great deal has been written, for example by V. Berlière (monk of Maredsous and historian,[33] who died in 1928) and C. Butler (Abbot of Downside, who died in 1934) about prayer, about mysticism even, the contemplative life, *lectio divina*, renunciation, work, obedience, but not about guidance.[34] This was considered to be a form of obedience and, as such, was to lead to docility, to the Spirit and to freedom.

The only common understanding which does seem to have remained intact down the ages is that found in Benedict's *Rule*. The evidence that can be discovered at different times in letters written to people outside the monastery demonstrates the same tendencies we discern in the guidance offered by people inside the monastery. This is the same whether it is given by monks or nuns. Such guidance is different from sacramental confession. It requires only the manifestation of those thoughts which can stir up the 'heart' so that they constitute an obstacle to progress towards God. This opening of conscience is either made to the abbot or abbess, or to members of the community. We may gather that in the past the situation was as has recently been described in these words:

> No doubt St Benedict understood the monk's guide to
> be the abbot; nevertheless, he was well aware of the
> difficulties which can inhibit this; he knew about the
> 'superior syndrome' which can, from time to time,
> make it impossible to get to the man. In fact, the abbot
> must fulfill the same conditions as any other spiritual
> guide. Nevertheless, even if he is able to give direction,
> in big communities he must ensure that there are
> enough of the brethren available who know what it is
> to guide others.[35]

Between a superior and his community there can be a communications problem, a form of inhibition which makes openness difficult.

Following St Benedict, the monastic tradition has always suggested that spiritual directors of whatever provenance should be kind, compassionate and full of 'mercy'.[36] This has been underlined in the case of, for instance, St Anselm.[37] Spiritual guidance has always been recognized as particularly useful in the first stages of monastic life; its purpose at that time being to help the newcomer to discern if he has a vocation. If this is the case, it will remain useful for the rest of his life and be received from the community as such or from one or other of the members. Because of its empirical nature, which means that it has neither a theory nor a method, Benedictine guidance is an experiential affair rather than a science; it presupposes no special training, but rather a gift whereby those who are able to give it are designated as 'spiritual' without anyone being particularly clear about what that means. Obviously this will mean taking a few risks. On the other hand, the fact that there is no special teaching means that ideas can be used from other spiritual traditions both past and present. All of this is relevant nowadays, at least for people in monastic orders. For them what is missing in the way of theory and techniques is compensated for by this essential fact: conventual life with its daily observances is in itself a school of the spiritual life.

Notes

[1] Mittermüller, R. (ed.): *Expositio regulae* (Ratisbonne, 1880), pp. 242–245.

[2] Spannagel, A. and Engelbert, P. (eds): *Smaragdi abbatis expositio in Regulam* (Siegburg, 1974), p. 83.

[3] Linage Conde, A. (ed.): *Una regla monástica riojana femenina del siglo X. El 'Libellus a Regula S Benedicti subtractus'* (Salamanca, 1973), pp. 38–39.

[4] *Ibid.*, p. 59.

[5] *Ibid.*, p. 55.

[6] *Ibid.*, p. 56.

[7] Quoted in Leclercq, J.: *Aspects of monasticism* (Kalamazoo, MI: Cistercian Publications, 1978), p. 220.

[8] Knowles, David (ed.): *The monastic constitutions of Lanfranc* (London), p. 104.

[9] *Ibid.*, p. 106.

[10] *Ibid.*, p. 107.

[11] *Ibid.*, p. 116.

[12] *De ordine vitae* n. 10, PL 184, 566–567.

[13] Schmitt, F. S. (ed.): *S Anselmi opera omnia*, vol. IV, epist. 167 (Edinburgh, 1949), p. 41.

[14] Radulfus: *Vita Petri Venerabilis*, 2, PL 189, 18–19.

[15] Caplet, A. M. (ed.): *Bernardi I abbatis Casinensis in Regulam Benedicti expositio* (Monte Cassino, 1894), p. 154.

[16] Lup, T. (ed.): *De imitatione Christi libri quatuor* (Rome, 1982), 1. III, ch. 20, p. 185. I have studied these texts and issues that arise in 'Un jalon dans l'histoire de la confession dans la vie religieuse', in *Vie consacrée*, 57 (1985), pp. 242–248.

[17] Colombás, G. M.: *Un reformador benedictino en tiempo de los reyes católicos García Jiménez de Cisneros* (Montserrat, 1955), p. 290.

[18] *Oeuvres spirituelles du Vénérable Louis de Blois*, trans. the Benedictines of St Paul de Wisques (Paris, 1913), vol. II, p. 142.

[19] Haeften, B.: *Disquisitiones monasticae*, tract V, disq. 1 (ed. Anvers, 1644), I, p. 311.

[20] *Ibid.*, pp. 392–396.

[21] *Holy wisdom or Directions for the prayer of contemplation* (London, 1876), pp. 73–86.

[22] *Ibid.*, pp. 73–86.

[23] *Ibid.*, p. 68.

[24] Martin, Dom Claude: *Conferénces ascétiques* (ed. J. R. Hesbert, Paris, 1956), vol. I, p. 196.

[25] *Ibid.*, p. 302.

[26] *Ibid.*, p. 191.

[27] Thibaut, R.: *L'union à Dieu dans le Christ d'après les lettres de direction de Dom Marmion* (Paris, 1941), p. xiii.

[28] Delatte, P.: *Commentaire de la Règle de S Benoît* (Paris, 1913), pp. 87 and 342.

[29] *Ibid.*, pp. 51 and 343.

[30] Hudleston, R. (ed.): *The spiritual letters of Dom John Chapman OSB* (London, 1935), p. 23.

[31] *Ibid.*, p. 84.

[32] *Ibid.*, p. 23.

[33] *L'ascèse bénédictine des origines à la fin du moyen âge* (Maredsous, 1927).

[34] Butler, C.: 'Benedictine monachism', in *Studies in Benedictine life and Rule* (London, 1924). This formula at least should be quoted: 'The abbot is the father in a much broader and more real sense than is suggested by the somewhat technical and professional connotation of the term "spiritual father"' (p. 193).

[35] Rosenthal, Anselm: '*Seniori spiritali patefacere.* Überlegungen zur geistlichen Begleitung des einzelnen in unseren Gemeinschaften', in *Monastische Informationen* Nr. 42 (15 March 1985), p. 15.

[36] RB 1980: *The Rule of St Benedict* (Collegeville, Minnesota, 1980).

[37] Sainte Marie, H. de: 'Les lettres de S. Anselme et la Règle de S. Benoît', in *Mélanges bénédictins* (Saint-Wandrille, 1947), pp. 317–319.

Translated from the French by the editor.
(vol. 27, no. 1, January 1987)

Soul-Friendship

Diarmuid O'Laoghaire SJ

There was a clerical student of Fearna, a foster-child of
Brigid, who used to bring her presents. He used to eat
with her in the refectory. Once when they were
together, said Brigid, 'Good young student, have you a
soul-friend (*anamchara*)?' 'I have indeed', said the
student. 'Let us perform his requiem', said Brigid.
'Why?' said the student. 'Just when you had half
finished your meal I saw he had died.' 'How did you
know?' said the student. 'Not hard to answer that', said
Brigid. 'I saw you half way through your meal without
a head, for your soul-friend was dead. And now, eat no
more till you find a soul-friend, for a person without a
soul-friend is a body without a head' (*Is colainn gan
cheann duine gan anamchara*).[1]

There we have a vivid illustration of a proverb that had
become a commonplace in ancient Ireland. Soul-friend is
rendered literally in Latin, *amicus animae*, or simply, *pater
spiritualis*, *confessor* or *pater confessionis*, and indeed it often
means just 'confessor', but it frequently means also 'spiritual
director'. We know from the pagan literature (passed on by
Christians) that wisdom was always highly esteemed and that
a king, above all, should have his counsellors. There is a great
amount of what we could call 'wisdom literature', which has
to do with that aspect of life. It may be of interest here to quote
from sayings attributed to Flann Fína mac Ossu, by which
name Alfrid son of King Oswy of Northumberland was
known in Ireland:

A teacher deserves honour; wisdom should be
reverenced; the beginning of wisdom is mildness;
wisdom is a good gift, which makes a king of a poor
man and a wise one of the foolish—good its beginning,
better its end.[2]

The seventh century Hiberno-Latin text, *De duodecim abusivis
saeculi*, attributed to, among others, St Cyprian, and very
popular in Europe, re-echoes the wisdom of the past: 'The
justice of the king consists . . . in having elders, wise men and
sober, as counsellors'.[3]

It is very important to realize that by the sixth century the
Irish Church was mainly a monastic Church, the monks being
actively engaged in pastoral work as well as leading a monastic
life. It was but natural, then, that religious literature should
have a monastic flavour. So too, doubtless, the practice of
soul-friendship was monastic in origin. It is interesting to note
that the Rule of St Columbanus seems to be unique among the
ancient monastic rules in having a chapter entitled 'On discretion'. The chapter is summed up in the final words: 'For
while we must always restrain ourselves from either side,
according to the saying, keep yourselves from the right and
from the left, we must ever proceed straight forward by
discretion, that is, by the light of God, while very often we say
and sing the victorious psalmist's verse, My God, enlighten
my darkness, since in Thee I am rescued from temptation. For
temptation is the life of man on earth.'[4]

In the next chapter of the same Rule, 'On mortification', we
have what we might call an apologia for the practice of soul-
friendship, for it is that which is implied here although not
specifically named:

The chief part of the monk's rule is mortification, since
indeed they are enjoined in scripture, 'do nothing
without counsel'. Thus if nothing is to be done without
counsel, everything must be asked for by counsel. Thus
we are enjoined through Moses also: 'Ask thy father
and he will show thee, thy elders and they will tell
thee'. But though this training seem hard to the hard-
hearted, namely that a man should always hang upon
the lips of another, yet by those who are fixed in the

fear of God it will be found pleasant and safe, if it is kept wholly and not in part, since nothing is pleasanter than safety of conscience and nothing safer than exoneration of the soul, which none can provide for himself by his own efforts, since it properly belongs to the judgments of others.[5]

Others than priests could be soul-friends. St Columbanus himself was ordered by an ancient anchoress to abandon the world. It was asked:

When is a person competent to answer for the souls of others? When he is competent to answer for his own soul first. When is he capable of correcting others? When in the first place he can correct himself. A person who converts his own soul to life everlasting, how many souls could he convert? The people of the whole world provided they were tractable he could convert them to life everlasting so that they would belong to the kingdom of heaven.[6]

The qualities of the soul-friend are frequently stressed. He should be 'learned in the rules of conduct laid down in scripture and the rules of the saints'[7] (although we are not told exactly what the rules of the saints are). We may note the gloss on 1 Corinthians 12:29 *Numquid omnes doctores?* (Are all teachers?)—'The soul-friends . . .'.[8] So we read that they instructed the young: 'Those children were baptized . . . and at the end of a month they were confirmed; and at the end of seven years they were taken to soul-friends, and with them they read their psalms and hymns and all the order of the Church.'[9] In the Rule of Mochuda there is comprehensive advice for the monk and the soul-friend: 'not to accept alms unless they [penitents] obey you'.[10] St Mael Ruain adds something to that: 'Laymen fancy that in order to get to heaven it is enough for them to give something to their soul-friends, and that their soul-friends will thenceforth be at their command. It is better then not to accept anything, save from one who is holy, or from one who accepts spiritual friendship.'[11] Mochuda warns lest 'their love be great about you, like a fire around your body',[12] a temptation of all times, lest what began as a soul-friendship should end as a body-friendship. We are reminded of the Curé of Ars or Padre Pio, perhaps, when we read: 'With fasting, with prayer you will pay their price. If you do not, you will pay for the crimes of many.'[13] 'Instruction of the ignorant, to yield to your direction that they may not fall into guilt through following you. Let there be no lasting love in your heart, only the love of God. Since pure is the Body to which you go, be pure who approaches it.'[14]

We have similar counsels for the monk and soul-friend in the Rule of St Ailbhe: 'Heavy is the burden he takes. Let his conscience be diligent, be keen, without proud lying, without vanity. Fewness of words . . . Let him be steady without a particle of weakness. Let him be an anvil for every profitable thing.'[15] The metaphor of the anvil was a favourite one, signifying perseverance, which was regarded as the highest of virtues, perseverance in prayer and service of God. We are reminded of what may well have been the source of the metaphor, the words of St Ignatius of Antioch to St Polycarp, urging him not to be frightened by false teachers: *Sta firmus ut incus qui percutitur*[16] (Stand firm as the anvil when it is struck):

Let him perform the desire of every person; let him
answer the sins of every soul [an expression of being all
things to all people, I suppose]. Let him be gentle, firm
and zealous, a serpent in deftness, a dove in filial
affection [a favoured metaphor]. The confession of
everyone he should closely conceal. Let him bewail
with everyone his sins; if it be a scandal he shall hide it;
the poor man, the needy man, as far as lies in his power,
he shall not refuse them. Without reviling, without
reproach, without rough reproof. Lest Satan carry him
off his track, let him act lowly against loftiness—that is
what the devil hates, that one should be gentle towards
a rough person. With affection, without any harshness,
without strife, without lust, humble, patient, with
mildness, gentle be his countenance.[17]

Constant is the reference in the Rules to the monk's own need for holiness before he can guide others. What are called 'Rules' are not so in the legal sense. They are rather counsels of perfection, with occasional precisions. So, when it comes to considering the function or requirements of the soul-friend, it is right to regard him in the full context of the Rule. Thus the Rule of St Ailbhe urges the monk to be:

> constant at prayer; let him not forget his canonical hours; his mind let him bow down without insolence or contentions. Their father is noble God, their mother is holy Church. Let it not be mouth-humility; let each have compassion on his brother. Let it not be too strict, let it not be lax. Let it not be a rule without knowledge, so that each may be able to bear his yoke, that he may not leave his enclosure.

Abruptly a word of advice may come for the soul-friend: 'A person who does not endure reproof and who admits not his blame, the soul-friend should warn him off to some other place'.[18]

When we realize that frequent confession was praised and practised—in one life of a saint we read, 'As the floor is swept every day so is the soul cleansed every day by confession'[19]—we are not surprised to find soul-friendships, in the broad sense of hearing confessions and in the narrower sense of direction of souls, as an integral part of the spiritual and pastoral literature.

There is constant counsel for the penitent; primarily, in the Rules, for the monk. Thus we have in a Rule from about the eighth century:

> Light, wonderful and mild is the yoke of the Lord. To go to a devout sage is good, to direct one's path. A devout sage to guide you, it is good to avoid punishment. Although you consider yourself very strong, be not your own guide.[20]

Wisdom in the soul-friend is often stressed. It is taken for granted that he will be one of the seniors. Seldom had the young the necessary wisdom—just through lack of experience (even in the modern language the word *críonnacht* means both old age and wisdom). 'It is better for you to avoid those whom you think could slay you, a fool, pious but ignorant, a sage impenitent and shameless.'[21] The choice of 'a humble, learned soul-friend'[22] is recommended, 'the selling of darkness for light'.[23] 'Study', the monk is told, 'with a well-spoken old man (senóir).'[24] To the soul-friend himself it is said: 'You do well to correct. You do not do well to reprove. The mind rebels against reproof. It is humble at being corrected. Wisdom without learning is better than learning without wisdom.'[25] It is the duty of the soul-friend to 'correct all impiety, without harshness, without shame; correction of all the proud [we are told, perhaps unexpectedly?] with humility, through laughter'.[26]

The penitent was to persevere in his repentance, yet steadily: 'The path of repentance if anyone should take, let him advance a step a day and not practise the ways of a charioteer. Make not a fire of bracken, it is quickly extinguished. Be not a sedge against the stream so that your piety will last.'[27]

For one who was serious in his desire for soul-friendship it was not considered a good sign to move from one soul-friend to another. Mael Ruain had no great desire to receive Mael Díthruibh, although an anchorite and a learned man, as his disciple or penitent. He said to him:

> 'Did you ask permission of those you left before
> coming here?' 'Yes.' 'Even artisans, smiths, carpenters
> etc., none of them likes a man of his household to go to
> anyone else.' 'What you say has been looked to', said
> Mael Díthruibh, 'I obtained authorization and
> permission.' Then he rendered his obedience to Mael
> Ruain. Now, till that time he had been under the
> spiritual direction [soul-friendship] of Echtguide.[28]

Mael Ruain added some advice that shows how seriously soul-friendship should be taken, and perhaps shows his esteem for Mael Díthruibh who was already well-advanced in holiness: 'When you place yourself under the judgment or control of another, seek out the fire that you think will burn you the fiercest [that is, him who will spare you least]'.[29]

Another soul-friend, Eláir, ended by sending all his penitents away:

> because he saw that their penance was not zealously
> performed, and also that they concealed their sins when

making confession. After that he finally refused to receive anyone at all to spiritual direction [soul-friendship]. However, he would sometimes allow holy persons to consult him.[30]

It was for the penitent, then, to seek out a good, learned and holy soul-friend. An impious teacher was regarded as one of the three enemies of the soul, the other two in scriptural terms being the world and the devil.[31] In a seventh century commentary on the Letter of St James we have the following remarks on chapter 5, verse 20:

> To what is the teacher [doctor] like when he converts a soul? He is like the sentry on the tower looking out and indicating the stratagems of the enemy. Then, not only does he save his own soul, but also those of the citizens. So a double good accrues to the teachers and their hearers who obey them and fight against the enemy.[32]

It is easy to see how those words would certainly be applied to the soul-friend as teacher.

Three women-saints in particular were noted for their guidance of souls, Brigid, Íde and Samhthann. It is related of Brigid that a feast was made for St Brendan, herself and her household and that

> they were thirty days consuming that feast together. And each of them confessed to the other. Brendan said first that since he became religious he had never gone over seven furrows without his mind on God.
>
> 'It is well', said Brigid, 'I thank God.' Brigid said however (that since she had fixed) her mind on God, she had never taken it from him at all. At which Brendan marvelled 'It is right, then', said Brendan, 'that you should surpass us in every respect'.[33]

Perhaps we have here an example of that mutuality we come across occasionally, a mutual soul-friendship. Mael Díthruibh when he sought Mael Ruain as his soul-friend has such a mutual sharing in mind when he spoke of his desire to have his fill of discourse with Mael Ruain. St Íde was known as the foster-mother of the saints of Ireland, and St Brendan, already mentioned, was said to have been her chief fosterling. An example of her wisdom is shown in the answer she gave one day to St Brendan. He had asked her what were the three works most pleasing and the three most displeasing to God. Íde replied:

> True faith in God with a pure heart; a simple life with piety; generosity with charity—those three things please God well. A mouth that hates men; holding on to evil dispositions in the heart; faith in riches—those three things displease God greatly.

And we are told that 'St Brendan and all who were there and heard those sentiments praised God for his handmaid'.[34] In many places in that same life we are told that the saint consulted St Íde before undertaking particular tasks.

St Samhthann who flourished in the eighth century, a couple of hundred years after Brigid and Íde, seems to have had a great reputation for her wise advice, and was connected with the general movement of reform in the eighth century, as was in particular St Mael Ruain. Her sayings merited recording:

> A certain monk once questioned St Samhthann about the way of praying; whether one should pray lying down, sitting or standing. To whom she replied: 'In every position', said she, 'should one pray'. Again, a certain teacher named Daircellach came to the virgin and said to her: 'I propose to give up study and give myself to prayer'. To whom (said) she 'What then can steady our mind and prevent it from wandering', she said, 'if you neglect spiritual study?' Then the teacher said 'I wish to go abroad on pilgrimage'. She replied, 'If God cannot be found on this side of the sea, by all means let us go overseas. But since God is near to all those who call on him, we have no need to cross the sea. One can reach the kingdom of Heaven from every land.'[35]

Another incident is told of her:

> There was a certain itinerant pedlar in Munster in the

time of Samhthann, who used to carry greetings from her to the 'sons of life' [i.e. religious] in that country. Once she called him to her and bound him not to add to nor take away a single word that anyone should say to whom he was sent. Then she said to him: 'Say to Mael Ruain for me', said she [—or to Fer Dá Chrích, and the latter is more likely, since Mael Ruain was more venerable than Samhthann], 'that he is my favourite among the clerics of the South, and another thing you will say to him: ask, does he accept women for confession and will he accept my soul-friendship?' The pedlar took this message. But when he told him that he was Samhthann's favourite, he rose at once and raised both hands as in a cross-vigil and gave thanks to God. When the pedlar asked him next whether women took counsel of him and whether he would accept Samhthann's soul-friendship, he blushed down to his breast, and made three genuflections, and fell silent for a long time. Then he said: 'Tell her', said he, 'that I will seek counsel from her'. Then the pedlar told all those sayings to Samhthann, and she said: 'I think', said she, 'something will come of that youth'. Then she draws her brooch out of her mantle and drives it into her cheek till it stuck in the bone, and then there came out two filaments of milk: yet not a single drop of blood came out. At that sight the pedlar began to weep and wail. Then she took the wound between two fingers and set to squeezing it for a long time, and not a drop was wrung from it. Then at last by reason of the long squeezing out came a little tiny drop. It was a little drop of water, and there was a little yellow on the surface, enough to change its colour. Then she put this little driblet on her nail, and she said: 'So long', said she, 'as there is this much juice in his body, let him bestow no friendship nor confidence upon womankind'.[36, 37]

• Nowhere is it clearer that soul-friendship was a serious matter than in the prescriptions for married people who placed themselves under a soul-friend:

From prime on Monday to matins on Wednesday, for

these two days and nights they are given exemption and licence both for meals and conjugal intercourse. After that time abstinence is imposed on them both from flesh and intercourse, from matins on Wednesday to matins on Thursday. They are given exemption again from matins on Thursday to matins on Friday. They must keep themselves again from intercourse from matins on Friday till matins on Monday, that is, they are to live separately for three days and three nights. Abstinence from meals is imposed on them on Friday and the following night, and on Saturday and Saturday night. They are given exemption, for meals only, on Sunday and Sunday night.[38]

The great principle in the guidance of souls was that borrowed from medicine and popularized by John Cassian, and after him, we might say, above all by the Irish in their Penitentials which exercised such an influence on the sacrament of penance in Europe: *Contraria contrariis sanantur* (contraries are healed by their contraries). In a way I suppose that is to show the negative side of soul-friendship, yet the need is nearly always there to remedy various spiritual ills. So we read:

Let the power of the physician become greater in the degree in which the fever of the sick man increases. Hence those who take care to heal the wounds of others are to observe carefully what are the age and sex of the sinner, what instruction he has received, what his strength, by what trouble he has been driven to sin, with what kind of passion he is assailed, how long he remained in sinful delight, with what sorrow and labour he is afflicted, and how much he is detached from worldly things. *For God despiseth not the contrite and humbled heart*. Wise men, in regulating penance, are to look carefully also to this: not to punish with the rod a crime worthy of the sword and to smite with the sword a sin worthy of the rod; and according to Gregory, great care is to be taken by pastors lest they carelessly bind what ought not to be bound and loose what ought not to be loosed.[39]

The principle itself is thus expressed in the Penitential of Finnian, the earliest of the penitentials, dating from the sixth century:

> By contraries, as we said, let us make haste to cure
> contraries and to cleanse away these faults from our
> hearts and introduce heavenly virtues in their place:
> patience must arise for wrathfulness; kindliness, or the
> love of God and of one's neighbour, for envy; for
> detraction, restraint of heart and tongue; for dejection,
> spiritual joy; for greed, liberality. For Scripture saith:
> *The anger of man worketh not the justice of God*, and envy
> is judged as leprosy by the law, detraction as anathema,
> as is said in the scriptures: *He that detracteth his neighbour*
> *shall be cast out of the land of the living*; Gloom certainly
> devours or consumes the soul; *covetousness is the root of*
> *all evil*, as saith the Apostle.[40]

It is easy to see how the principle fits in with the virtue of discretion, as expounded, for instance, by Columbanus, and indeed for him they are intertwined. In our day it could well be profitable to take up the principle seriously and perhaps lay aside the polysyllables. The principle, after all, is timeless in matters of the body or the soul, no matter how it may be disguised or hidden under jargon. Certainly, whatever fault we may find with the old Irish or other ancient Christians, we can rarely fault them for lack of clarity.

We noted earlier that the soul-friend was expected to be 'learned in the rules of conduct laid down in scripture and in the Rules of the saints'. On reflection I think these must be the monastic Rules to which we have referred repeatedly. As I said, they are not Rules in the legal sense (although Columbanus has also a communal Rule which is penitential in character), but rather 'rules of conduct', prefaced by the great Rule of love of God and the neighbour. That last phrase occurs very very often in all the religious literature, whether in the Latin *dilectio Dei et proximi* or in the Irish (and incidentally is common in the traditional prayers that have come down to our own day). I have no doubt (considering also the fact that every ordained monk, at least, was also expected to be a soul-friend) that these Rules, as I have already hinted, had the soul-friend in mind. It is a subject which would deserve deeper study, but a few further excerpts will show how the constant growth of the soul seems to be always in view. From the sixth or early seventh century text, *Apgitir Chrábaid* or Alphabet of Piety, cognate to the Rules, we note the following: 'Three things expel a vacillating spirit and make for a steadfast mind: vigil and prayer and labour.[41] There are four things that obscure the truth: sexual love and fear, partiality and necessity. So long as a person is unjust, he cannot proclaim the truth in its propriety.'[42] Moderation and wisdom and true holiness, together it is that a man attains them. When does a man attain them? When his truth is faultless? When his heart is in its proper condition, then truth is therein as if he had not been born of man.'[43] The first part of the answer to the question, 'What should be learned by a person?' is 'Perseverance in holiness'.[44] One of the rules already quoted says: 'Through fear is the love of the King who heals every misery. It is from love of him that his will and his commandments are cared for.'[45] And again: 'Fear controls repentance, love determines piety'.[46] 'This is the virtue that causes long consolation, that in all your desires you exercise patience.'[47]

There was variety of discipline in the old Irish monasteries, even within the same monastery. 'Different is the condition of everyone, different the nature of the place. . . .'[48] Fostering that spirit and springing from it was surely the practice of soul-friendship.

Notes

[1] *Félire Oengusso (The Calendar of Oengus)*, February 1.

[2] *Anecdota from Irish Manuscripts* III, pp. 10–20.

[3] Migne, PL 4, 947–990.

[4] Walker, *Sancti Columbani Opera*, pp. 135–139.

[5] *Ibid.*, pp. 139–141.

[6] 'Apgitir Chrábaid' no. 18 in *Celtica* VIII (1968), ed. Vernam Hull.

[7] *The Rule of Tallaght*, ed. Edward Gwynn, *Rule of the Céli Dé*, 37.

[8] *Thesaurus Palaeohibernicus*, ed. Stokes and Strachan, vol. 1, p. 574.

[9] *Life of Colmán son of Luachán*, ed. Kuno Meyer, no. 8.

[10] *Irish Ecclesiastical Record* XXVII (1910), p. 505.

[11] *Ut sup.*, 7, p. 61. It is interesting to note that Thomas Merton wrote in 1960 in *Spiritual direction and meditation* that only if the layman 'has

special work to do for the Church or is in a situation with peculiar problems' ought he to have a spiritual director (quotation in Sellner, Edward C.: 'Soul Friend: guidance on our sacred journeys', in *Spiritual Life*, Summer 1982, p. 75).

[12] *Ut sup.*, 10, p. 505.

[13] *Ibid.*

[14] *Ibid.*

[15] *Ériu*, III (1907), p. 97.

[16] Quoted in Roman breviary, *heb. xvii per annum, fervi, lectio altera.*

[17] *Ut sup.*, 15.

[18] *Ut sup.*, pp. 99, 103, 105.

[19] *Vitae Sanctorum Hiberniae*, ed. Plummer, *Molua* xxx.

[20] *Ériu*, I (1904), p. 197.

[21] *Ibid.*, p. 198.

[22] *Ériu*, II (1905), p. 64.

[23] *Ibid.*, p. 65.

[24] *Ibid.*

[25] *Ut sup.*, 6, no. 36.

[26] 'Anmchairdes Mancháin Léith' (The Soul-friendship of M. L.), *Zeitschrift für Celtische Philologie*, VII (1910), p. 311.

[27] *Ut sup.*, 20, pp. 200, 194.

[28] *The Monastery of Tallaght*, ed. Gwynn and Purton, no. 24.

[29] *Ut sup.*, 7, no. 77.

[30] *Ut sup.*, 28, no. 23.

[31] *Ut sup.*, 6, no. 20.

[32] *Scriptores Hiberniae Minores*, I, ed. R. E. McNally SJ, p. 22, 763–767.

[33] *Ut sup.*, vol. 2, p. 324.

[34] *Ut sup.*, *Ite* xxii.

[35] *Ibid.*, *Samhthann* xx.

[36] *Ibid.*, xxiv.

[37] Kathleen Hughes in *The Church in early Irish society*, p. 177, footnote 6, remarks that the *Life* of Samhthann 'shows a more enlightened attitude. The story expresses the views of Mael Ruain rather than the views of Samhthann.'

[38] *Ut sup.*, 28, no. 50.

[39] *The Irish Penitentials*, ed. Bieler, p. 199.

[40] *Ibid.*, p. 85.

[41] *Ut sup.*, 6, no. 20.

[42] *Ibid.*, no. 14.

[43] *Ibid.*, no. 16.

[44] *Ibid.*, no. 9.

[45] *Ut sup.*, 20, p. 195.

[46] *Ibid.*

[47] *Ibid.*, p. 196.

[48] *Ut sup.*, 10, p. 511.

(vol. 25, no. 2, April 1985)

The Carthusians

Gordon Mursell

To the poor of the world we give bread or whatever
else our resources afford or goodwill suggests: we
rarely receive them under our roof, but instead send
them to find lodgings in the village. For it is not for the
temporal care of the bodies of our neighbours that we
have fled to this desert, but for the eternal salvation of
our souls. Therefore it is not surprising if we give more
friendship and assistance to those who come here for
the sake of their souls than to those who come for the
sake of their bodies. [1]

This extract from the earliest Carthusian customary (c. 1125),
the *Consuetudines Cartusiae* of Prior Guigo I, may appear somewhat chilly to those acquainted with St Benedict's injunction
to receive the poor as though receiving Christ himself (though
in fact, as Guigo subsequently points out, the monks did give
generously of what little they had to be distributed in nearby
villages). But it underlines one of the most striking features of
the early Carthusians, the 'unworthy and useless poor men of
Christ who dwell in the desert of the Chartreuse for love of the
name of Jesus', as another early prior of the Grande Chartreuse
put it:[2] the careful and coherent way in which, from the very
start, they set about creating a manner of life that would be
appropriate in every particular to the vocation they had
embraced. The first charterhouses were, like the Chartreuse
itself, in distinctly inhospitable (though not always uninha-
bited) places; the monks sought to be self-sufficient as far as
they possibly could, and one of the distinctive features of the

early communities was the way they set about clearing or purchasing the land around the monastery (within the *termini* they themselves specified) in order to guarantee the solitude they needed. This might seem to imply that the 'poor men of Christ' had little to do with the poor men and women of this world.

Yet the contradiction is more apparent than real. One of the striking features of the early Carthusians, as with the Cistercians and others, was the way in which, even from their mountainous retreats, they took part in the affairs of the world outside. Like St Bernard (with whom he corresponded), Prior Guigo I did not hesitate to tell the Church how to behave itself, and to use his influence to espouse the principles of the Gregorian reform,[3] and the early monks of the nearby monastery of Portes, one of the first to affiliate to the fledgling order in the early twelfth century, wrote a number of letters offering detailed spiritual guidance both to religious and lay people.[4]

For all the rigour of their asceticism, then, the early Carthusians did not see themselves as entirely cut off from the needs of the Church as a whole: indeed they saw their vocation not so much as a flight *from* the world as a flight *for* the world, and their way of life, centred upon what Guigo I called the *quasi bina dilectio* (almost twofold love, of God and of neighbour), as a challenge and even a witness to their contemporaries. The reluctance to help the physically poor was part of this asceticism, part of a means to a greater end: those who sought to live with the utmost simplicity and in the utmost poverty themselves would have little material wealth or property to share with others. What they could share was something altogether deeper: a *philosophia*, or 'lived wisdom', that might touch hearts and change lives far beyond the bleak *termini* of the charterhouse.

From the beginning, then, what the Carthusians had to offer was not material wealth (they have succeeded, perhaps to a greater extent than any other monastic order, in avoiding that altogether), not even gems of individual guidance, but the witness of their lives. The Grande Chartreuse itself was founded by St Bruno, formerly chancellor of the cathedral at Rheims, in 1084; and it is clear that the distinctive lineaments and rhythm of the Carthusian life owe their origins to him, even though it was the fifth prior, Guigo I, who (as we have seen) first committed their customs to writing. The life was a coherent and carefully worked out blend of the cenobitic and eremitic, each fulfilling the other; and it was made possible by the institution of *conversi* who were not so much servants as lay *monks*, and whose lives involved more manual labour than that of the choir monks, yet who from the start were clearly seen to be integral and full members of the whole community.

There were no novice masters in the early charterhouses, and monastic formation took place in the cell; Guigo I says that one of the experienced monks (as well as the prior) would be deputed to visit the novice there 'to instruct him in necessary things'.[5] The life of a Carthusian choir monk was minutely prescribed, and with good reason: the balance of solitude and community, the blend of prayer, physical work, recreation and study was carefully structured and maintained. From the start, then, spiritual guidance in the charterhouse was primarily a group affair, not an individual one: the whole community, in their corporate liturgy, chapter meetings and recreation as well as in their long hours in solitude, took responsibility for one another; and their founder described their life as 'His [Christ's] school, under the discipline of the Holy Spirit'.[6] Tilden Edwards has pointed out[7] that group spiritual direction is in fact the standard form of guidance in the Christian tradition; and the Carthusians were and still are among its exemplars. What this meant in practice is the subject of most of the remainder of this article.

First and foremost, and notwithstanding the emphasis on the community already noted, the Carthusian monk or nun[8] had to develop a considerable capacity for self-knowledge and awareness. In a remarkable set of meditations, written in about 1115, Guigo I reflected constantly and critically on his own experience and reactions. This is what he wrote about a disaster at Vespers:

> Notice how, when you recently tripped up in front of
> the brethren by saying one antiphon instead of another,
> your mind tried to think of a way of putting the blame
> on something else—either on the book itself, or on
> some other thing. For your heart was reluctant to see

itself as it really is, and so it pretended to itself that it
was different, inclining itself to evil words to excuse its
sin. The Lord will reprove you, and set before you
what you have done; you won't be able to hide from
yourself any longer, or to escape from yourself.[9]

Some of the meditations are extremely short, such as the pithy
Meditation 87: 'Insult any harlot you like—if you dare'. Invariably, however, the emphasis is upon self-scrutiny:

There are certain tastes, like that of honey; and there are
certain temperaments and passions, like those of the
flesh. When these things are either taken away or
damaged, notice how this is for you (*quomodo sit tibi
vide*).[10]

It is also worth noting that this self-scrutiny involves a genuinely pastoral concern for others:

Notice how you can, in the hope of what is to come,
love the harvest in the young shoot, and the twisted
tree-trunk. In the same way you must love those who
are not yet good. . . .
    Not much is gained if you take away from a person
something that he holds onto wrongly; but it is if, by
our words of encouragement and by your example, you
get him to let it go of his own accord. . . .[11]

This is not unhealthy self-absorption, but the indispensable
precondition, not only for the Carthusian life, but for any life
centred upon love: indeed the psychological acuteness of Guigo's emphasis on understanding yourself and reflecting on
your reactions to all that happens to you is remarkable. To
know ourselves, as Guigo makes clear throughout his 476
meditations, is to become aware both of our inherent predis-
position to run away from the truth, and of the divine love
existing deep within us. Yet to face this truth will invariably be
painful: for it is not just the truth, but the truth *crucified*, that
we are called to worship (*Sine aspectu et decore crucique affixa,
adoranda est veritas*);[12] and by discovering what it means to love
God without condition or strings attached, we are freed from
the dependence on (or possessiveness of) others in order to

love them as we should do—to seek their true good, not simply what we think is good for them. The theology of love underpins the whole of St Bruno's and Guigo's conception of the Carthusian life, and informs its most practical prescriptions; and this constant and rigorous probing of one's own interior intentions and reactions is its most fundamental prerequisite.[13]

Second, the Carthusian life was characterized by the coherent interweaving of theology and lifestyle, of the individual and corporate, that is embodied by the Latin word *utilitas*. In his meditations Guigo I wrote:

> Happy is the person who chooses somewhere he may work without anxiety. Now this is a sure choice and worthwhile thing to work at (*labor utilis*)—the desire to do good to all, so that you want them to be people who do not need your help. For the more people seem to be concerned with their own interests (*propriis utilitatibus*), the less they are doing what is good for them. For this is the distinctive good (*propria utilitas*) of each individual—to want to do good at all. But who understands this?
>
> Whoever, therefore, seeks to work for his own good, not only does not find it, but also incurs great harm to his soul. For while he seeks his own good, which cannot be sought at all, he is rejected by the common good, that is, by God. For just as there is one nature for everyone, so also there is one common good (*ita et utilitas*).[14]

It is worth noting in passing Guigo's psychological perception here too: the emphasis upon seeking to set people free from being dependent on your help is a fundamental aspect of all spiritual direction. The emphasis on the *common* good, on the essentially corporate aspects of Carthusian spirituality, is even more important however, and underlines the stress on group support and guidance referred to above. And the integrated nature of their lives went further than that: both Guigo I and the Carthusians of Portes, writing letters of spiritual guidance, stressed the interweaving of what was traditionally called 'spiritual exercise' (the fourfold monastic pattern of reading, meditation, prayer and contemplation) with public liturgical worship, physical exercise, study and other aspects of the common life. This is a crucial point: whereas later Carthusian (and other) writers, such as Guigo II (whose *Scala claustralium* or 'Ladder of Monks' became very popular after his death in c. 1190[15]), explored in great detail the relationship between the four different ingredients of 'spiritual exercise', Guigo I shows no interest in that at all, instead concentrating on emphasizing the relationship between all of them and the other, more corporate, aspects of the Carthusian life, as well as to the heart of the monastic vocation itself.[16] Love of God, and of neighbour—the two parts of the *quasi bina dilectio* belong together: by devoting his life to those exercises which, in the context of solitude and poverty, dispose him to receive and be transformed by the love of God, the monk who has apparently renounced his neighbour discovers instead the surest possible means of loving him.

This exploration of the practice and theology of the early Carthusians may appear to have very little to do with the wider subject of spiritual guidance within the Carthusian tradition as a whole. In fact, however, it has everything to do with it: the distinctive features of Carthusian spiritual guidance are not to be found by examining later works which happen to have been written by Carthusians but which in most cases could as easily have been written by members of any religious order, but by coming to see that it was their whole lives, and above all their *common* life, which was their primary contribution to the lives of others. When Guigo I wrote his life of St Hugh of Grenoble (and, to a considerable extent, when Adam of Eynsham wrote the life of another early Carthusian, St Hugh of Lincoln), he was not producing just another work of hushed hagiography, but offering what is in effect the essence of the Carthusian life as it could be (and was) lived by busy Christians 'in the world': both Hughs were bishops, both were described as incarnating the theology of love which lay at the heart of the Carthusian vocation, and as seeking, in lives unconditionally devoted to God alone, to be free to discern others' true worth as well as to issue prophetic warnings about social and ecclesiastical evils. Instead of simply giving the world aims, the Carthusians gave it people: a significant number of bishops and others emerged during the centuries from the *termini* of the charterhouses. Instead of compromising their own form of life, they offered its virtues, suitably adapted, for those living in the world.

Not everyone, then, has to renounce everything and don the white Carthusian cowl in order to recognize, and live, the distinctive principles and dynamic which informed and still inform their vocation. The slow and costly process of reflecting regularly on your own experience and reactions, and above all on your own motives and intentions; the concern to foster a thoroughgoing openness, even passivity, towards God in order to be more free to love other people without seeking to dominate or manipulate them; the willingness to work away at creating (and helping others to create) a pattern of life that integrates both solitude and common life in such a way as to fulfil each; and the readiness to seek a genuine simplicity of life which might help you live in loving and hidden identification with the physically poor and deprived— all these are essential dimensions of any authentic Christian spirituality. And to achieve them we will need guidance; not only, or even primarily, the one-to-one individual guidance that has in recent years become popular, but also the kind of critical yet loving mutual support and encouragement that a group, family or Christian parish community can offer its members, not by the eloquence of its speech or even by the quality of each person's private piety, but precisely by the openness and attentive love which informs its common life.

The spirituality of the Carthusian life was influenced, like that of any other order, by the prevailing insights and circumstances of the times; and most of the authors and texts mentioned in the remainder of this article wrote letters and treatises on spiritual guidance which in large part could have been written by members of any contemporary enclosed order. The 1972 Statutes of the Order contain restrictions in this respect which not all former Carthusians have observed. The Statutes explicitly say, for example:

> We never give spiritual direction by letter; nor may any
> of us preach in public. If seculars do not benefit from
> our silence, much less will they from our speech.[17]

From earliest times, however, the Carthusians were able to reach people without speaking: Guigo I himself describes in detail the distinctively Carthusian form of *praedicatio muta*, which was the copying of manuscripts, a form of apostolate peculiarly well suited to contemplative monks. This practice continued thereafter: Michael Sargent has pointed out the way in which late-medieval Carthusian monks, particularly (though not only) in England, translated and copied earlier spiritual texts, partly in order to make them available to a wider literate (but not Latin-reading) lay audience, partly to combat the spread of Wycliffite and other forms of heresy.[18] This is important: the Carthusians have never entirely separated theology from spirituality, and have never entirely lost their concern for truth, even in periods when the practice of prayer was at its most affective. The 'Mirrour of the Blessed Life of Jesus Christ' by Nicholas Love (c. 1410), a Carthusian of Mount Grace, Yorkshire, is a good example of this: it is a translation of an earlier work by the Pseudo–Bonaventure, and its popularity suggests that it served both a devotional and a propagandist purpose.[19]

The writings of some later Carthusians certainly suggest that their *praedicatio* was anything but *muta*—and (as has already been said) much of it contains little that is distinctively Carthusian. Ludolph of Saxony, for example, who was a monk of the charterhouse of Coblenz and who lived from 1295 to 1377, wrote a Life of Christ which (to judge by the number of manuscript copies and printed editions) was widely disseminated: its emphasis on *imitatio Christi* was typical of the age, though Ludolph's reflections on the delights of natural beauty recall similar passages in the beautiful letter of St Bruno to his friend Raoul le Verd.[20] Others produced works that were more explicitly concerned with spiritual guidance. Robert, a monk of the charterhouse of Le Parc-en-Charnie in France who died in 1388, wrote *Le chastel perilleux*, a treatise written to his cousin, who was a Benedictine nun: it is full of practical advice about contemplative prayer, praying in common, the sacramental life and other subjects likely to be of interest to both religious and lay readers.[21] Others seem to have acquired something of a reputation as spiritual guides: the prolific Denys, a Dutch Carthusian who lived from 1402 to 1471, wrote innumerable letters of counsel, only a few of which survive, and also complete sequences of sermons, both for religious and for those 'in the world': his complete works fill over forty substantial volumes. Finally, Richard Methley (1451–1528), also of Mount Grace, wrote a number of treatises on the monastic and spiritual life, and appears to have been in some demand as a director.[22]

As time passed, then, the Carthusians became involved in the practice of spiritual guidance to a degree far greater than was envisaged either by their founders or by their modern successors. And yet the *primary* concern of the Carthusians has never been spiritual guidance, but the way of living which, as we have seen, was their most distinctive act of witness. The establishing in 1984 of the first Carthusian monastery in the Third World, in southern Brazil, illustrates this point: their principal contribution to the poor among whom they now live is likely to be this hidden and loving identification, in the crucified *pauper Christus*, that is articulated in the Carthusian vocation, rather than any commitment to an active apostolate. And to a society less committed than ours to the pursuit of privatized perfection, such an apostolate might be infinitely more fruitful than we suppose. Why? Because, better than any frantic activist, it may help us all to rethink our values: in the desert, waiting and passivity and silence are inherently creative, not useless; apparent redundance in the world's eyes and your own can allow God to use you for his purposes; in and through the poor, the solitary and the powerless, God ushers in the kingdom of heaven. The most recent Statutes of the Order express this with simple eloquence:

> In choosing this, the 'best part', it is not our advantage
> alone that we have in view; in embracing a hidden life
> we do not abandon the great family of our fellow men;
> on the contrary, by devoting ourselves exclusively to
> God we exercise a special function in the Church where
> things seen are ordered to things unseen, exterior
> activity to contemplation. . . .
>   If, therefore, we are truly living in union with God,
> our minds and hearts, far from becoming shut up in
> themselves, open up to embrace the whole universe and

the mystery of Christ that saves it. Set apart from all, to all we are united, so that it is in the name of all that we stand before the living God.[23]

Notes

[1] Guigo I, *Consuetudines Cartusiae* (hereafter CC), 20:1; Latin text with French translation in *Sources Chrétiennes*, vol. 313 (1984), p. 206.

[2] Prior Basil, in a charter dated 1156.

[3] See his letters, with French translation, in *Sources Chrétiennes*, vol. 88 (1982), especially nos 2–6.

[4] Edited, with French translation, in *Sources Chrétiennes*, vol. 274 (1980).

[5] 'de necessariis instruat', CC 22:3.

[6] Letter to Raoul le Verd, 10; text with French translation in *Sources Chrétiennes*, vol. 88 (1962), p. 74.

[7] *Spiritual friend* (New York: Paulist Press, 1980), ch. 7.

[8] The first community of women religious to join the Carthusians was Prebayon, in 1140.

[9] *Meditations*, 282; Latin text with French translation in *Sources Chrétiennes*, vol. 308 (1983), pp. 190–192. It is hoped that a new English translation will appear in the not too distant future.

[10] *Meditations*, 306.

[11] *Meditations*, 167 and 297.

[12] *Meditations*, 5.

[13] A much fuller exploration of the theology of love and its implications for each aspect of the Carthusian life will be found in my *The theology of the Carthusian life* (Salzburg: *Analecta Cartusiana* series, vol. 127 [1988]).

[14] *Meditations*, 106.

[15] It is available in English translation by Edmund Colledge and James Walsh: Guigo II, *The ladder of monks and twelve meditations* (London: Mowbray, 1978).

[16] See especially *Meditations*, 390, where Guigo I explores the relationship of love of God and love of neighbour with reference to the monastic life in some detail.

[17] *Statutes* (1972), ch. 1:6.

[18] Sargent, Michael: 'Ruusbroec in England: the chastising of God's children and related works', in *Historia et Spiritualitas Cartusiensis* (Acta of the Fourth International Colloquium on this theme; Belgium: Destelbergen, 1983), pp. 303–312.

[19] For Nicholas Love, see the study by Elizabeth Salter in *Analecta Cartusiana*, vol. 10 (1974).

[20] For St Bruno's letter see note 2 above. For Ludolph, see Conway, Charles Abbott, Jr: 'The *Vita Christi* of Ludolph of Saxony and late medieval devotion centred on the Incarnation: a descriptive analysis', in *Analecta Cartusiana*, vol. 34 (1976); and Bodenstedt, Sr Mary Immaculate: 'Praying the life of Christ' (a translation of the prayers that

conclude Ludolph's 'Life', many of which are full of implicit spiritual guidance), in *Analecta Cartusiana*, vol. 15 (1973).

[21] *Le chastel perilleux* has been edited by Sr Marie Brisson with full introduction and commentary, in *Analecta Cartusiana*, vol. 19 (1974), 2 vols.

[22] See Hogg, James: 'A mystical diary: the *Refectorium salutis* of Richard Methley', in *Kartaüsermystik und -Mystiker*, vol. 1 (*Analecta Cartusiana*, vol. 55 [1981], pp. 208–238).

[23] *Statutes* of the Order (1972), ch. 34.

(vol. 29, no. 3, July 1989)

The Cloud of Unknowing

David Lonsdale SJ

Personal spiritual guidance, in the form of direction of one person by another by way of a series of conversations over a period of weeks or months, remains relatively rare and, some would say, an expensive luxury. Many people would not acknowledge its value; others would modestly and wrongly think their own efforts at Christian living too lowly to merit such attention; some shirk the self-revelation that seems to be implied; the vast majority, unfortunately, simply lack opportunity, though the practice of spiritual direction as a ministry open to lay people as well as clergy is beginning to gain ground in some countries. The present proliferation of books on prayer, meditation and the Christian life shows that very many people search the shelves of bookshops and libraries to find spiritual guidance and encouragement. The medieval *Cloud of unknowing* has become part of that trend. One popular paperback translation alone of *The cloud* has been reprinted fourteen times since it was first published in 1961.

The author's intention was quite particular: to write a long letter of guidance in prayer and contemplation to a young friend who was probably an enclosed monk or nun with inclinations towards a solitary form of life. Naturally he also foresaw that if the book proved helpful it might be passed on to others, and while he was sure that it would be useful to some he was also clear about the people for whom he was not writing: 'the worldly chatterboxes . . . the rumour-mongers, the gossips, the tittle-tattlers and the fault-finders of every sort' as well as those, 'however excellent they may be', who are absorbed in the 'active life' (Prologue). Nowadays, commercial publishing means that in suburban homes and tropical ashrams, in colleges and railway stations, Christians and non-Christians, agnostics and unbelievers look to *The cloud* for guidance and encouragement. Here I want to examine, in the light of some questions thrown up by present-day experience, aspects of what *The cloud* has to say about spiritual direction.

In what has been called 'educative spiritual direction' an experienced director guides a comparative neophyte in prayer or other aspects of the Christian life by giving appropriate theological, moral or spiritual information, encouragement and advice. *The cloud* seems to fall into this category. Not everything that is in a book is helpful to all, and the writer of *The cloud* is aware of that. Spiritual direction by means of a book, while enabling the direction to be systematic and ordered, misses the give-and-take and continuing discernment of a series of conversations. The author of *The cloud* knows that his friend is meeting a spiritual director regularly, and he would like his own recommendations to be discussed in these meetings, which become a way of determining whether the book's guidance is truly for the individual's good at a particular time. Of course, since the readership of *The cloud* has widened immensely, this kind of check would not now be available to most of its readers.

Spiritual directors approach their task with a theoretical framework of beliefs about how the human person is structured and operates and about how God relates to this human reality. This framework may be more or less implicit and unconscious or explicitly articulated. The author of *The cloud* naturally uses the psychology current in his own time, with the theory of the various powers of the soul (chapters 62–66), and the belief that the right ordering of the person is for the body–spirit unity to be governed and led by the Spirit. In locating contemplation so firmly in the will, as a response of love to God in the affective rather than the cognitive dimension of a person, *The cloud* is a helpful corrective to those who would make contemplation a matter of the mind's knowledge of God, an intellectual vision. Contemplation here is also primarily grace, a movement originated by God in the depths of the person: 'the impulse of love, this is the work of God alone' (chapter 26). Our part is to dispose ourselves as far as possible for this gift and to allow it to happen: 'Be the tree: let it be the carpenter. Be the house and let it be the householder who lives there' (chapter 34).

Prayer

One of the persistent questions that requires skill on the part of a spiritual director is the point at which it is right for a directee to move into a simpler, more passive and 'contemplative' form of prayer. Sometimes the transition takes place naturally and smoothly; sometimes the directee is afraid to move into what may seem comparatively arid, empty and formless. This transition is not merely a question of changing one's way of praying, a matter of method or technique. The movement into a more passive, contemplative form of prayer indicates an invitation to a more complete surrender to God not only in prayer but also in everyday living; an invitation to allow God increasingly to lead. To block this transition is to impede growth, and that is why John of the Cross, for example, takes it very seriously.

The cloud offers various signs by which a person's readiness for contemplation can be known. A basic condition is a serious attempt over a period of time to live the Christian life, arising out of and accompanying sorrow for sin, repentance and confession. Beyond this, the author also presupposes that the readers will not be absolute beginners in a life of prayer, but will already have spent time in the regular practice of 'many sweet meditations . . . on their own wretched state, on the passion, the kindness and the great goodness and the worthiness of God' (chapter 7). They will also be spending time regularly in the threefold occupation proper to the contemplative apprentice: reading, reflecting and praying (chapter 35).

A further sign of readiness will be the experience of a persistent 'leash of longing' for contemplative life and prayer (chapter 1), and a 'true affinity for the effect of this exercise'. Not all those who have a congenial feeling for this form of prayer, however, are necessarily called by God to be contemplatives or ready to move into contemplation. The feeling must be tested, and a more reliable indication is a persistent desire that 'is always pressing on their minds more regularly than is so with any other exercise' so that nothing else seems of any value in comparison with this 'little secret love' (chapter 75). Even so this impulse is unlikely to remain continuously. For various reasons it is sometimes withdrawn for one's own good (chapter 75). So when the withdrawal of the desire for this contemplation causes great pain and then the return of the desire gives even greater joy, this is a most authentic sign that the person is being drawn by God into this way of contemplation (chapter 75). It is a common experience in spiritual direction that a change into a new way of praying that seems to have been indicated by such signs as these brings a new taste for prayer and revives the joy of praying.

It is rare to meet a book that is as committed as *The cloud* to an apophatic approach to prayer. Contemplation means loving rather than knowing: 'because (God) can certainly be loved but not thought. He can be taken and held by love but not by thought' (chapter 6). Because God is not accessible to thought, this kind of contemplation is experienced as darkness for the mind and imagination. All thoughts, even 'good and holy thoughts' about God and his creatures, are to be hidden in a 'cloud of forgetting', as one reaches out with a 'dart of longing love' in darkness to God (chapter 7). Even so, it would be inaccurate to think that *The cloud* is recommending an entirely imageless and wordless form of prayer. The use of a short word or image such as 'God' or 'love' is advised. This word, as it were, arises from within the praying person and sums up in a very expressive way the love and the longing. But discursive thought and the active use of imagination in dwelling on images are seen as a waste of time in contemplation and even a positive hindrance to growth.

Discernment

One difficulty about writing a book designed to guide others in prayer is the fact that what suits one person may be wrong for another, and what is right for a person at one time may not be right at another. Discernment of these things does not work by rule. Of silence and strict fasting and retiring into solitude the same author writes in another place:

> they are sometimes good, sometimes bad; sometimes for you, sometimes against; sometimes a help, sometimes a hindrance. It could be that were you always to follow the particular urge that would bind you to silence, strict fasting and solitude, you would often be dumb when you ought to be speaking, fasting when you ought to be eating, and on your own when you should be with others.[1]

And so of other choices and activities in all walks of life besides the monastic. What *The cloud* offers are some guidelines towards a method of discernment, based on such classic teaching as the following:

> And do not be afraid of the devil, for he cannot come so close. He can never come to move a man's will except very rarely, and very indirectly, no matter how clever he is. Nor can a good angel move your will effectively without an intermediary. In short, nothing can move it except God. (chapter 34)

> But the consolations . . . which come suddenly from outside, even though you do not know whence, I beseech you hold all these suspect. For they can be either good or evil. If they are good, they are produced by a good angel, and if bad, then by an evil angel. (chapter 48)

For the actual practical application of *The cloud*'s teaching on discernment it is not necessary to adopt the author's theoretical framework of the activities of good angels and bad angels. But the 'sharp, two-edged, awesome sword of discretion' (chapter 33) is a necessary gift. One particularly interesting insight of *The cloud* is that contemplation itself teaches discernment. By giving her/himself 'immoderately' (chapters 41, 42) to loving God in this contemplation, which is 'the one thing necessary' chosen by Mary,[2] a person increasingly knows with growing certainty which options, courses of action and styles of life are in harmony with this love and which are not.

Then that very thing you are experiencing will know
how to tell you when to speak and when to be silent. It
will govern your whole life with discretion and
certainty, and will teach you mystically how to begin
and how to cease in all these natural matters with great
and supreme wisdom.[3]

The human heart ordinarily runs after many things in the
course of even a short span of time and experiences many
different desires and fears, attractions and revulsions. In
prayer as in the rest of life we become aware of various levels
of affective experience ranging from surface emotion to profound feeling. In this complexity, our tradition holds that
there are fundamentally two kinds of feeling that are important for discernment of spirits: what might be called positive
feeling towards God and his will ('consolation'), and negative
feeling towards God and his will ('desolation'). At root, both
of these are states of personal being which manifest themselves
in our affective experience. Consolation includes such experiences as a felt love for God, a profound sense of peace and joy,
of being in harmony with oneself and one's own most authentic truth. Desolation is the opposite of this, and can include
experiences of darkness, stress, anxiety, inner conflict and
turmoil, as well as an attraction to what is likely to draw one
away from God. Both consolation and desolation, it should be
remembered, can be productive of growth. Only sin is truly
evil and God brings good even from that.

The author of *The cloud* naturally wants to help his friend to
interpret the different 'stirrings' that he is likely to experience
in the course of learning contemplation, and to discriminate
between helpful and unhelpful attractions, desires and other
kinds of feeling. He suggests that in order to know which
kinds of pleasurable feeling, superficial or profound, can be
trusted and acted upon, one should look at their origin. The
true wellspring of contemplation is a 'devout stirring of love
which dwells in pure spirit'. This love will sometimes be felt
pleasurably in the emotions and 'bodily senses'. This kind of
consolation can be welcomed as a gift because of its origin in
the 'stirring of love'. Felt consolations, however, sometimes
have another origin: 'sounds, gladness and sweetness which

come suddenly from outside' (chapter 48). Here *The cloud* advises the contemplative to 'hold all these suspect' because they can be either aids or hindrances to growth and need further discernment. This further discernment is learned through consultation with a spiritual director and the practice of contemplation itself (chapter 48). The author of *The cloud* also hands on the traditional teaching about what our attitude to pleasant feelings towards God should be. Their presence is not in itself a sign of the quality of holiness. What is important is to be as God wishes, to welcome pleasant and positive feelings towards God when they are given and not to be dependent on them (chapter 50).

The writer of *The cloud* is also concerned to warn his pupil of likely pitfalls and misleading experiences that he might encounter in his future growth. Some of these seem to be part of a kind of popular mysticism of the time, experiences on which people in the current contemplative world tended mistakenly to set great value, perhaps partly under the influence of the spread of the writings of Richard Rolle. These pitfalls include a tendency to strain after certain kinds of feelings and emotional states, believing that these are somehow 'mystical' or signs of growth in holiness. Rather than straining 'like a greedy greyhound', the true contemplative will 'wait patiently on the will of our Lord with courtesy and humility' and 'learn to love God with quiet, eager joy, at rest in body as in soul' (chapter 46).

Other possible dangers are due to misunderstanding the language of spirituality. This misunderstanding, which may be intentional or simply naive, consists of giving a 'physical' meaning to what is intended 'spiritually' (chapter 51), thus emphasizing superficial emotion and some physical phenomena associated with piety at the expense of genuine contemplation. Further dangers mentioned include exhibitionism, hypocrisy, obduracy, self-righteousness and extreme moral zeal which leads to a constant habit of condemning others. *The cloud* helpfully shows how external behaviour in these cases is indicative of a person's deeper attitudes. These false paths are also examples of evil's well known tendency to appear disguised as good. The disguises are suited to the person and the age in which they occur, and our own current ones are probably not the same as those noted in fourteenth-century England. But the spiritual direction principle remains the same: religious experiences are to be evaluated by the results they produce in terms of how a person actually lives. *The cloud's* chief touchstone for this evaluation is the fact that genuine contemplation springs from and engenders Christian love. So the signs to look for are those of love (chapter 24), following the guidance of St Paul (1 Cor 13:1–8).

Evaluations

The charm, the wisdom and the appealing literary gifts of the author go a long way towards explaining the continuing popularity of *The cloud*. Its spiritual guidance is profound and encouraging and is especially valued at the present time because its apophatic approach to prayer seems to provide points of contact with Eastern Christian and some non-Christian mystical traditions which have been enjoying a revival of interest in the West.

Some of the limitations of *The cloud* are those of the apophatic tradition in general. In downplaying the role of knowledge and imagination in prayer, this tradition sometimes seems to imply that these are inimical to true contemplation and do not really enter into a person's profound relationship with God. This is clearly an unacceptable position to hold. Genuine contemplation implies a personal response to God in which the different 'faculties' eventually come into harmony and have a part to play. Neither understanding nor imagination is irrelevant to prayer, though even the kataphatic traditions insist, as does *The cloud*, that they are to be ruled and guided by love. Another limitation, too, of the style of contemplation advocated by *The cloud*, as of any form of prayer, is that it probably suits certain temperaments and types of person rather than others. Some are happy with a prayer that is relatively non-conceptual and free from images; others ask for more scope for understanding and especially imagination. We need both the apophatic and the kataphatic approaches, and it is important for a modern spiritual director to appreciate the value of both and to be able to assist different kinds of people to find their true path of prayer.

Most people who take prayer seriously experience some form of darkness at different stages in their growth. This may be associated with experiences like bereavement and grieving, illness, loss of confidence in oneself and/or God, conflict and turmoil within or in relation to others or periods of intellectual, moral and spiritual doubt. The times when accustomed ways of praying and of relating to God no longer seem valid can also be very dark indeed. At such times *The cloud* can be both a very informative guide and a real encouragement. It shows clearly that darkness and forms of 'unknowing' are to be expected in a life of prayer and that they can in fact be welcomed as a positive if painful invitation to deepen and integrate more fully one's love for God and people.

The cloud belongs to a monastic tradition which holds solitude and contemplation in special esteem. There is a real danger, however, that behind some forms of spiritual advice about treading all creatures underfoot and placing them in a 'cloud of forgetting' there lies an unhealthy disparagement of God's creation. Withdrawing from 'creatures' in order to find God, whether physically into a monastery or desert or in a 'cloud of forgetting' in prayer, can imply a mistaken, world-denying view that God cannot really be found in the midst of his creation. Though this is not necessarily the outlook of the writer of *The cloud*, it is not uncommon in some forms of Christian spirituality, and needs to be balanced by another strand of the Christian tradition which emphasizes that created reality itself is sacramental, the primary revelation of God to humanity. This would mean that living in 'the world' and contemplating God's creation and human history as they evolve are also recognized as a valid pathway to God. Creation and history mediate the presence and nature of God to the contemplative person. *The cloud* focuses almost exclusively on the individual's person-to-person, contemplative relationship with God. This is no doubt largely due to the circumstances and the age in which it was written. It would be unfortunate, however, if modern readers assumed that this is the only relationship to be considered in spiritual direction, and that interpersonal and social-structural issues are unimportant or even irrelevant. The author of *The cloud* is clearly aware of the interpersonal dimensions of his guidance; this is obvious from what he writes about charity. But the modern attention to the social, structural and political dimensions of spirituality is a sign of a more recent maturing of the Christian consciousness. Once again, therefore, the teaching of *The cloud* has to be supplemented and rounded off by an approach to spiritual direction which seriously takes account of the social and political structures of the world and of current issues of social justice.

Notes

[1] 'The discernment of stirrings', in *A study of wisdom*, trans. and ed. Clifton Wolters (Oxford: SLG Press), pp. 27–28. Cf. 'The assessment of inward stirrings', in *The pursuit of wisdom*, trans. and ed. James A. Walsh SJ, preface by George A. Maloney SJ (New York/Mahwah, NJ: Paulist Press,1988).

[2] *A study of wisdom*, p. 35.

[3] *Ibid.*, p. 36.

(vol. 26, no. 2, April 1986)

Themes in Carmelite Spiritual Direction

Michael Brundell OCarm

The primary source of the Carmelite tradition of spirituality is the Rule, or *vitae formula*, written some time between 1206 and 1214 by Albert of Avogadro, Patriarch of Jerusalem resident at Acre. This document was written at the request and following the proposals of a community of hermits already living on Mount Carmel under the leadership of an anonymous 'Brother B'. The Rule of St Albert, as it has come to be called, is remarkable for its brevity, and for the saturation of its lines with both direct and indirect quotations from and allusions to the sacred scriptures.[1] It does not concern itself so much with the minute prescriptions of daily living as with the style and quality of the collective enterprise called 'a life of service or allegiance to Jesus Christ'. The nucleus of the Rule is clearly based on the passages of the Acts of the Apostles frequently referred to as 'summaries' (Acts 2:42–47; 4:32–35). Therefore the celebration of the Eucharist, fraternity, constant prayer, and poverty or the common life are the basis for the way of life desired by the hermits of Mount Carmel.

Although the Rule of St Albert is clearly an attempt to be an alternative to the detailed structural models found at the time frequently in the way of life of the monks, yet it is above all else a document of spiritual guidance for those who wish to learn how to live a life 'meditating on the law of the Lord day and night'. Among other general directives concerning work, silence, humility and the proper understanding of obedience as a listening, attentive heart, the Rule underlines the importance of dialogue—on Sundays as a minimum but as often as necessary—in order to preserve the community commitment to a way of life and for the spiritual well-being of all. Conformity to the will of Christ, transformation in Christ, is the principle which the community, and through it the individual, must begin to practise. This includes adapting the way of thinking to the way Jesus thinks, since this truth leads to free service in love and from love. Development in love requires simplicity and sincerity of spirit and a heart constantly becoming more centred on Christ, that is, a heart becoming pure. What a person is and does will reflect whether that person is living in obedience to Christ. To this end also, the cultivation of a good conscience, which is the quality of interior dispositions, will lead to correct love and service of God and consequently to love and service of neighbour. The spiritual guidance of the Rule therefore centres upon the celebration of the Eucharist, recalling the paschal mystery of Christ's death, resurrection and glorification, and entering into that mystery through faith and love. The presence of God always in the oratory 'in the middle of the cells' is a constant reminder of the call to contemplation and thanksgiving which should reflect something of the joy of Christ. A developing love of scripture and the liturgy through constant pondering of God's living word leads to the practical expression of the ideal of sharing all things together, and makes of it a true witness to the Lord in an apostolic and Spirit-filled sense. The Rule seeks to guide the Carmelite to a real experience of what it means 'to live in Christ'.

The flaming arrow

The constant state of war with its unsettled and unsettling conditions in the Holy Land eventually led to the migration of some of the hermits from Mount Carmel towards the end of the third decade of the thirteenth century. Between 1238 and 1242 settlements were made in Cyprus, Sicily, England and southern France. Circumstances and conditions in these countries led the Carmelite migrants and refugees to petition the Pope for mitigation of the Rule in order to make adequate adaptations to the changed situation in which they now found themselves. Pope Innocent IV, with the Bull *Quae honorem conditoris* of 1 October 1247, approved some small changes in the Albertine Rule.[2] Yet small though these changes may have been, they in fact wrought a profound change in the lifestyle of the hermits, eventually leading to the complete adoption of the Carmelites by the Church as mendicant friars. This momentous event, which took place during the period from the arrival in Europe to the end of the thirteenth century, was not without opposition, and indeed it may be claimed that the subsequent history of the Order has been affected by the continual need to come to grips with its eremitical origins and contemplative status in an ever-changing and challenging world.

Nicholas of Narbonne, General Prior from 1266 to 1271, wrote a passionate defence of the eremitical–contemplative tradition in his *Ignea sagitta*, a letter addressed to all the brothers of St Mary of Mount Carmel. This prophet of a return to the sources addressed his impassioned plea to a fidelity to the spirit of the Rule of St Albert. If you want to guide people on the road of holiness, he says, then you must first be holy and learned yourself in the sphere of knowledge and love of God, and only then can you presume to pass on to others what you have known and experienced yourself. What Nicholas objected to was not involvement in the apostolate, since he acknowledged that such was a part of life on Mount Carmel from the beginning, but that the lure of immersion in apostolic activity was attracting men who were not properly prepared intellectually or spiritually.

> Where among you, tell me, are to be found preachers, well versed in the word of God, and fit to preach as it should be done? Some there are, indeed, presumptuous enough, in their craving for vain glory, to attempt it, and to trot out to the people such scraps as they have been able to cull from books, in an effort to teach others what they themselves know neither by study nor by experience. They prate away before the common folk—without understanding a word of their own rigmarole—as bold-faced as though all theology lay digested in the stomach of their memory, and any tale will serve their turn if it can be given a mystical twist and made to redound to their own glory. Then, when they have done preaching—or rather tale-telling—there

they stand, ears all pricked up and itching to catch the
slightest whisper of flattery. But not a vestige do they
show of the endowments for which, in their appetite
for vain glory, they long to be praised.[3]

Strong words are these, and they become even stronger when
Nicholas turns to the subject of hearing confessions and the
giving of spiritual counsel. And yet the letter is not just a
negative catalogue of woes. Beautiful passages express the joy
and delight of contemplation, the direction of the Holy Spirit
in the lives and hearts of people called to praise God in union
with all creation, and the example of the solitude of Mary's
chamber being the place where the Word of God became flesh.
Many commentators have seen in the letter of Nicholas of
Narbonne the seed of the doctrine of St John of the Cross, and
many of his expressions are echoed in the sixteenth-century
doctor's works. Above all else, Nicholas of Narbonne is
concerned to be faithful to the spiritual guidance of the Rule of
St Albert, which teaches the necessity for study, both intellectual and spiritual, of the following of Christ, as portrayed in
the scriptures, and, especially, experience. The ascent of the
Mount of Carmel, which is Christ, is both personal and
communal, and true solitude is found in the fraternal living
out of the Rule. This contemplative attitude both gives
personal direction and enables such a soul to be a vehicle of
guidance for others.

The institution of the first monks

Nicholas resigned his office in 1271 and was succeeded by the
Englishman Ralph de Fryston who, on his death in 1276, was
buried at Hulne in Northumberland—a foundation which
remained very much a contemplative one until its dissolution
in 1538. The Carmelites appear to have heeded the warnings
and advice of the *Flaming arrow* however, for Carmelites began
to become known as learned and holy men by the end of the
thirteenth century. This period coincided with a problem
about origins: the Marian character or patronage of the Virgin
Mary was with the Carmelites from the beginning, and it is
with little difficulty that this was adequately upheld and well

defended. But the claim of a link with the prophet Elijah was quite another matter, and much ink was spilt in the fourteenth and succeeding centuries attempting to prove direct succession from Elijah, Elisha and the 'sons of the prophets' to the hermits who received the Rule from St Albert of Jerusalem at the beginning of the thirteenth century. Among the many works written in defence of this succession was a four-part classic of Carmelite spirituality by a Catalan, one Philip Ribot, in 1370. Ribot claimed to be editing and commenting on four works from antiquity, the first of which, called *The book of the institution of the first monks*, was held to be the rule before that of St Albert, and written by John, the forty-fourth Bishop of Jerusalem. The value of this particular work is certainly not historical; but its spiritual influence has been extraordinarily profound and pervasive, including among others St Teresa of Jesus who had access to a copy in the library of the monastery of the Incarnation at Avila.

Part one of *The institution of the first monks* consists of nine chapters which present the Carmelite call as the eremitical–contemplative ideal lived out after the example of the prophet Elijah. In the manner of the day, the interpretation of the scriptures is largely allegorical but the spiritual values are clearly universal:

> The goal of this life is two-fold. One part we acquire, with the help of divine grace, through our efforts and virtuous works. This is to offer to God a holy heart, free from all stain of actual sin. We do this when we are perfect and in Karith, that is hidden in that charity of which the wise man says: 'Charity covers all offences' (Prov 10:12). God desired Elias to advance thus far, when he said to him: 'Hide yourself by the brook Karith'. The other part of the goal of this life is granted us as the free gift of God: namely, to taste somewhat in the heart and to experience in the soul, not only after death but even in this mortal life, the intensity of the divine presence and the sweetness of the glory of heaven. This is to drink of the torrent of the love of God. God promised it to Elias in the words: 'You shall drink from the brook'.[4]

Further chapters reveal how important it is to achieve detachment, purity of heart, conformity of the will with God, in order to reach perfect charity. This journey or movement of the soul is, however, crowned by the absolutely free gift of God which lifts it into divine union. The spiritual life is never a static affair; the soul must constantly strive for humility and total detachment so that it may be more disposed to receive God's grace and his gifts. The truly prophetic vocation becomes one of abandonment to the Lord which itself has to be learnt; the prophet Elijah in the Books of Kings provides the proper example of abandonment and subsequent filling by God with his presence. Elijah's experiences therefore are the model of Carmelite spiritual guidance both in terms of the spiritual preparation of oneself and in learning how to prepare and guide any other soul who is seeking deeper union with the Lord.

A recent study has brought out more fully the importance of the liturgy given by the author of *The institution of the first monks* to a fully integrated spiritual life.[5] The proclamation of the scriptures, the singing of the psalms, the centrality of the oratory among the cells (continued according to the author by St Albert) all point to the necessity for the interiorization of liturgical texts as the principal sources for meditation and contemplation. It becomes clear that the spiritual journey of the soul is both personal and communal, which follows closely the pattern of both the Rule of St Albert and the letter of Nicholas of Narbonne. Guidance for the soul then is not something spasmodic or a matter of chance, but directed according to the sound principles of the Church throughout its journey of discipleship. In this way, the idols which lead people astray from true worship of God may be combated with the prophetic zeal of Elijah, the contemplative in the service of the living God, and in communion with other disciples of that same God.

Practice

It has been said that the heritage of these three principal sources of Carmelite spirituality, together with various editions of the

Constitutions and other less well-known works, has been to make Carmelite history a constant series of reforms and calls to renewal. In 1413 was the first organized reform which grew into the Congregation of Mantua, and at the end of the same century a renewal movement in France, centred at Albi, returned to a strict observance of the Rule.

The twenty-year generalate (1451–1471) of the French Carmelite Blessed John Soreth saw the establishment of monasteries of contemplative nuns within the Order, and the consequent development of the need for good spiritual directors for these enclosed groups of women. The monastery at Vilvoorde in Belgium, founded by Soreth in 1468, is still in existence and maintains the link with its founder's reforming activity of renewing and strengthening the commitment to prayer in the Order. Soreth felt that in addition to communities of men in Carmel, the many groups of beguines and other women associated with the churches of Carmelites should be placed on a surer footing. His reasoning was that while the communities of men needed to be constantly alert to the retention of pristine observance, and while, too, a healthy tension between the eremitical–contemplative basis and the active apostolate contributed to a constant dialogue with the Order's origins, nevertheless groups of enclosed women associated with the Order would be a necessary reminder of the first duty of the Order as being contemplation. It is possible to discern in the writings of Soreth a similar inclination to the values of his predecessor Nicholas: the absolute priority which must be given to prayer and personal development and maturity in the spiritual life, before ever presuming to direct others or lead them 'to the holy mountain, Christ our Lord'. The idea of a journey or pilgrimage to God is present in Soreth as with so many other early Carmelite writers, perhaps reinforced by the facts of their early history when they became refugees from persecution on Mount Carmel, and had to discover the value of adaptation to changed circumstances and conditions. In adapting they also discovered the value of renewal of life and apostolate as well, claiming Mary's *fiat* (Luke 1:38) as the example and model.

Sixteenth-century reform

Undoubtedly, St Teresa of Jesus (1515–1582) of the Spanish monastery of the Incarnation, Avila, brought the renewal of Carmel to unprecedented heights of awareness of the primacy of contemplation. With the encouragement of John Baptist Rossi, General Prior from 1564 to 1578, she restored the commitment to the true spirit of the Rule of St Albert, influenced certainly by *The institution of the first monks* and probably also by the *Flaming arrow*. From the point of view of spiritual guidance, St Teresa's most important cry was for good and wise directors for her nuns. She herself had suffered much from the unlearned and the unwise, and she was emphatic about the need for discerning, wise and proper direction for those seeking to make progress in the spiritual life. She was not prepared to accept holy men if they did not know what they were talking about or dealing with in terms of experience along the spiritual path. Her own works were written at the request of others and they provide a guide in themselves to correct spiritual awareness of the variety of developments which can occur to the soul on its journey to the Lord of all. Teresa clearly understood fully the ramifications of St Albert's Rule, and is in sympathetic continuity with Nicholas of Narbonne, Ribot's *The institution of the first monks*, Soreth and others like them. For her, the awareness of the humanity of Christ, and the experience of suffering in the spiritual life, brought the soul to the dimension of love of God as Father, and linked the life of grace to the natural growth occasioned by deepening knowledge of the mystery of Christ, saviour and redeemer. But the need for good direction is paramount:

> I beg every superior, for the love of the Lord, to allow a holy liberty here: let the bishop or provincial be approached for leave for the sisters to go from time to time beyond their ordinary confessors and talk about their souls with persons of learning, especially if the confessors, though good men, have no learning; for learning is a great help in giving light upon everything. It should be possible to find a number of people who combine both learning and spirituality, and the more

favours the Lord grants you in prayer, the more needful
is it that your good works and your prayers should
have a sure foundation.[6]

St John of the Cross (1542–1591), associated with St Teresa in
the reform of Carmel, with his poetic soul has given to the
Church a depth of understanding of what it means to be a
follower of Christ the true shepherd and guide. His poetry
relates the mosaic pattern of a soul's experiences on the journey towards the liberating, transforming union in Christ. The
desire of which he wrote as being the kernel from which
spiritual development ensues found form and expression in his
poetic genius. Comprehension of the poetic art form was,
however, difficult to realize by those with whom he shared his
spiritual itinerary. Therefore, at their request, John of the
Cross wrote his theological commentaries on the poetry to
expound the principles from which the poetic revelatory experience grew. Again the idea of pilgrimage is evident, not
only in the psychological development, but even more in the
spiritual growth towards a deeper life of grace. John is sometimes seen as a highly complex theologian, too profound and
indeed advanced for ordinary souls seeking further guidance
along the spiritual paths. But his works, while theologically
complex, are still comprehensible to those who really take the
journey of the spiritual life seriously. Poetry must be savoured
meditatively; his maxims are pithy, relevant and very much
down to earth; his letters are replete with practical guidance
for the individual and related to the concrete situation. The
commentaries explain for the soul wandering the paths of
darkness to light the different phases of transforming union
and the activity of grace on nature. Applications may vary, but
the essential is the same. John of the Cross realized that
sometimes written guides are needed in the absence of good
and holy learned directors.

Although he did not write a manual for directors, and his
remarks on the role and duties of the spiritual guide are often
indirect and frequently negative, yet it is possible to find a
positive picture of the spiritual director in his works. Experience, wisdom and discretion are the three principal characteristics of a good director:

Certainly experience and knowledge, deep faith and wisdom are necessary in spiritual direction, but in the actual direction situation it is the virtue of discretion that surfaces. In a specific case the discreet director can draw on his knowledge and personal spirituality to judge and communicate with the person who comes for counsel. Therefore, for John of the Cross the spiritual director 'needs to be wise, discreet and experienced'.[7]

Renewal in the seventeenth century

When, in 1593, after the death of Teresa of Jesus and John of the Cross, the reformed monasteries and convents asked for and received complete autonomy, becoming two juridically distinct Discalced Carmelite congregations based in Spain and Italy, once again the Carmelites began the renewal process in conjunction with their historical roots. The heritage of Nicholas, Soreth, Teresa, John and others began to coalesce in a new movement centred upon a group belonging to the French Province of Touraine. The guiding lights of the movement were Philippe Thibault and Pierre Behourt who developed the stricter observance which spread throughout all the French Provinces, the Provinces of Belgium and Holland, Germany, Poland, Russia, Lithuania, Italy and finally to Spain and Portugal via the Provinces of Brazil. Thibault, Behourt and their companions were influenced by the earlier reform movements in Carmel, including the Teresian, and one of the aspects of considerable importance to them was the desire to have well-trained religious who would not only be committed to the development of their own spiritual life, but would also be qualified to teach and direct others. Therefore, we find much of their apostolic activity taken up with spiritual guidance, not only of the Carmelite nuns, but indeed of many different types of people, from princes to the workers in the towns where they were established.

The spiritual heart of this renewal movement was the blind brother, John of St Samson (1571–1636). A gifted musician, blind from the age of three, he spent most of his life in the novitiate of the Province, where his influence on the novices was profound. A mystic with a strong emphasis on the practice of the presence of God through the aspirative approach to prayer, his advice and guidance were sought by many, both within and without the Order. He was consulted with regard to the case of possession in connection with the community of Ursulines at Loudun, and Maria de'Medici sought his guidance among others in her various political schemes. But it was in regard to the general trend of spiritual renewal in France that John of St Samson was most widely influential. His guidance of bishops, priests and laity was based on his own deeply experienced methods of prayer and union with God. He never ceased to repeat to the novices the need for proper spiritual awareness based on the knowledge of scripture and tried and tested spiritual masters.[8] John's effect was most pronounced and obvious in the large numbers of holy men who, as his disciples, propagated and developed his teaching. Dominic of St Albert, who wrote the manual for correct direction and training of novices for the Stricter Observance, stressed constantly the primary duty of anyone seeking to be apostolic to have a profound and constant life of prayer. Maur of the Child Jesus and Mark of the Nativity among others spent much time in the direction and guidance of souls, but always from within the framework of personal awareness of the action of grace in souls derived from constant meditation and reflection on the scriptures. Such meditation and reflection must be in the first place applied to one's own personal spiritual life and corrected and refined by reference to the spiritual masters.

With the spread of the renewal movement into the Low Countries, a blossoming of holy men and women noted for their learning and piety, and consequently their importance in the realm of spiritual guidance, arose especially in Flanders. Among the most notable of these was the many times Provincial Michael of St Augustine (1621–1684), whose activities were most widely acclaimed in the area of direction of souls. His many written works included a treatise on maturing in the spiritual life, and an interesting example of the trend of seeing the Virgin Mary as the prime exemplar and model of Christian faith, hope and love. Michael of St Augustine saw Mary as the true contemplative who spent her life pondering the words and deeds of her Son and growing in her love for and appreciation of God's all-powerful actions in history. His interesting book on the Mariform life of devotion and spiritual slavery or service to the Virgin predates the better-known work by St Louis-Marie Grignion de Montfort by some twenty years, probably both being the inheritors of an earlier tradition. One of Flanders' greatest mystics, Maria of St Theresa Petijt (1623–1677), attained the highest peaks of transforming union with Christ in her prayer life, and is remarkable in that she was not a nun but a lay woman—a member of the Carmelite Third Order. In contact with Michael of St Augustine, whose penitent she was, she advanced towards perfection with the assistance of the saintly priest who encouraged her to write down her experiences. As with so many great spiritual friendships, influence was a two-way affair, the one helping and encouraging the other. Maria was primarily interested in proclaiming that the importance of the real spiritual director for souls is God, in Christ, through the action of the Holy Spirit. Her awareness of the activity of the triune life within and also without, led her to an increasing certainty of perfection and well-being based on fidelity: an absolute trust in the caring presence of the Lord in all spheres of life.

Maria Petijt was an outstanding example of the direction or spiritual guidance of lay people which was carried out by the development of the Carmelite Third Order—which enabled them to develop full spiritual lives according to their own circumstances. Primarily the guidance of the Third Order was communitarian, that is, there were frequent meetings with the priest who was spiritual director, at which aspects of spiritual development were expounded. Particularly important were the Third Order groups in Portugal and Brazil, where these lay Carmelites grew to be very strong and had a wide and influential following. During the periods of suppression and exclaustration of religious in the nineteenth century, Carmelite churches and chapels in Brazil and Portugal often remained open in the hands of dedicated groups of these lay Carmelites. The most important element in the development of the Third Order was the emphasis on periods of quiet prayer based on knowledge of the psalms and other scripture passages and explained to the members by the director. The idea of groups of lay people attached to religious orders is not unique, but what was somewhat novel was the emphasis on the communitarian aspect of spiritual progress. This was no doubt due to the idea that being enrolled in the scapular made a person a part of a much larger group or family, with commitments to God, through devotion to the Virgin Mary, and commitments to the group or confraternity within which this devotion was carried out. Scapular confraternities emphasized personal holiness to be sure, but yet it was always in the context of a group; the group or community dimension was essential.

The disaster of the suppressions of the late eighteenth century, and the nineteenth century, reduced the Carmelite Order to little more than a remnant. But fidelity to the primitive tradition remained with the few survivors and brought about a further renewal in the twentieth century. The outstanding example of Titus Brandsma (1881–1942), martyred at Dachau concentration camp, is one which, in continuity with those ancient principles, reawakened Carmel's commitment to spiritual guidance in line with its prophetic and Marian roots.

Notes

[1] Recent excellent studies of the Rule of St Albert include: Secondin, Bruno, OCarm: *La regola del Carmelo* (Rome, 1982); Steggink, Otger, *et al.*: *Carmelite rule* (Almelo, 1979).

[2] Smet, Joachim, OCarm: *The Carmelites: a history of the Brothers of Our Lady of Mount Carmel*, vol. I (Rome: Carmelite Institute, 1975), p. 13. Many of the historical details of the present article are taken from this work, and vols II and III (1976; 1982).

[3] Staring, Adrianus, OCarm: 'Nicolai Prioris Generalis Ordinis Carmelitanus Ignea Sagitta', in *Carmelus*, 9 (1962), pp. 237–307.

[4] 'Liber de Institutione Primorum Monachorum', chs 1–9 reprinted in *Analecta Ordinis Carmelitarum*, 3 (1914–16), pp. 346–367. For an excellent study of the place of the prophet Elijah in Carmelite tradition, see Joseph Chalmers, OCarm: *The prophetic model of religious life: the role of the prophet Elijah in Carmelite spirituality* (Rome, 1982) (pro manuscripto).

[5] Valabek, Redemptus Maria, OCarm: *Prayer life in Carmel* (Rome: Institutum Carmelitanum, 1982), pp. 32–5.

[6] St Teresa of Jesus: *The way of perfection*, ed. E. Allison Peers (London), ch. V, p. 23.

[7] Graviss, Dennis R., OCarm: *Portrait of the spiritual director in the writings of St John of the Cross* (Rome: Institutum Carmelitanum, 1983), p. 197.

[8] See, among others: Bouchereaux, Suzanne-Marie: *La réforme des Carmes en France et Jean de Saint-Samson* (Paris: J. Vrin, 1950); Healy, Kilian, OCarm: *Methods of prayer in the directory of the Carmelite reform of Touraine* (Rome: Carmelite Institute, 1956).

(vol. 25, no. 3, July 1985)

St Teresa of Avila and Spiritual Direction

Joseph Chalmers OCARM

The central theme of the writings of St Teresa is the attachment to the person of Christ through prayer and the central theme of her whole life is the love of God. She viewed prayer as the privileged means of communication with God.[1] She considered spiritual direction as a means of primary importance for making progress in the ways of the Spirit and a significant help in avoiding the dangers and overcoming the difficulties inherent in striving for the goal of the spiritual life—union with God. Teresa's experience of being on the receiving end of spiritual direction made her value a good director when she found one because she had suffered much from incompetent directors. She was convinced that if she had had a good director from the beginning of her journey to God, she would have given herself to God's service much earlier and she would have reached her goal of union with God much sooner.

The ministry of spiritual direction has received new life in recent years because of the experience of the need for sure guides in the search for a more authentic faith and in the search for a deeper experience of God in prayer. Teresa's experience of direction from both sides—receiving and giving—can teach us much about the spiritual life, about how we can advance in the love and knowledge of God and how we can help others on their journey towards God.

Teresa stressed the importance and the need for spiritual direction. For herself, she feared that her own experiences in prayer might not be from God. As the Inquisition was only too eager to root out false visionaries, she had good reason to fear. However, she had great difficulties in finding anyone who understood her. When she was writing her *Life*, her fears had largely disappeared. Gradually she became the spiritual director of some of her own directors and of many other people too.

The qualities of the spiritual director

What did Teresa look for in a spiritual director? She stressed the need for a director to be experienced in the spiritual life[2] especially for those who were beginning to give themselves to prayer. Teresa had the opportunity of consulting some of the most famous theologians of her day and several saints. She greatly valued learning in directors[3] but she also came across people who were learned in a rather superficial way. If learning remains only in the head and does not penetrate to the heart, it is rather arid. Academic knowledge of theology and scripture is important because it provides a sure foundation for faith but it is far more important to have a knowledge of God's ways, that is, the ability to translate academic knowledge into real life.

A director who is careless about his or her own life can be very dangerous because he or she can encourage carelessness in others. A director will often be a model for those who come to him or her for help. Therefore, according to Teresa, it is necessary for a director to seek holiness because:

> it is a great encouragement to see that things which
> were thought impossible are possible to others and how
> easily these others do them. It makes us feel that we
> may emulate their flights and venture to fly ourselves,
> as the young birds do when their parents teach them;
> they are not yet ready for great flights but they
> gradually learn to imitate their parents.[4]

Teresa as spiritual director

Through the experiences which she had, Teresa came to grasp certain principles about prayer and the spiritual life. She wrote her major works either for her spiritual directors at their request to help them understand her better or for her own nuns. Amongst her nuns, there were several with very high spiritual gifts and who were advanced on the path of holiness. However the majority were ordinary women with normal problems. Therefore Teresa took pains to point out that prayer was only part of the Christian life; the normal Christian virtues must accompany prayer and growth in the virtues authenticates growth in prayer. She very strenuously advises that we must not always be looking in on ourselves to check our spiritual pulse as it were. Instead we must look outwards towards God and to the needs of other people. As she wrote in her *Interior castle*:

> When I see people very diligently trying to discover
> what kind of prayer they are experiencing and so
> completely wrapped up in their prayers that they seem
> afraid to stir, or to indulge in a moment's thought, lest
> they should lose the slightest degree of the tenderness
> and devotion which they had been feeling, I realise how
> little they understand of the road to the attainment of
> union. They think that the whole thing consists in this.
> But no, sisters, no; what the Lord desires is works.[5]

We are called to love which has very practical consequences. However I cannot exercise love outside God. Prayer is an opening to God whereby I consciously allow him into my life. St Paul urges us to pray always.[6] If we take this seriously, we must see that our prayer goes beyond the times we set aside for formal prayer. My prayer expresses my relationship with God. My practical care and concern for other people authenticates my love for God. If my relationship to other people is not going well, then I should not be surprised when my relationship with God does not seem to go well either. Prayer and daily life are inextricably connected.

Teresa was always very practical. She deals with the first steps towards God as well as the most sublime states of union with him. When the decision is taken to give oneself to the Lord, the first step of the journey is the struggle against sin. Teresa says that one should be prepared to die rather than commit a grave sin.[7] Also one must avoid with the greatest diligence any venial sin. The best way of defending ourselves is prayer which helps us get up after a fall and not to fall again.

Along with the struggle against sin, there must be the practice of the ordinary Christian virtues. Teresa wrote *The way of perfection* for the nuns of St Joseph's, the first convent she had founded. They had asked her to write about prayer but she prefaced it by a short explanation of the practice of the virtues. There are two versions of her book, *The way of perfection*. The second version was probably written when Teresa realized that many of her nuns in other convents wanted to read it too. She tells her sisters that prayer cannot be accompanied by self-indulgence. Prayer is a going out of oneself to God while self-indulgence is a concentration on self. Teresa lays down three attitudes which are vital in a life of prayer: love of neighbour; detachment from earthly things; and humility. The way to test whether we are advancing on our journey towards God is to look at our lives. Are we growing in love for those around us? Are we becoming less possessive and grasping of material goods? Are we growing in true humility, that is a true knowledge of ourselves, that we are sinners in need of God? Teresa stresses often that we cannot merit anything from God. It is his will that he fills us with his love but before he can do so, he must break down the barriers which we have set up against him. This can be a very slow process.

Teresa tells her nuns that they must not only be detached from exterior things but also from themselves. This latter detachment is much more difficult than the former because it is more difficult to see one's attachment to self. We can seek ourselves in many things and even in seemingly holy pursuits like prayer. Why do we pray? Is it to advance in the spiritual life or is it simply to give time to the One whom we love and whom we know loves us? Do we seek consolations in prayer and abandon it when prayer becomes more difficult? We need a great deal of honesty and so this detachment from self must go hand in hand with true humility. Teresa is careful to point out that this detachment must be practised in little things because by being faithful in little things, we tend to become faithful in bigger things.

The best way, according to Teresa, to obtain the virtues of

love, humility and detachment is through prayer. She does not waste much time trying to explain the nature of love but she takes great pains to determine what it means in practice.[8] Perfection consists in the conformity of our wills with the divine will and this is attained by loving God and our neighbour.

> The highest perfection consists not in interior favours or in great raptures or in visions or in the spirit of prophecy, but in the bringing of our wills so closely into conformity with the will of God that as soon as we realise he wills anything, we desire it ourselves with all our might, and take the bitter with the sweet, knowing that to be His Majesty's will.[9]

God does not look only at external works but he looks at the love which lies behind them.[10] He alone can see to the heart. The Lord wants to give himself to us in love but he will not force this. God wants all to reach perfection but it is necessary that the individual actively disposes himself or herself by freeing his or her heart in order to receive God. Therefore the person must free his or her heart from all other things. Detachment is the preparation of the soil for the seed which is the love of God and given the right conditions, this seed will grow and flower into full union of the human and divine. Humility prepares the way for detachment. It prepares the soul to be empty so that it can receive the love of God. Humility is the foundation of the spiritual edifice and the Lord will never raise a person up much if that virtue is not very secure.[11]

Teresa puts prayer at the beginning of the spiritual life and it accompanies the whole development of the person producing ever more perfect fruit up to the fullness of holiness. To begin on the way of perfection means to begin on the way of prayer. Prayer is an intimate relationship of friendship with One whom we know loves us. The person who decides to give himself or herself to prayer must have a firm resolution not to stop at any obstacle. To this point Teresa often returns. This means that one must never give up prayer for any motive— false humility, sin, illness, criticism etc. The person must not think of consolations but only to conform his or her will with the will of God. Authentic prayer is recognized by its fruits and a continual life of prayer attracts the gifts of God. If we are content with mediocrity, then we will never progress very far. It is so easy to think that we are very good people when we have hardly begun to walk the road which leads to God. We must never be complacent or even content. God has created us for much, much more and he wants to give us much more if only we are willing to receive it.

The interior castle

Teresa's masterpiece is *The interior castle* because there we have her most profound thoughts on the spiritual life worked out in a systematic fashion. Fr Gracian, Teresa's great friend, asked her to write a book on prayer as the manuscript of her *Life* was in the hands of the Inquisition.

First mansions

The interior castle is the symbol of the human being.[12] The door of the castle is prayer and it is through prayer that one enters into oneself. Within this castle there are many rooms and the Lord himself lives in the innermost room at the very heart of the castle. God calls us to himself and we respond by entering into an intimate dialogue with him. Those who are deaf to his call, live outside the castle among the reptiles and insects. The first rooms of the castle are the rooms of self-knowledge. Humility is a natural consequence of a growth in self-knowledge.

Second mansions

In the second set of rooms or mansions are those who have made an earnest start in giving themselves to God, that is in Teresa's terms those who have begun to pray seriously. These people have a resolution to do God's will although it is still weak. The important thing at this time is to persevere because God is very patient with us even though we fall often. The danger at this stage is to return to the things which we have been called to leave behind. The second mansions are a vital stage of growth because here begins the parting of the ways between those who will live for God and those who will settle for mediocrity.

Third mansions

In the third mansions are those people who seem to be on the straight road to God. They desire very much not to sin, even in small ways and they generally live very good lives. There seems to be no good reason why these people should not progress much further in the spiritual life. However sometimes God sends these people little tests and immediately they begin to believe that they are martyrs. Yet God only withdraws his help a little to let them understand how imperfect they are. God wants to fill people with his love but first of all they must be made capable of receiving him. The capacity of the person for God in the third mansions is still very fragile.

The third mansions are a springboard for further progress but this stage can be rather dangerous. It is precisely because this state is so good that it can provide a stumbling block to further goodness. People at this stage can feel a secret satisfaction with themselves and they can think that they are spiritual people. Generally people do not commit gross sins at this point in their spiritual lives but their state is similar to that of a garden which has been recently weeded. The garden looks lovely, but just below the surface the roots of the weeds are busily preparing a new assault on the surface. People in the third mansions order their lives very well; their generosity is kept under control by good sense.

Often we expect God to reward us for our goodness. This is seldom a conscious idea because in our heads we know that we can merit nothing from God since all is gift. However in prayer, we can expect some consolations and when they do not come, we can easily become disgruntled. Why do I feel empty at prayer? Why does God not do his part, after all I am hardly a beginner? At this stage we have not grasped with the heart that all is grace and that we can only receive humbly and gratefully. We still lack the ardent love for God which would make us willing to put up with boredom in prayer and inconvenience etc. in life in general. So this is a dangerous state because it is so easy to become complacent. We can get used to the way we are and we can fail to see that there is still a long way ahead.

Fourth mansions

The fourth mansions are of great beauty and Teresa finds it very difficult to explain what there is to see here. She says that really to understand this state, one must experience it. Normally before entering these mansions, one will have spent a considerable time in the other mansions. Teresa points out that the way to make much progress is not to think much but to love much. Since that is the case, one must feel free in prayer—'do, then, whatever most arouses you to love'.[13] Teresa stresses that love is not an emotion but a decision—'for love consists not in the extent of our happiness but in the firmness of our determination to try to please God in everything, and to endeavour in all possible ways not to offend Him . . .'.[14]

It is in the fourth mansions that Teresa says 'we begin to touch the supernatural'.[15] This is where we enter the strange world of mysticism. God has made the person who enters these mansions capable of receiving him to a certain extent and now he begins to touch that person at the very core of his or her being. God is now preparing the person to be united with him in a way which surpasses all human understanding. This way is not for a privileged few but is offered to all. One modern writer stresses that the mystical way '. . . means being wholly possessed by God and that is holiness. One cannot be holy unless one is a mystic and if we do not become mystics in this life we become such hereafter.'[16] Many of the experiences which Teresa talks about are by no means normal. They are the effects of mystical graces in very few people. The more usual experience of mystical prayer is one of darkness in which the person is aware that God is powerfully at work but in no way 'sees' what God is doing.

The genuineness of any experience in prayer must be measured by its fruits. There must be a growth in humility and in the love of God and others. The important thing is to strive to love God simply because he is God and not because of anything he can give us. This is to love the God of all consolations and not the consolations of God.

What we find in the fourth mansions is not a deepening of what has gone before but is something completely new. This 'something new' is the beginning of a process which continues in the fifth and sixth mansions and is completed in the seventh. God continually offers us divine intimacy and by this time the person has accepted this offer and has done and continues to do all in his or her power to be open to receive this gift of God. Teresa says that it is in the fourth mansions that God begins to give us his Kingdom, not that he did not want to do so before this point but simply that before this, we were incapable of receiving it.

Fifth mansions

From now on, human language fails. There are simply no words adequately to explain what is going on in the depth of the soul. Teresa uses the analogy of the silkworm for the person who has travelled thus far.[17] At the beginning of its life, the worm grows by means of the natural helps which God offers. It is in the fifth mansions that the soul begins to spin its cocoon around itself. Within the cocoon great changes take place so that a beautiful butterfly may emerge. There is still suffering to be endured here. The little butterfly has left its old home, the cocoon, but it has not yet reached its true resting place in God. It flies around not knowing quite where to settle.

The person can still be led astray at this stage in very subtle ways. Self-love is always ready to eat away at us. We can think that we are loving God and others when in fact we are really self-seeking. Therefore this stage is one of growth in love. If there is no growth, there is something seriously wrong.

Sixth mansions

In these mansions, the person wants nothing else than to be eternally united with God. Suffering can be caused at this time by all sorts of things. Some people will praise such a one and this causes suffering because he or she knows that no merit attaches to him or her since all is grace. Furthermore the person realizes how little he or she has responded to the immensity of God's love. There can also be periods of great aridity when the feeling is that God has forgotten him or her. It is only the Lord who can relieve this distress. He does so by visiting the soul and wounding it by love. The person realizes that God is present but is unable to look upon him and this causes a sweet distress. The person feels at the same time deep distress and joyful tranquillity.

Looking back from this stage, the soul sees all its sins as dreadful. The person loves God so much that the slightest infidelity of the past seems gross and utter madness. He or she knows that if God were to allow him or her to fall from his hands, all would be lost since all the virtues which are possessed come as a free gift from God. There is generally great growth in the love of God at this time until the moment of total surrender into his hands.

Seventh mansions

This is the moment of the spiritual marriage between God and the soul. The two are united, never to be separated. The soul is brought into the intimate life of the Trinity and it experiences the mystery of faith that the One God is a trinity of persons. This is the stage of wholeness, of holiness, when the person becomes what he or she was created to be. Whatever the person does at this stage is done in, with and for God. The person's whole attention is on the Lord's will. Everything that happens is seen as coming directly from the hands of God. The love of such a one is truly great and he or she becomes a slave of God and of other people. There is less and less outward rest but normally there is great tranquillity within, no matter what is happening outside.

Conclusion

The spiritual direction which can be gleaned from the writings of St Teresa is always of a very practical manner. The acid test of any supposed experience or progress in the spiritual life is whether the person is becoming a better human being. The foundation of all progress is humility which makes us trust only in God and not in anything of our own. The basic Christian virtues are vital for a life of prayer and they authenticate it. Teresa gives her readers an ambition. Why should we settle for mediocrity when God is calling us to an intimate friendship with himself? 'Anyone who fails to go forward, begins to go back, and love, I believe, can never be content to stay for long where it is.'[18]

Notes

[1] Cf *Life*, 8, 5.

[2] *Life*, 13.

[3] *Ibid*.

[4] *Interior castle*, 3, 2, 12. All quotations from the works of St Teresa in this article are taken from the translation of E. Allison Peers.

[5] *Interior castle*, 5, 3, 12.

[6] 1 Thess 5:17.

[7] *Way of perfection*, 41, 3.

[8] Cf. *Foundations*, 5, 5.

[9] *Foundations*, 5, 10; cf. *Interior castle*, 5, 3.

[10] *Interior castle*, 7, 4, 18.

[11] *Ibid.*, 7, 4, 8.

[12] For an interesting modern interpretation of this and other symbols in the writings of St Teresa, see Welch, John: *Spiritual pilgrims: Carl Jung and Teresa of Avila* (New York, 1982).

[13] *Interior castle*, 4, 1, 7.

[14] *Ibid*.

[15] *Ibid.*, 4, 1, 1. See also *Spiritual relations*, 5 for Teresa's explanation of what she meant by 'supernatural prayer'.

[16] Burrows, Ruth: *Guidelines for mystical prayer* (London, 1976), p. 10. See also her *Interior castle explored* (London, 1981).

[17] *Interior castle*, 5, 2.

[18] *Ibid.*, 7, 4, 10.

(vol. 26, no. 4, October 1986)

'Our Conversation is in Heaven': An Introduction to the Spirituality of Fray Luis de León

Jane Tillier

Unless you have had the good fortune to study Spanish literature at some stage in your life to date, it is unlikely that you
will have heard of the sixteenth-century Augustinian Fray
Luis de León. At best you will have seen him mentioned in
passing, as in the comprehensive book entitled *The study of
spirituality*, where the chapter on John of the Cross and Teresa
of Avila is followed by a short section headed 'Other Spanish
spiritual writers'.[1] Whilst not wishing to make exaggerated
claims for Fray Luis by placing him alongside these well-
known Spanish spiritual 'greats', I feel sure that there is nevertheless a good deal to be gained from reading and reflecting on
his life and work. I offer the following pages by way of
introduction, in the hope that some insights may arise from
my observations which will lead to further acquaintance with
the work of this rather neglected spiritual guide.

The one anecdote which just about every Spaniard knows
about Fray Luis is probably merely a popular fabrication. I say
'merely', and yet the very fact that a legend should grow up
around someone suggests that his life has some enduring
significance. To this day Spaniards will report how, after a
four-year imprisonment by the Inquisition, Fray Luis
returned to the lecture theatre in the University of Salamanca
and restarted his lecture series with the customary words
Dicebamus hesterna die—'As we were saying yesterday...'.
Such understated defiance of the powers that be obviously has
considerable appeal and encapsulates something of the tenor of
the life of this unusually gifted man. In 1541, at the age of
about fourteen, Luis de León began his studies in Salamanca
and his association with the Augustinians. He was formally

admitted to the order in 1544 and by 1561 he had been elected to the Chair of St Thomas Aquinas at the University of Salamanca.

At a time when Latin was the only acceptable language of theological study and the Vulgate the 'official' translation of the Bible, Fray Luis increasingly found himself in conflict with the authorities, both as a Hebrew scholar critical of the Vulgate, in defiance of the edict of the Council of Trent, and as a spiritual teacher committed to the accessibility of scripture and theology in the vernacular. It is important to remember throughout the coming pages that this underlies the whole of Fray Luis's spirituality. In him we find an inspiring example of courageous critical dialogue with tradition arising from his commitment to the whole people of God. We might perhaps find modern parallels for such a concern in, for example, the work of some liberation theologians or Christian feminists.

Among other things Fray Luis had written a commentary on his own Spanish translation of the Song of Songs for his cousin Isabel Osorio, a nun. It seems to have been intended only for her private reading but a copy fell into the wrong hands and was to be used in evidence against him by the Inquisition. He had anyway been known to be openly critical of the Vulgate and he was not without enemies on account of his outspokenness and intellectual integrity. It was, therefore, not so very surprising that he should be denounced to the Inquisition and arrested. This was in 1572, and it was not until 1576 that he was finally pronounced innocent. Although sick and frail on his release he nevertheless returned to active intellectual debate and to his committed involvement in both secular and religious affairs. It is well worth keeping in mind all the indications of Luis de León's active secular life as we come later to look at his emphasis on retreat and withdrawal. It is clear from the biographical detail that we have about him that in his own life the two were not mutually exclusive but went hand in hand. His contemporaries obviously held him in very high regard and he was awarded the Chair of Moral Philosophy in 1578 and that of Biblical Studies in 1579. Just nine days before his death in 1591 he heard that he had been elected Provincial of the Augustinian order in Castile.

Nowadays Luis de León is best known as a poet and his

small corpus of works is frequently studied. This was not the case during his lifetime. His poems were published posthumously in 1631 by Francisco de Quevedo as an example of the classical virtues of poetry that is restrained and concise. Quevedo hoped that they would prove to be something of a corrective to the affected style fashionable in poetry of the time. Among his contemporaries Fray Luis was renowned primarily as a scholastic theologian. The main focus for attention in these pages will be his vernacular treatise *De los nombres de Cristo (The names of Christ)* which is often cited as a landmark in the development of Spanish prose.[2] In it one can detect not only the hand of the poet and that of the trained academic theologian but also the depth of a man of prayer committed to assisting others to follow a spiritually enriching path. Besides being central to Fray Luis's thinking and teaching this work has the added advantage that it is readily accessible in an English translation. In the coming pages I propose to consider how this treatise is presented as well as what it is saying. It will be seen that to some extent the two are inseparable in that the very nature of the presentation of the material constitutes a tangible expression of beliefs. Underlying both of these areas of concern will be the question of why the work might be of significance as we examine traditions of spiritual guidance today.

The language of scholarly debate and theological reflection in sixteenth-century Spain was Latin and it is a mark of Fray Luis's breadth of understanding and commitment that he undertook to compose more than one substantial treatise in the vernacular. His expressed aim in the dedication which heads *The names of Christ* is 'to write something for the people of Christ'.[3] The result is a stimulating fusion of theological and spiritual exploration and teaching in which the insights of academic study rub shoulders with those of prayerful devotion, both bearing equal weight and emphasis. Luis de León's prose is rich and elegant, his thought complex and profound, and yet the work is exemplary in its accessibility and lack of pretension. (Many a modern writer on spirituality could learn much from this alone!)

The book takes the form of a relaxed conversation between three friends who have chosen to spend some time away together at the Augustinian retreat of La Flecha in the country-side a little way from Salamanca. The beauty of the surround-ings provides a natural setting for the group's reflections on the nature of God as revealed in the person of Jesus Christ. A clear structure is given to these insights by the systematic exploration of each of a list of names attributed to Christ in the Bible. The written list, held by Sabino, one of the friends, acts as a prompt to discussion. It includes names derived typologi-cally from Old Testament references as well as those used directly in the New Testament. It is not clear—nor is it important—how far the group of friends is fictitious and how far it is based on real individuals. Sabino is the sensitive poet who is easily moved by the sights and sounds around him. Juliano has an enquiring mind, and is never afraid to interrupt the flow of conversation in order to clarify a point or to ask a searching question. Marcelo is the experienced academic theo-logian and teacher who leads the others in their reflections and acts as a knowledgeable resource during their deliberations. Many see this last as the character most likely to represent the author himself.

It is clear then that the style of this 'retreat' is slightly different from the sort of thing we might be used to. Fray Luis often suggests that we can best approach God through the natural world, in solitude, by withdrawing from the demands of the daily round. His most famous poem, *La vida retirada*, is a meditation on this very theme based on Horace's ode *Beatus ille*.[4] On numerous occasions city life is characterized as noisy and distracting and life in the countryside is presented as a welcome contrast. This is most noticeable in the section of *The names of Christ* where the name 'shepherd' is under discussion:

> In the first place, pastoral life is a tranquil one, which flows far from the noises, vices, and pleasures of the city. We find in this tranquil life a great innocence, similarly in its labor and the activity to which it is attached. It has its pleasures, born from things simpler, purer, and more natural: from the view of the open sky, from the purity of the air, from the forms of the countryside, from the green of the grass, from the beauty of the roses and the flowers.[5]

It may seem a little idealized, but what Fray Luis is suggesting is that it is in natural surroundings that we can find conditions conducive to responding to the peace offered to us by God. I found an echo of such a sentiment, though without the explicitly Christian content, in the introduction to a book of walks which I used whilst visiting the Lake District earlier this year:

> In the natural beauty of the countryside one can find an oasis of reassurance in the confusing desert of changing modern values. . . . All we have to do is to awaken our senses and willingly accept nature's messages in sight, scent and sound.[6]

The quotation could almost have come from Fray Luis; the sentiments expressed are so close to his own thinking. This is an area where insights certainly seem as relevant to twentieth-century England as they were to sixteenth-century Spain. It is also important to remember that in his case such convictions were coupled with his day-to-day life of challenging engagement.

The section of the treatise entitled 'Prince of Peace' is one of the most beautiful in the book and those who are interested may like to note that it provides something of a commentary on one of Fray Luis's most accomplished poems, *Noche serena*. In the following passage we see how Marcelo makes use of his surroundings to help his friends to understand a point he wishes to make:

> 'Let us define this peace, this grace, and its effect upon us,' Marcelo said, and while he was speaking he was gazing at the flowing current of the river, pure and shining, a mirror to all the heavenly stars, and then, pointing out toward the river with his hand, said, 'This flowing river, this dark water reflecting the stars which seems like a second starry sky, can help us understand the meaning of God's grace. The same way that the sky is reflected in the water, which acts as a mirror, and turns the river into something very similar to the sky, in the same fashion divine grace coming down to our souls and taking over our minds turns us into an image of God. . . .'[7]

Such insights are normally found in solitary contemplation and Fray Luis writes frequently about the importance of solitude. His understanding of the nature of solitude is broad. For example, one does not normally expect to find solitude by going away with a group of friends. And yet Fray Luis presents the group's experience as one of solitude, as they find themselves so united in a common purpose. Extroverts like myself, who find themselves nourished and energized by interaction with others, will doubtless join me in welcoming the fact that what we have here is tantamount to an articulation of a sort of 'group work' spirituality. Nor is it even as contrived as that suggests. It is simply that the pleasant company of good friends is seen as a valid place of withdrawal and a stimulating environment for profound spiritual and theological reflection. The friends share not only thoughts and feelings, quotations from scripture and passages from the Church Fathers, they also read and comment on poetry, tease one another and laugh together. And these timeless activities take place on a sunny June day in the shade of trees and by a river or in the cool of the evening as the first stars appear in the sky.

It is beneficial to be reminded of the enormously positive results which can be achieved when a group of friends are given time and space to reflect together in this way. For a number of years I took a group of students out of Cambridge for a day in June after they had finished their exams. We went to the community at Little Gidding and the day had no fixed plan or agenda. Perhaps these groups of students would be able to say that their experience on these occasions reflects to some extent that of the friends of La Flecha? Perhaps one year I should have tried suggesting to them that they look at the names of Christ together in a group?

The conversation between friends which we have in *The names of Christ* is derived from the classical dialogue form. It has been placed in a distinctive setting and is used in the service of Christian reflection. The eclectic mind of the Renaissance humanist draws on a wealth of knowledge from a wide range of sources. These include not only the classical and the Christian but also, some scholars suggest, the Kabbalah and Sufi mystic tradition. Fray Luis writes not just as an academic but also as a member of a religious order and as a poet of considerable talent. His way of presenting his work demonstrates that all of these aspects are gifts from God which can be placed in the service of others. With this particular combination of interests Fray Luis was not slow to recognize the merits of a near contemporary writer. He offered us a considerable service by preparing a posthumous edition of some of the work of Teresa of Avila which he published in 1588. He never actually met her but it is clear that he had a great admiration for the woman and her work.

Like Teresa one of the things which Fray Luis endorses in his work is the free use of imagery in response to spiritual truths. This is partly a product of his poetic imagination and partly an indication of his affirmation of the validity of an individual's spiritual freedom before God. He is consistently and repeatedly clear about the inadequacy of any of our language about God. We shall only be able to know and name God when we finally stand in God's presence. One of the reasons for looking at the names attributed to Christ is that they provide a means of exploring some of the facets of God's self-revelation to us. In the following passage Marcelo concludes his introduction to the topic under discussion:

> Let us approach the subject proper of our undertaking . . . and see why Christ is given so many names. This is so because of his limitless greatness and the treasury of his very rich perfections and with them the host of functions and other benefits that are born in Him and spread over us. Just as they cannot be embraced by the soul's vision, so much less can a single word name them. It is like someone pouring water into a glass with a long narrow neck, who adds it drop by drop; so also the Holy Spirit, who knows the narrowness and poverty of our understanding, does not give us that greatness all at once but offers it to us in drops, telling us, at times, something under one name, and some other thing, at other times, under another name.[8]

To acknowledge our inadequacy in naming is not to offer an excuse for complacency in seeking to know God. Fray Luis presents us with a gracious and gradual self-revelation of God through the Spirit offered in a way that is tailored to each individual. The passage is beautifully written, giving us a commonplace, concrete image for faith seeking understanding by the grace of God.

One of the indications of the clarity of the imagery used by Luis de León is the fact that it stands the test of translation and the passage of time. He communicates with ease the nature of the truths he is seeking to expound. In the section of the book in which the friends examine the significance of Christ calling himself 'the way' we find the following image used by Marcelo:

> Have you not seen some mothers, Sabino, who holding with their two hands the two hands of their children, make them put their feet upon theirs and so carry them forwards and embrace them, and are thus their ground and their guide? Oh, what goodness is God's! In the same way You act, Lord, toward our weakness as children.[9]

This portrayal of Christ as our ground and our guide is attractive and inspiring both through its content: a God who is tender and gentle with us; and through the manner in which it is presented to us: in the homely image of a mother playing with her child. I write at a time when feminists have awakened us to the great wealth of the often ignored stores of feminine images for God and Christ in the works of the great spiritual writers through the ages. It is a pleasure to be able to add another refreshing example of this to the sometimes over-worked group of well-known examples (such as that of Julian of Norwich), especially since I feel that it is a more satisfying and complete image than many of those already available to us.

I hope that it is not difficult to see why I feel that the writings of Fray Luis have an enduring spiritual appeal. The relationship with God which he describes is one of open childlike trust. The God he portrays is understanding and multi-faceted, accessible to us in the person of Christ and in the many names by which he is known. Our capacity for comprehension of God is limited but we are to take heart as a result of the ways in which we can increase and develop our understanding by knowledge of Christ, by acquaintance with the scriptures, by enjoyment of the world which God has created and through sharing with friends.

By way of conclusion I should like to look briefly at the title I have chosen for this short introduction to the spirituality of Fray Luis de León. It is a literal rendering of the Vulgate translation of a verse from Philippians: *Nostra autem conversatio in caelis est...* (3:20). It is significant that when Fray Luis quotes it he does not question this version but translates it literally. He was enough of a biblical scholar to challenge it if he chose. And we have seen that he was not afraid to be critical of the Vulgate if he thought it necessary. In this particular instance this rather idiosyncratic rendering of what is normally translated as 'commonwealth' or 'citizenship' suits his purpose rather well. 'Conversation' stands as an image for social interaction comparable with 'commonwealth' or 'citizenship'. Throughout *The names of Christ* we are witnessing a conversation between friends. In turn these friends, by the nature of their subject, are in conversation with the Word of God. Finally, as readers and as Christians, we ourselves are also engaged in a process of interaction with the text and with God. The main focus of the book, the crucial tenet underlying the spirituality of Fray Luis de León, is the importance of communication. His presentation of a three-way conversation, his subject matter and his vivid use of imagery all illustrate this. He is concerned to show the ways in which God communicates with us, the ways in which we seek to communicate with God, and the essential God-given unity which we will find when we truly communicate with one another.

Notes

[1] *The study of spirituality*, ed. Cheslyn Jones, Geoffrey Wainwright and Edward Yarnold (London: SPCK, 1986; New York: Oxford University Press, 1987), p. 377. The present study is by nature only introductory. Anyone interested in further reading should consult Bell, Aubrey F. G.: *Luis de León* (Oxford: OUP, 1925) and the comprehensive study by Thompson, Colin P.: *The strife of tongues: Fray Luis de León and the Golden Age of Spain* (Cambridge: CUP, 1988) which is the most authoritative and inspiring English study of his work.

[2] Fray Luis de León, *De los nombres de Cristo*, ed. Federico de Onís (Clásicos Castellanos, vols 28, 33 and 41; Madrid: Espasa-Calpe, 1966–69). For an English translation see: Luis de León, *The names of Christ*, trans. Manuel

Durán and William Kluback (The Classics of Western Spirituality; London: SPCK, 1984; Mahwah, NJ: Paulist Press, 1984). Quotations from the text are taken from this translation with minor alterations (based on my own translation of the original) where necessary for ease of comprehension.

[3] *The names of Christ*, p. 39.

[4] For the poetry see: *The unknown light: the poems of Fray Luis de León*, trans. Willis Barnstone (Albany: State University of New York Press, 1979).

[5] *The names of Christ*, p. 88.

[6] Parker, John: *Walk the Lakes*, Bartholomew Map and Guide (Edinburgh: Bartholomew, 1983), p. 5.

[7] *The names of Christ*, p. 224.

[8] *The names of Christ*, pp. 52–53.

[9] *The names of Christ*, p. 81.

(vol. 28, no. 4, October 1988)

St Ignatius of Loyola and
Spiritual Direction

Philip Sheldrake SJ

A contemporary writer has suggested that the *Spiritual Exercises* of St Ignatius of Loyola are 'the foundation for the development of a whole school of spiritual direction'.[1] I would suggest, however, that we must be very careful about uncritically removing certain items from the text of the Exercises in order to construct a model for spiritual direction in the widest sense. It is true that the Exercises have produced generations of spiritual directors. Such people are not limited to members of St Ignatius's religious order, the Society of Jesus, nor indeed to members of the Roman Catholic Church. However, it must be borne in mind that much that appears in the Exercises or in the early collections of notes on giving them (called the 'directories') refers to the very specific context of a retreat.

Having said this, it remains true that the basis for spiritual direction in the Ignatian tradition must be, first of all, the observations and practical notes contained in the *Spiritual Exercises*,[2] and in the early 'directories'.[3] These notes are disparate comments on specific points rather than an organic body of definitive guidance for spiritual directors.

In writing this article I have confined myself to the ideas of St Ignatius and other early sources rather than discussed the subsequent history of Ignatian spiritual direction. For this reason I have not considered the 1599 'official' directory as a resource.[4] It must always be remembered that 'the Exercises are essentially a point of departure'.[5] It is therefore important to link the basics of direction in the Exercises with what Ignatius has to say in his letters and in the *Constitutions* of the Society of Jesus if we are to arrive at a more rounded picture.[6]

Finally, I would suggest that Ignatius's vision was that the *Spiritual Exercises* and the spirituality which came from it could only be transmitted in a vital way from person to person, for he saw the Exercises as an *experience* rather than a collection of spiritual maxims. Thus Ignatius sought to form people who would *live* the Exercises until their minds were simply reflections of its spirit. If this is the case it may be argued, perhaps, that it is futile to attempt to present a systematic approach to giving the Exercises or to spiritual direction in general. I have not attempted to do this. What follows is no more than a collection of notes on a few important aspects of direction in general (rather than in the retreat experience): the nature of the relationship between director and the one directed; the focus or content of spiritual direction; and finally, some reflections on Ignatius's teaching on prayer.

Although Ignatius never used the words 'director' or 'directee', and although much of the traditional language of spiritual guidance can give a very false impression, I have reluctantly continued to use such words in this article for the sake of brevity and because they are still commonplace.

The relationship of director with directee

A number of contemporary writers have described the primary aim of Ignatius as helping an individual to true inner freedom.[7] Certainly he himself describes the Exercises as 'every way of preparing and disposing the soul to rid itself of all inordinate attachments . . .' (Exx 1). Again, in the preamble to the text proper he describes the purpose of the Exercises as 'the conquest of self and the regulation of one's life in such a way that no decision is made under the influence of any inordinate attachment' (Exx 21). Spiritual direction, therefore, is to be a context for this vital freedom to grow.

Without any doubt this desire for the inner freedom of an individual colours the way in which Ignatius envisages the relationship with a director. The absolute foundation, the 'presupposition' without which the relationship cannot function properly, is mutual trust (Exx 22).[8] In his 'presupposi-

tion' Ignatius draws attention to the very real danger of cate-
gorizing, judging or misinterpreting people. Prejudice is out
of place. One should always put a good interpretation on what
is said. Confrontation is to be avoided: if a person seems to be
wrong one should first clarify whether one has understood
correctly and if correction seems necessary it should be gentle.
In other words, a director needs to become aware of his or her
own inner reactions.

The person being directed will only arrive at the openness
about inner feelings that Ignatius sees as vital for spiritual
direction if there is real trust. If a person appears to have no
such feelings or 'spiritual experiences' the director is instructed
to ask questions (Exx 6). For it is only if there is a faithful and
honest account of thoughts, feelings, experiences and distur-
bances that a director can 'propose some spiritual exercises in
accordance with the degree of progress made and suited and
adapted' to the needs of the individual (Exx 17). Ignatius
points out in his Rules for discernment that there is often a real
temptation not to be honest with a director when difficulties
arise. This must be resisted (Exx 326).

Openness in direction is also mentioned by Ignatius in the
Jesuit *Constitutions*. In dialogue with the superior, Jesuits
should keep nothing hidden, whether interior or exterior, 'in
order that the superior might better direct them along the path
of perfection' (*Const* 551). From the very beginning, novices
should open themselves in confidence to superiors or to their
spiritual guide in order to receive 'counsel and aid in everything' (*Const* 263).

The importance that Ignatius attached to spiritual guidance
is underlined by the fact that all Jesuits were asked to give a full
account of themselves at least once a year (*Const* 97). This was
seen as being of 'great or even extraordinary importance'
(*Const* 91). It was presupposed that every Jesuit, from novice
to professed, had someone to whom they went for spiritual
guidance. In the case of novices this was either the novice-
master or 'whomever the superior appoints as being more fit
for this charge' (*Const* 264). Rectors of communities had the
duty to appoint someone to superintend spiritual matters for
young Jesuit students (*Const* 431). The Jesuit superior himself
also had the role and authority of a 'spiritual father' and could

advise on the prayer life of individual Jesuits (*Const* 341, 583). Professed Jesuits could deal either with the superior or with a regular confessor on such matters (*Const* 584). Ignatius often uses the word 'obedience' in reference to the attitude of Jesuits to their superior or confessor in spiritual matters. There is a sense, too, in which this also applies in spiritual direction in general, for the relationship cannot function if a person continually refuses to follow advice or suggestions. 'Obviously anyone who refuses to obey the director and wants to follow his own judgement should not continue to make the exercises.'[9]

A director should always remember that the fundamental relationship is that between God and the person coming for direction. So the director is to allow 'the Creator to deal directly with the creature, and the creature directly with his Creator and Lord' (Exx 15). Directors must be careful not to impose their own ideas but should entrust directees to God 'that he should not permit that for the sins of one who gives the exercises any soul should be ensnared'.[10] The editor of Ignatius's autobiography, da Camara, records in his own diary that 'the Father [Ignatius] said to me that there can be no greater mistake, in his view in things of the Spirit, than to want to mould others to one's own image'.[11] As a modern experienced director has suggested, to stand off and to be patient and objective in direction is a very difficult role to maintain. It is easy to become either too close (over-identification) or to become too impatient.[12]

Because the role of a director is secondary and supportive of the fundamental relationship with God, he or she should be a balance without 'leaning to one side or the other' (Exx 15) and should be extremely careful not to put undue pressure on someone to undertake any course of action (Exx 14).[13] This does not mean that the director's role is negligible because it is not a matter of being merely a passive sponge! It is perfectly valid, humbly and sensitively, to help a person to follow what best serves God.[14] This search for what is 'better' in a relationship with God is a frequent reference point in the Exercises and is at the centre of spiritual direction in general as well.

The human guide must avoid seeking, unconsciously perhaps, to do what is God's work. Direction is not primarily a classroom and should not be over didactic (Exx 2).[15] Interviews should not be too frequent for there is a danger of creating over-dependence by seeing a directee too often.[16] The emphasis, too, should be less on intellectual input or talking 'learnedly about God' than on guiding people towards self-discovery and the meaning of their own experiences.[17] For as Ignatius succinctly comments, 'it is not much knowledge that fills and satisfies the soul but the intimate understanding and relish of the truth' (Exx 2). In other words the director's task is to help the individual 'to articulate, clarify and distinguish what is occurring within him'.[18]

Ignatius's comments about brevity of explanation also imply that what people discover for themselves has a deeper effect. If a person is prone to fluctuations of feelings (what Ignatius terms 'consolation' and 'desolation') and finds this confusing, the director is to explain the various rules for discernment (Exx 8). In other words, people must be helped to discern for themselves instead of relying merely on the director. Ignatius clearly wanted the development of self-awareness in people. 'Our Father wanted us, in all our activities, as far as possible, to be free, at ease in ourselves, and obedient to the light given particularly to each one.'[19] The discipline of reporting to a director is itself an education in discerning for oneself, for what is reported is already sifted and assessed as important. The *Constitutions* indicate that Ignatius anticipated that spiritually mature people would be able to function to a great extent on their own, but even those at an earlier stage were to be trusted to some degree with the conduct of their own spiritual lives. In his remarks on penance in the Exercises, Ignatius suggests that people should experiment for themselves 'for he [God] often grants each one the grace to understand what is suitable for him' (Exx 89).[20]

A director should not seek unnecessary information for while openness is vital, the privacy of each must be respected (Exx 17). The focus should be on the present and most especially on inner experiences or feelings for direction is essentially a response to these (Exx 6, 17).[21] Yet it is also true that 'the particular inner movements . . . only take on meaning for direction against the background of the personal, spiritual and relational structures of his concrete life and experience'.[22]

So Ignatius would not have objected to a director seeking to know the directee reasonably well. It has been argued that his concern was more with the director's *motivation* in seeking information.[23]

In the end, the aim of any information is to help the director to speak helpfully to a particular person's needs and to adapt what is said to the right level or stage of growth. Generalizations, spiritual maxims or universal rules for the spiritual life are not part of Ignatius's method. In a letter to Francis Borgia in 1548, Ignatius strongly affirms the need for flexibility. Sometimes a person needs penance or a certain kind of prayer, at others he or she needs something different. Likewise progress necessarily makes methods which were once useful no longer so.[24]

This attitude of flexible response by the director is reinforced by some of the observations in the Exercises that allow for adaptation of material (Exx 4, 18, 19, 20). Likewise, in the *Constitutions* Ignatius returns to the same theme in his treatment of prayer. Those who do not seem to be advancing by one method should be guided by the superior towards some alternative. Spiritual directors should always keep in view the 'circumstances of persons, times and places' (e.g. *Const* 343).

Ignatius is clear that a director should be neither too firm nor too lenient. If a person is suffering distractions or dryness it may help to suggest more prayer (Exx 13).[25] In the Exercises the director should always encourage perseverance in prayer particularly if there is a temptation to give up or to cut corners (Exx 12). Yet the director must also be sensitive to weakness. When someone is in difficulty or suffering from temptation or desolation the director is to be gentle and kind and always encouraging, thus offering the necessary hope 'to prepare and dispose him for coming consolation' (Exx 7). One of the early directories adds that a director should not press 'melancholic types'. 'Rather be careful to keep them open.'[26]

Focus of direction

St Ignatius affirms both that prayer and life should be integrated and yet that the primary focus of spiritual direction is 'religious experience' and a person's relationship with God. In his own practice, Ignatius's aim was always 'to discover the concrete will of God and to bring it to completion'.[27] He was primarily concerned 'with leading those entrusted to him to a spiritual experience. . . . The person should receive an inner sense for the workings of God's grace.'[28]

Thus the introductory notes in the Exercises fix the attention both of the director and of the directee firmly on prayer. That being said, should spiritual direction limit itself purely to prayer? Certainly spiritual direction outside a 'closed retreat' (whether ordinary direction or the 'Exercises in daily life') will not be detached 'from all friends and acquaintances and from all worldly cares' (Exx 20). Quite the contrary! However, even within the Exercises, there is implicit reference to the fact that 'religious experience' is not to be limited to the time of explicit prayer. For example the general examen of conscience presents a way of reflecting on what happens in daily life (Exx 43).[29] Likewise the 'Contemplation to attain the love of God' at the close of the Exercises offers a form of prayer that focuses explicitly on the ways in which prayer acts in the world and in daily life (Exx 230–237).

The Exercises clearly assume that certain fundamental attitudes that lie behind what happens in prayer will also be an important focus in direction. The most important is generosity which enables a person to offer self to God. Obviously generosity will never be total and will appear as an issue at various times in direction (Exx 5). One of the early directories also mentions another attitude—the gradual purification of motives in prayer so that one does not seek consolation or anything else for its own sake.[30] A most important attitude is to centre on the 'here and now' rather than on an unhealthy and introspective stirring around in the past. This is one interpretation of an aspect of the introductory notes that is suggested by a modern commentator (Exx 17).[31]

As we have seen, Ignatius's emphasis in prayer is very much on the 'affective' and on inner feelings. It is not so much ideas that matter as 'the intimate understanding and relish of the truth' (Exx 2). A modern commentator has suggested that Ignatius learned from his own process of conversion that the alternation of 'affective experiences' or inner reactions was the main criterion for determining how God is leading a person. It is this awareness of the significance of such experiences that led Ignatius to affirm strongly that God must be allowed to deal freely with the individual and that the director should question carefully about them.[32]

Because Ignatius believed that there was an intimate link between prayer and externals such as environment, preparation, place and posture, he suggests that a director should ask about such things, especially if prayer is dry or distracted. The details of these 'externals' are to be found in what are called the 'additional directions' (Exx 73–90). Equally, Ignatius, in line with his philosophy that the physical is important in prayer, has a number of remarks about diet (Exx 210–217). This insight that the whole of life, including food, should be in proper order to aid inner growth finds an echo in other traditions—not least in such non-Christian ones as yoga or Zen where diet is part and parcel of the way to enlightenment.

Much the same motivation (that the body and external environment play a part in spiritual growth) lies behind Ignatius's concern that austerities or penance should also be in proper order. The director is exhorted to keep an eye on this while at the same time allowing the individual to experiment freely (Exx 82–90). Certainly no penances must be imposed. The aim is not in any sense a rejection of the body as a hindrance but the search for a proper balance in living. In a letter to Borgia, Ignatius emphasizes that in the end inner gifts are to be preferred to outward austerities. The body is not to be abused. 'We should love the body in so far as it is obedient and helpful to the soul, since the soul with the body's help and service is better disposed for the service and praise of our Creator and Lord.'[33] In another letter to a Spanish nun he exhorts her to take great care of the body, to take proper nourishment, recreation and adequate sleep.[34]

In all these matters moderation is the key. 'If one fails to observe this moderation, he will find that good is turned to evil and virtue to vice.'[35] And so a director is to keep a careful eye on this danger.[36] For the same reason Ignatius exhorts Jesuits to follow the superior's judgement in order to avoid vanity.[37]

Finally, a central focus of spiritual direction is the development of discernment, particularly that which is appropriate to different stages of spiritual growth (Exx 8, 10, 14).[38] The one who comes for direction needs it even to establish what should be mentioned in dialogue with the director as we have already seen. A director can help by showing the directee how to make a brief period of reflection after prayer and how to keep notes on this (Exx 77).[39] The main body of Ignatius's teaching on discernment, however, is contained in the Rules which appear in the Exercises and which the director should explain as appropriate to the directee (Exx 313–336). There is no room to discuss these in such a brief article and in any case there are several good commentaries available in English.[40] The Rules help both director and directee to understand the significance of inner feelings or reactions—in other words how to sift experience in order to distinguish the true and helpful from the false and misleading.

It is clear that Ignatius did not see his teaching on discernment as limited either to a closed retreat or to an early stage in spiritual growth. He felt it helpful to discuss it (especially the nature of consolation, desolation and scruples) in his dealings even with people who had made considerable progress.[41] There do remain serious questions about the practical validity of the Rules in the later stages of growth in prayer. The great analyst of mysticism, Poulain, implies that at least the teaching on consolation and desolation remain useful.[42] Ignatius himself recognizes a difference between what were traditionally called the purgative and illuminative ways (Exx 10). The strong oscillation of feelings is associated with the First Week (or earlier stage in the spiritual journey). As commitment deepens, Ignatius suggests that deceptive good or the 'enemy' posing as an angel of light will be more significant. The dangers become those of false humility or spiritual élitism.[43] The greater subtlety of the remarks in the Rules for the Second Week seem to me to indicate that movement or interior feelings will be much less obvious. If so, this indicates a need to be very careful in the application of Ignatius's remarks (Exx 17) about the director questioning the absence of such movements.

St Ignatius and prayer

Because a person seeking spiritual direction will as a matter of course wish to discuss prayer experiences and will hope for guidance in this area, it seems useful to look briefly at St Ignatius's teaching on prayer. It is important to allay fears that Ignatius had a narrow view of prayer or that directors in the Ignatian tradition are bound to impose particular forms of prayer on those being directed.

Obviously it is helpful to begin with some brief remarks about prayer as it is presented in the book of the *Spiritual Exercises*. The one being directed should be taught about the importance of preparation and recollection. Although the remarks on recollection (for example calling to mind the material for the day's prayer upon rising) are tailored to a closed retreat, the general principle is still valid in a wider context. The specific activity of praying needs to be rooted in some general cultivation of awareness and reflection. Likewise it is helpful, even in daily life, to prepare for prayer by deciding what one is going to do and why (cf. Exx 73–74).

Ignatius, in addition, points out the importance of place for prayer, without specifying where it should be. But he does seem to imply that it need not be a chapel or church (Exx 79). In practice it is important for each person to decide what is the best place. Wherever the 'holy ground' is, Ignatius suggests that a physical act of reverence (perhaps a profound bow) may be useful. There is considerable stress on the importance of posture. Again each person should discover the one which is most helpful and Ignatius's wide range of suggestions indicates a great freedom in this regard (Exx 76). Apart from place and posture, he also points out that the use of light or darkness should be varied as seems appropriate or helpful (Exx 79).

With regard to the length of prayer, Ignatius certainly seems to insist on the space of one hour in the context of the Exercises (Exx 12–13). However, as we shall see, he was far more flexible when it came to prayer in everyday life. The remarks in the Exercises do have some importance and that is to emphasize the need for faithfulness to what has been decided before prayer about the length. Otherwise the danger is that one cuts corners, or gives up when times are hard. There is the possibility of important growth in perseverance.

When we turn to the structure of prayer as proposed in the Exercises it may seem that it is over-detailed and something of a strait-jacket. However, one has to bear in mind two things. Firstly, that Ignatius's great principle was flexibility and adaptation in the light of the needs of the individual. Secondly, the presentation in the Exercises is a form of shorthand for the director and there is a danger in treating it in an over-literal or 'fundamentalist' way. Throughout the various phases of the Exercises there are indeed certain constants which Ignatius clearly feels are of special value: a preparatory prayer (which amounts to a conscious act of presence to God); focusing on the 'subject matter' of the prayer (or, in other words, what I am about to do), and asking for what I desire or sense I need. The latter is not some way of twisting God's arm or limiting his freedom. It is an acknowledgment that prayer is God's action and that I need his grace. It is also an explicit acknowledgment of the needs that have already been revealed to me by God's grace and therefore indicates a kind of purposefulness in my prayer. But my desires are always in need of refinement and therefore I place what I know before God, trusting that his Spirit will act upon them and transform them if this is necessary.

Throughout the Exercises, the methods or structures of the subsequent periods of prayer vary a great deal. It is vital to keep in mind Ignatius's principle that one should remain where there is 'fruit' or benefit and not feel bound to move on (Exx 76). There is no justification for supposing that Ignatius thought of prayer as a syllabus or some set of hoops to jump through!

Contrary to popular mythology in the not so distant past, Ignatius did not promote any *one* method of prayer (even in the Exercises) and one should be extremely cautious about talking about '*the* Ignatian method'. At the very beginning of the Exercises he defines 'spiritual exercises' as '*every* method of examination of conscience, meditation, contemplation, of vocal and mental prayer...' (Exx 1). If one lists the many approaches that appear in the pages of the Exercises, it will be seen that they represent a great range of possibilities: the two forms of 'examen' (Exx 24–26, 43); discursive meditation of the three powers of the soul (cf. for example, Exx 45–54); gospel contemplation with the use of imagination (Second to Fourth Weeks, for example Exx 110–117); the prayer of finding God in the world and in life called the 'Contemplation to attain the love of God' (Exx 230–237); the three methods of prayer (Exx 238–260) which include a measured repetition of words linked to breathing. One might also include the 'colloquy' that appears at the end of every period of prayer throughout the Exercises. Although this is presented as part both of meditation and contemplation rather than as a method on its own, it does underline that Ignatius saw familiar conversation with God as a valid aspect of prayer.

Finally, the Exercises provide evidence for the fact that Ignatius anticipates a process of simplification in prayer. The 'repetitions' throughout the Exercises are a form of simpler prayer, in which the person is invited to concentrate on less 'material'. 'We should pay attention to and dwell upon those points in which we have experienced greater consolation or desolation or greater spiritual appreciation' (Exx 62). The 'Application of the Senses' which is introduced in the Second Week as the final period of prayer in the day is once again a form of simplified prayer with more emphasis on the 'affective'. The process of simplification is further underlined by the fact that Ignatius suggests less and less material as the basis for each day's prayer as the Exercises progress.

W. H. Longridge, the Anglican translator and commentator on the Exercises, argued strongly that, both within the framework of the Exercises and elsewhere, Ignatius provided sufficiently for all types of people—even for those who are genuinely contemplative and (using traditional language) in the illuminative or unitive ways.[44] He pointed out that even in the earlier stages of the Exercises the 'repetitions' demand that the understanding 'be restrained' in order to give more scope to the affections. 'Repetitions should in fact be made more after the manner of affective prayer than of meditation so called.'[45] Longridge felt that Ignatius placed considerable importance on 'repetitions', particularly after the middle of the Second Week because 'without them our meditations would often be in danger of becoming shallow, scarcely going beyond the intellectual exercises, and missing that interior savour of the truth which St Ignatius is so anxious that we should enjoy'.[46] The Application of the Senses does not proceed by reasoning at all but simply 'rests'. 'Hearing' is of the heart rather than of the understanding.[47] While Longridge felt that there was a distinction between 'gospel contemplation' in the Exercises and the way that contemplation is understood in the mystical tradition as a whole, he nevertheless believed that Ignatian prayer may be a preparation for what is called the 'prayer of simple regard':

> Especially if we take into account what he says about repetitions and application of the senses, a soul can hardly help being led on from meditation to affective prayer, and that in increasing degrees of simplification till it arrives at last, if God so wills, at the prayer of simple regard.[48]

He quotes Suarez (who certainly did not belong to the purely 'ascetical' school of Jesuits) in support of his views and he seems to be in accord with much that Poulain, the writer on mysticism, says.[49]

Outside the context of the Exercises, there is plenty of evidence that Ignatius taught a very broad understanding of prayer and recognized a development towards simplification and contemplation. In his famous letter to the Spanish nun, Sister Teresa Rejadell, he comments for example:

> Every kind of meditation in which the understanding is engaged wearies the body. There are other kinds of meditation, orderly and restful, which are pleasant to the understanding and offer no difficulty to the interior faculties of the soul, and which can be made without interior expenditure of effort.[50]

Poulain cites this letter as an example of Ignatius pointing towards a genuinely simple form of prayer.[51] He also points out that the primary aim of the Exercises is not to provide a system of prayer but to free a person who wishes to be generous with God. Thus, by implication, the rather methodical approach is appropriate to the experience of the Exercises but it is to be hoped that there a person will have learned to pray more freely.[52]

It is important to note that Ignatius's principle of flexibility in the light of the needs of an individual meant that his advice on prayer in his letters varied a great deal. Thus, in some cases, he was prepared to insist on a daily pattern of formal prayer, as in the case of the layman, Anthony Enriquez: 'Set aside some time each day so that the soul will not be without its nourishment and you be led to complain like him who said "my heart is withered because I forgot to eat my bread"'.[53] Yet in other places he accepts that different circumstances demand different remedies. To priests and students at Coimbra who were in danger of excess he commented:

> The demands of your life of study do not permit you to
> devote much time to prayer, yet you can make up for
> this by desires, since the time you devote to your
> various exercises is a continuous prayer, seeing that you
> are engaged in them only for God's service.[54]

While the desire for prayer and contemplation is valid, for those dedicated to the apostolate, works of charity and a Christian life in the world, prayer can never be an end in itself. There should be a dialogue between contemplativity and activity. Those who resent the lack of time for prayer because of the 'distraction' of activity are advised that this 'distraction which you accept for his greater service' can be 'the equivalent of the union and recollection of uninterrupted contemplation'.[55] The growing ability to 'find God in all things' is in some ways better than a long time spent in formal prayer.[56] And in a letter to Fr Brandao concerning younger Jesuits Ignatius offers the widest possible teaching on prayer: These young Jesuits should:

> Seek God's presence in all things, in their
> conversations, their walks, in all that they see, taste,
> hear, understand, in all their actions, since his divine
> Majesty is truly in all things by his presence, power and
> essence. This kind of meditation which finds God our
> Lord in all things is easier than raising oneself to the
> consideration of divine truths which are more abstract

and which demand something of an effort if we are to
keep our attention on them. But this method is an
excellent exercise to prepare for great visitations of our
Lord, even in prayers that are rather short.[57]

In his *Constitutions* Ignatius's prescriptions for Jesuit prayer
were equally flexible. For students he talks of one hour each
day, but the hour is understood as a total rather than one
continuous period. The actual form of personal prayer was not
specified. In the case of the professed, Ignatius makes no
detailed requirements. He presupposed that these men were
spiritual by nature and sufficiently advanced to know what
they required (but always in dialogue with their superior).[58] It
was not until sometime after Ignatius's death that a daily
period of one hour's continuous mental prayer was introduced. This was part of a more general tendency to narrow the
understanding of Ignatian prayer. The more affective or contemplative dimension, in official circles at least, gave way to a
preference for discursive meditation. The causes of the narrowing of perspective and practice were complex but a major
one was the desire to bring Jesuit practice into line with what
was acceptable in the new atmosphere after the Council of
Trent. There was a tendency towards a kind of 'reductionism'
in favour of conventional practices in other religious orders—
including a more structured approach to 'times of prayer'.
Equally there was a suspicion of anything that smacked of the
mystical or 'inner lights' and movements of the Spirit which,
it was felt, could all too easily slide into the heresy of 'illumi-
nism'. This narrowing of the understanding of prayer (and the
Exercises in particular) naturally spilled over into the kind of
instruction that Jesuit spiritual directors gave to those who
sought guidance. There always remained some Jesuits, however, who continued to promote a more flexible or more
contemplative approach—sometimes in the face of considerable opposition.[59]

Conclusion

It now seems possible to indicate in summary the fundamental
principles of spiritual direction in the mind of St Ignatius. We

have seen that the primary focus is on the particular religious experience of the person being directed. For Ignatius this means not simply the activity of prayer (although this is a vital element) but, because he has what in contemporary terms would be called a 'holistic' approach, it also involves developing an awareness of the way God is to be found in all the experiences of life. By implication too, the life of the Spirit is not to be reduced to a series of ascetical exercises common to all. Direction therefore, is essentially a response to an experience of God's presence and action as reported by the person who comes for guidance. A director cannot know in detail what he or she should say beforehand.

To respond to what a person reports and also to one's perception of that person's character and needs also means that what is offered by the director must be as fully adapted as possible. This is Ignatius's principle of flexibility—that all instruction or advice should be what helps this particular person at this particular moment. This demands a great deal of patience on the part of the director, not a little intuition or sensitivity and a non-judgmental approach. Directors should avoid any temptation to measure people against objective norms. This attitude of being 'as a balance at equilibrium' (Exx 15) led some people to accuse Ignatius of heresy because it seemed to give a dangerous prominence to the interior guidance of the Spirit in each individual and to prevent the director from correcting false doctrinal or ethical stances.[60] In fact, of course, Ignatius did see the possibility of correction but this should be sensitive and gentle and not dogmatic confrontation (Exx 22). The important thing for Ignatius was to help each person to grow in an inner freedom to respond to God's call and demands. For what is appropriated personally is likely to go deeper than what is imposed.

Notes

[1] Leech, K.: *Soul friend* (London: Sheldon Press, 1979; New York: Harper & Row, 1980), p. 58.

[2] References in this article are to *The Spiritual Exercises of St Ignatius*, trans. L. Puhl (Chicago, 1951), cited as Exx. While I have tried to avoid exclusive language throughout this article, all direct quotations are given in their original form.

[3] The early directories appear in *Monumenta Historica Societatis Jesu*, 76. In this article I have referred to an English translation, *Autograph directories of St Ignatius Loyola* in the series 'Program to adapt the Spiritual Exercises', ed. Thomas Burke (Jersey City, no date). In this there are three directories associated with St Ignatius himself which I have cited subsequently as: *Autograph*, *Tradita* and *Calveras*.

[4] This also appears in *MHSJ*, 76 and in a good English translation in *The Spiritual Exercises of Ignatius Loyola*, ed. W. H. Longridge (London, 1930).

[5] Veale, J.: 'Ignatian prayer or Jesuit spirituality', in *The Way Supplement*, 27 (Spring 1976), p. 8.

[6] For Ignatius's letters I have referred in this article to the selection entitled *Letters of St Ignatius of Loyola*, trans. William Young (Chicago, 1959), cited as *Letters*. For the Constitutions, see *The Constitutions of the Society of Jesus*, trans. George Ganss (St Louis, 1970), cited as *Const*.

[7] Cf. Fleming, D.: 'The Ignatian Spiritual Exercises: understanding a dynamic', in *Notes on the Spiritual Exercises of St Ignatius of Loyola*, ed. D. Fleming (St Louis, 1981), pp. 4–5. And English, J.: *Spiritual freedom* (Guelph, 1982), *passim*.

[8] Cf. Fleming, *op. cit.*, pp. 4–5.

[9] *Tradita*, notes.

[10] *Calveras*, 407.

[11] Quoted in Veale, *op. cit.*, p. 9, n. 28.

[12] English, *op. cit.*, pp. 56–68.

[13] *Autograph*, 7.

[14] *Autograph*, 8.

[15] *Tradita*, Manner of giving Exx, 1.

[16] *Calveras*, 412. *Cf.* also English, *op. cit.*, comments on Exx 2, pp. 56–68.

[17] Cf. Bernadicou, P.: 'The retreat director in the Spiritual Exercises', in Fleming, *op. cit.*, pp. 27–38.

[18] Robb, P.: *The retreatant in a directed retreat*, in the series 'Program to adapt the Spiritual Exercises', p. 1.

[19] Quoted in Veale, *op. cit.*, p. 9, n. 27.

[20] *Tradita*, 2.

[21] *Autograph*, 5. Cf. also English, *op. cit.*, on Exx 17, pp. 56–68.

[22] Robb, *op. cit.*, p. 1.

[23] Robb, *op. cit.*, p. 5.

[24] *Letters*, p. 179.

[25] *Letters*, p. 179.

[26] *Calveras*, 431.

[27] Wulf, F.: 'Ignatius as a spiritual guide', in *Ignatius Loyola, his personality and spiritual heritage 1556–1956*, ed. F. Wulf (St Louis, 1977), p. 36.

[28] Wulf, *op. cit.*, p. 37.

[29] Nowadays most directors favour a broader approach to this, popularly called the 'examen of consciousness' which focuses not merely on faults but on the whole of life. Cf. Aschenbrenner, G.: 'Consciousness

examen', in *Review for Religious*, vol. 31 (1972), pp. 14–21, reprinted in Fleming, *op. cit.*, pp. 175–185.

[30] *Calveras*, 408.

[31] English, *op. cit.*, pp. 56–68.

[32] Robb, *op. cit.*, p. 3.

[33] *Letters*, p. 180.

[34] *Letters*, pp. 24–25.

[35] *Letters*, p. 126.

[36] For example, *Calveras*, 431.

[37] *Letters*, pp. 159–162.

[38] *Autograph*, 11–12.

[39] *Tradita*, Manner of giving Exx, 4.

[40] Cf. for example: Toner, J.: *A commentary on St Ignatius's Rules for the discernment of spirits* (St Louis, 1982); Futrell, J.: 'Ignatian discernment', in *Studies in the spirituality of Jesuits*, vol. II, no. 2 (April 1970); Buckley, M.: 'Rules for the discernment of spirits', in *The Way Supplement*, 20 (Autumn 1973), pp. 19–37.

[41] Cf. *Letters*, pp. 18–24.

[42] Poulain, A.: *The graces of interior prayer*, trans. L. Yorke Smith (London, 1950), pp. 368–369.

[43] Cf. *Letters*, p. 19.

[44] Cf. Longridge, W. H.: *The Spiritual Exercises of Ignatius Loyola* (London, 1930), pp. 258f. *passim*.

[45] Longridge, *op. cit.*, pp. 228–229.

[46] Longridge, *ibid.*

[47] Longridge, *op. cit.*, pp. 253–256.

[48] Longridge, *op. cit.*, p. 258.

[49] Cf. Poulain, A., *op. cit.*, pp. 34–35.

[50] *Letters*, p. 24.

[51] Poulain, *op. cit.*, p. 45.

[52] Poulain, *op. cit.*, p. 29, footnote.

[53] *Letters*, p. 333.

[54] *Letters*, p. 129.

[55] *Letters*, pp. 254–255.

[56] *Letters*, pp. 235–236.

[57] *Letters*, p. 240.

[58] For Ignatius's legislation on the prayer of Jesuits, see *Const* 340–343, 582–585.

[59] Cf. Veale, *op. cit.*, pp. 5–6, 7, 13.

[60] Cf. Veale, *op. cit.*, p. 5, n. 8.

(vol. 24, no. 4, October 1984 and vol. 25, no. 1, January 1985)

Pierre de Bérulle

Anne M. Minton

Much of the spirituality of the Roman Catholic Church in the sixteenth and seventeenth centuries was noted for its attention to method in prayer. From the *Spiritual Exercises* of Ignatius and the treatises of John of the Cross, through the devotional writings of Francis de Sales, we find detailed descriptions of how to pray and how to direct those who pray.[1]

However, the 'French School' of spirituality and especially its founder, Pierre de Bérulle (1575–1629), is the exception.[2] Among all his writings, Bérulle has no systematic treatment of prayer or spiritual direction. But it is possible to describe his ideas about spiritual direction from an analysis of his writings and a look at how he functioned as a director himself.

Bérulle was a secular priest, a founder of the French Oratory and a cardinal whose thinking has deeply influenced Roman Catholic spirituality, but whose work has not been translated and is seldom read among English speakers. Bérulle was actively involved in prayer circles of his time. He was a spiritual director to Vincent de Paul and the Queen of England, Henriette-Marie, wife of Charles I, among others. His spirituality helped form the French Carmelites and Ursulines, the French Oratory and the Sulpicians. He was a man of prayer whom others sought out for advice. Descartes was one of those who came to seek his counsel. He was a man of learning, a theologian of the spiritual life as well as a practitioner and a contemplative. Bérulle studied theology at the Sorbonne and had a good foundation in the Christian spiritual tradition, having read extensively in the fourteenth- and fifteenth-century German mystics and the sixteenth-century Spaniards, John of Avila, Teresa of Avila and John of the Cross. Educated by Jesuits, he made the Spiritual Exercises in a directed retreat and was exposed from his youth to the spiritual tradition of Ignatius and his men. Besides Ignatius, the single most pervasive influence upon him was Teresa of Avila, and Bérulle was instrumental in bringing the Discalced Carmelite nuns into France. The sustained spiritual relationship he had with the Carmelite nuns from 1604 until his death was crucial to his own development and piety.

Thus Bérulle has a rich background in the classics of the spirituality and spiritual direction from various traditions. One of his contributions to Christian spirituality is a synthesis of many different writers and a reworking of their ideas to fit his own time. This is equally true of his ideas on spiritual direction.

Although there is no text dealing with 'spiritual direction' as such in his collected works, there is a treatise written in 1624 for the superiors in the houses of the Oratory which he founded. Since much of their work involves leading others on 'interior paths' the treatise is very useful for our purposes in describing how he envisions spiritual direction. This *Mémorial de direction pour les supérieurs* was intended to give superiors advice on fulfilling their office. This text, correlated with Bérulle's letters of direction to men and women and his numerous meditations and works of piety form a pattern. From these combined writings one can get a fairly detailed description of the purpose of spiritual direction and the role of the director.

There are certain basic presuppositions of Bérullian spirituality which underlie all his ideas on spiritual direction. The first is that we are all creatures of God, dependent upon God and in relationship with God. Relationship as creatures is at the very core of human life. For the Christian it is more specified as living Christ's life, living with Christ's attitudes in relationship to God. How that relationship with God is to be lived out has been modelled for us by Christ.

Another fundamental conviction of Bérulle is that the goal of our life is to allow Christ to live in us. Bérulle appropriated as his motto the words of Paul, 'I live now not I, but Christ lives in me'. This life of Christ in the person is the lived out realization of what occurs sacramentally in Baptism. We are baptized into Christ's death and resurrection. We are led by

God's grace to 'strip off the old man and clothe ourselves anew', 'to live on earth for Christ and not for ourselves', to live 'not by our own spirit but by the Spirit of Jesus constantly renouncing our own inclinations in order to follow the movements and the leading of his Spirit in us'.[3]

Our life's goal should be to seek first the Kingdom of God and God's glory. Our attention is directed to God and the Kingdom of God not to ourselves or our own virtue or good works. 'We are on earth only to establish the reign and announce the glorious coming of Christ.'[4] He says that the 'foundation and the goal of our ministry . . . is to prepare and hasten the last coming of the Son of God as the prophets prepared for his first coming'.[5] One of the fundamental tasks of the Christian is to wait for and long for the coming of Christ.

Although Bérulle customarily writes to and directs the spiritually mature and advanced, there is nothing anywhere in his writing to suggest that only the advanced, the ordained or the educated can hear this teaching. Bérulle proposes the same goal of the Christian life for everyone, regardless of rank, state in life, sex, age or education. For a Christian the goal is to put on Christ and live Christ's life on earth. God 'draws us to him in order to live with him, and to live in him another sort of life from what we live on earth; this is a heavenly and divine life, an immortal and happy life and a life in which our eternal happiness consists'.[6] Most of the work of transforming us into Christ and leading us to God is done by God's grace. We have only to remove the obstacles to grace. This is the human role in what is otherwise a somewhat passive experience. Clearly there are many pitfalls and difficulties and much danger of self-delusion in something so unspecified as cultivating the attitudes necessary to receive and embrace God's grace. Fortunately, according to Bérulle, one does have help available. We have the life and example of Jesus Christ and we have the assistance of spiritual guides.

All Christians have available to them the life and example of Christ. Bérulle says that one of Christ's purposes on earth was to teach us how to become holy. For this purpose Christ established a school where we can learn the secrets of heaven. This is Bérulle's way of thinking about Christ as wisdom and sanctity. The school of Jesus stands in stark contrast to the school of this earth whose spirit is cold and dry and proud. The school of Jesus is marked by a spirit of abnegation and discipline. Those in the school of Christ are characterized by a spirit of piety. In his school there is 'care to acquire and exercise true and solid virtues'.[7] In the school of Jesus people learn about God and the ways of God. Only in Jesus, our sole mediator, do we find the way to God.

For Bérulle the way to holiness was solely through the example and teachings of Christ. People came to know this Christ through the cycle of New Testament readings in the Mass and the Divine Office. However, the image of Christ that Bérulle presents in his writing, and one may assume also in his spiritual conferences is a pray-er, a contemplative. Jesus is not portrayed with an active ministry, with a group of disciples, preaching, teaching and healing. He is almost always seen in relationship to God the Father, and very rarely in relationship to other people. Presumably, this was the Christ whom Bérulle wanted everyone to appropriate in their own lives.

In addition to the life and example of Christ to guide us, we also have spiritual directors. Bérulle has certain presuppositions about the role of the director and the qualities that the director should possess. The director is told that his task is to form Jesus Christ in souls: '. . . our ministry leads us to form Jesus Christ in souls'. The call is to give a new birth to Christ. 'Jesus is the fruit of our labours, and our ministry leads to producing him just as the Father produces him in eternity.'[8] Bérulle writes that since the incarnation,

> heaven and earth have been renewed in grace and blessing and our ministry . . . leads to birthing and forming Jesus in hearts; it leads to giving a new birth to him who was born from all eternity in the bosom of the Father, and in the fullness of time in the womb of the most holy Virgin, and it leads to giving us the sort of relationship with the Son of God that this same Son of God honoured, celebrated and exalted in these great words: 'whoever does the will of my Father is my brother and my sister and my mother' (Matthew 7:21).[9]

The director should be characterized by a breadth of spirit, a tolerance and charity towards others. The director should honour everything which comes from God, aware that there is nothing too small or insignificant, 'there is nothing little in the house of God'.[10] Since failure is one of the most common human experiences the director should be particularly attentive to how to regard other people's faults. The director should avoid an authoritarian attitude and false zeal in correcting people.[11]

How does the director accomplish such an awesome task? He must learn from the Spirit the care of souls which Bérulle describes as the 'art of arts'. 'The Spirit is the doctor of this science and the director of this work.'[12]

> The Spirit teaches this art in the school of Jesus. This art
> is a science, not of memory but of spirit, not of study
> but of prayer, not of discourse but of practice, not of
> contention but of humility, not of speculation but of
> love and the love of Jesus which is delivered and
> abandoned, forgetting itself and poured out for the
> salvation of souls.[13]

There is great care taken to make clear that this science of the care of souls is higher than all other sciences. It confounds philosophers and theologians who are vain and arrogant. (It is important in all of this to remember that Bérulle held a theology degree from the Sorbonne.) This science is learned from the book of life at the foot of the cross, not from the books of the academics. Bérulle asserts that this science of the care of souls encompasses everything because it is based in Christ and in his cross and ultimately this science arrives at the end of all things, that is, Jesus. It is a holy science which he describes as 'the daughter of prayer, the disciple of humility and the mother of discretion'.[14]

In his century which saw the beginning of the modern scientific revolution it is significant that Bérulle has used the term science throughout his treatise. He expands on this idea when he writes:

> Now God who wished to perfect in this century all
> other kinds of science, dispersing the shadows of past

centuries, wishes also to renew and perfect in this
century truly and properly his own science by his life
and by his Spirit. . . .[15]

It is clear that Bérulle has a very exalted understanding of the
work of direction and has described it all as fundamentally the
work of God. But God uses human mediators for the care of
souls. The director must prepare himself for this work by
abasement before God, continual prayer, preparing himself to
be a living instrument animated by the Spirit of Jesus. The
director ought to renounce his own spirit in order to live in the
power and the guidance of the Spirit of God. He ought to
'illuminate others in consuming himself', as though he were a
burning candle.[16] The two central virtues which should
characterize the director are those which are fundamental to
Christianity, humility and charity.

More practically, how does Bérulle suggest that the director assist the person who comes for help? The director listens
attentively to all the relevant details of the person's life, no
matter how small or insignificant these details may seem.
Bérulle believes that God's grace and redeeming love per-
meates all of life and with Ignatius he holds that God's action
can be discerned in many aspects of a person's life, not just in
their prayer.

The director's role is to assist the person in becoming ever
more abandoned to God and possessed by God. The test of
this surrender and possession is obedience and living with the
attitudes of Christ. As mentioned above the Christ who is
being formed and brought to birth in this system is Christ the
contemplative. The French School formed people of prayer in
the firm belief that real contemplative prayer would create
holy apostolic people. But the emphasis in direction was on
the contemplative not the apostle.

The Bérullian model of spiritual direction has a contribution to make to the spiritual tradition of the Church and some
limitations to be noted. Its contribution is first that it is a
contemplative model. In an era of considerable emphasis upon
methods and steps and stages, Bérulle's ideas are refreshing.
This shows some of his debt to Teresa's interior castle where
one may go from room to room with some ease. Everyone

would agree that the work of spiritual direction is a work of grace and that the partners must be attentive at all times to God's action. What Bérulle's system does is to take this idea seriously and to focus on God's work without much stress on human activity.

The second is that the heart of the Christian life is to die and be raised up in Christ. Bérulle took that reality to be the goal of his own life and his spirituality. Practically in the spiritual direction relationship this meant a concentration on dying to oneself, making oneself into nothing, a central motif in his writings. Although it is often understood ascetically as self-abnegation and acts of humility, it is more profoundly a way of being in the world ever more ready to be filled with God. The human person is a pure capacity for God, according to Bérulle, and the work of direction is to cultivate the attitudes of receptivity. In concrete terms this means getting out of one's own way! It refers to focusing on God and not oneself, rooting out self-centred, destructive, grandiose, rigid attitudes that prevent God's uninhibited action. The work of direction is also intended to help the person prepare to be raised up in Christ, in the sense of learning and growing in the attitudes of Christ, living as one reborn in him. Thus much of direction is concerned with learning Christ's attitudes, talking about the Jesus whom we meet in the scriptures and the liturgy of the Church.

Another contribution is the metaphor of spiritual direction as birth and midwifery. Instead of an image of achieving certain goals or reaching certain levels, we have an image of birth. A person reborn in Christ is brought to a qualitatively different life in this process as life in the world is different from life in the womb. The director has the uniquely feminine role of midwife, being present, lending support, using skill to avert danger or to bring comfort and strength, but essentially waiting and being attentive until Christ is formed in the person and a new Christ is brought forth. The director is an attendant at a birth.

The limitations of this model of spiritual direction are that it can lead to a very privatized piety. The individual and the director are concerned with the person living with Christ's attitudes in relationship to God the Father. There is very little emphasis on the wider Church community or the secular world. It is assumed that people will make the necessary connections between interior attitudes and building the Kingdom of God but this can degenerate into a very solitary enterprise. Because of the very lack of specificity, and absence of a series of benchmarks, there is a great potential for self-delusion. As was pointed out above, the Christ whose attitudes one appropriates is a very specific distillation of the Gospels. The Jesus whom Bérulle presents is a man without disciples, ministry or community. He was a perfect adorer of the Father. This is not the whole Christ, and there is a real danger of an incomplete appropriation of Christ when the director is not skilful enough or aware enough of the limitations of the Bérullian portrait of Christ.

Although his model is not limited to any class or group of people in itself, it is clear that it would be much more effective with the spiritually mature and advanced. To speak of 'nothingness' with someone who has not done some of the purgative, ascetical groundwork would not be helpful. People must have come to a certain point in their Christian lives even to desire what Bérulle is talking about, much less to seek to deepen and expand this way of life. This contemplative, radical, Christocentric model presupposes certain kinds of people and would not be effective with beginners in the spiritual life, unlike the model of Ignatius and Francis de Sales.

The model also exalts contemplation over action and assumes a precedence temporarily at least. One needs to begin with prayer. The danger is that the person will never understand the mutual interdependence of prayer and ministry and will always see prayer as central and ministry and apostolic lives as expendable. It is also the case that people who do not have the environment conducive to contemplative prayer, married women, people in business and politics, diocesan priests, will experience a continual frustration in this method because they will never be able to give themselves over to contemplation as they feel they should because of the distractions of life in the world! Bérulle was able to avoid some of these pitfalls in his own life, but the system lends itself to these dangers in less than skilful hands.

Perhaps the single most important contribution that Bérullian direction can make to contemporary ideas about spiritual direction is its contemplative, theocentric focus. In an era dominated by psychological models and the pursuit of human health and fulfilment, Bérulle's model provides an alternative and a challenge. There is a radical difference between a theocentric and psychological/human potential model. Ironically, the goal of joyful freedom is often achieved as a result of the theocentric model, a goal sought by the psychological model. With Bérulle's form of direction the joy and the freedom that are experienced are the result of seeking first the Kingdom of God and God's glory, knowing that everything else will be given to us besides.

Notes

[1] For a good overview of Counter-Reformation spirituality see Evennett, H. Outram: *The spirit of the Counter-Reformation* (Notre Dame: University of Notre Dame Press, c. 1968).

[2] There is no substantial study on Bérulle in English. The best sources for further reading are Dagens, Jean: *Bérulle et les origines de la restauration catholique (1575–1611)* (Paris: Desclée de Brouwer, 1952), and Chochois, Paul: *Bérulle et l'école française* (Paris: Editions du Seuil, 1963).

[3] Bérulle: *Mémorial de direction pour les supérieurs, Oeuvres complètes*, Bourgoing, éditeur (Paris: Migne, 1856), pp. 807–808.

[4] *Ibid.*, p. 833.

[5] *Ibid.*

[6] *Ibid.*, p. 815.

[7] *Ibid.*, p. 820.

[8] *Ibid.*, p. 816.

[9] *Ibid.*, pp. 816–817.

[10] *Ibid.*, p. 826.

[11] *Ibid.*, p. 817.

[12] *Ibid.*, p. 817.

[13] *Ibid.*, p. 818.

[14] *Ibid.*, p. 819.

[15] *Ibid.*

[16] *Ibid.*, p. 830.

(vol. 30, no. 1, January 1990)

Evelyn Underhill, a Companion on Many Journeys

Joy Milos CSJ

When I grow up I should like to be an author because
you can influence people more widely by books than by
pictures. . . . Goodbye sixteen years old. I hope my
mind will not grow tall to look down on things, but
wide to embrace all sorts of things in the coming year.[1]

With this journal entry on the eve of her seventeenth birthday,
Evelyn Underhill offered an uncanny prophecy of the path her
life and career would follow. Acclaiming Underhill as a writer
with 'an insight into the meaning of the culture and of the
individual gropings of the soul that was unmatched by any of
the professional teachers of her day',[2] *The Times Literary
Supplement* would testify after her death to the fulfilment of
her adolescent vision. She had indeed come to 'embrace all
sorts of things' as the years passed and, with apparently uner-
ring insight, touched countless lives in the process, chiefly
through her role as 'spiritual director to her generation'.[3]
Recognized as such an influential guide, Underhill deserves
retrieving in the contemporary search for meaningful spiritual
guidance.

A prolific early twentieth-century British spiritual and
theological writer, Evelyn Underhill (1875–1941) was the first
woman to lecture on theology at Oxford, the first woman to
assume leadership in retreat work in the Anglican community
of her day, and among the first to be involved in ecumenical
dialogue. Although best known for her two classic works,
Mysticism (1911, 1st edition) and *Worship* (1936), Underhill's
written corpus includes poetry and novels from early in her

126

career, more than thirty books on various aspects of mysticism and the spiritual life, as well as numerous articles, lectures, essays and book reviews. The partial eclipsing after her death of the contribution she had made to the spiritual life of the Church of England has been vindicated by the recent decision of the Episcopal Church to add Evelyn Underhill to the liturgical calendar as 'mystic and theologian'.[4]

Underhill's youth gave little indication of the spiritual concerns which would occupy her later years. Growing up in a family where she 'wasn't brought up to religion really—except just in a formal way',[5] she would progress through a period of eight or nine years where she believed herself to be an atheist, to a time of involvement with the Hermetic Society of the Golden Dawn, to a time of growing toward a rather generic sense of Christian belief, which culminated in a profound conversion experience in 1907. Even that event would take years of sorting on her own before she made a formal commitment and shared that struggle as she sought spiritual direction herself. The significance of faith and the need for companions on the journey proved a gradual revelation to Underhill. And yet, had Underhill emerged from a more religiously orthodox upbringing, her generation might not have had her as a pathfinder for so many searching souls. Someone who had to discover her own way would develop an instinctive empathy for those struggling with similar questions.[6]

Underhill as guide

Having established something of Underhill's credibility as a commentator upon and model of spiritual guidance, the remainder of this article will examine her actual practice in such a role.[7] Although Underhill had a frequent stream of directees approaching her, much of her guidance was offered through regular correspondence. An analysis of her extended correspondence with one particularly close directee,[8] additional letters to others seeking guidance and comments by others about her approach to direction will illustrate her style and themes. The concluding segment will synthesize what appear to be Underhill's most effective and relevant characteristics as a contemporary role model.

Lucy Menzies, the most intimate of Evelyn Underhill's 'family' of directees, spent the first six years of their relationship meeting her director only through letters. Menzies began writing to her during World War I and in 1923 the two correspondents finally met. The relationship between these two women was deepened by Menzies' assumption of the role of Warden of Underhill's beloved retreat centre at Pleshey. The letters during the ten-year period testify to Underhill's growing concern over her friend's over-conscientiousness in fulfilling her duties and her own sense of inadequacy in offering direction to individuals who approached her. Lucy Menzies found Underhill's advice a continuing support and challenge and, to the end of her life, never ceased her accolades. To a correspondent in 1946 Menzies wrote:

> How glad I am to hear from anyone who reads Evelyn Underhill. She was, and is, my greatest friend. To me, too, her writings opened a new world. No one else ever made me conscious of God as she did. Everything she wrote somehow helped me on.[9]

A case study of direction

In her correspondence with Lucy Menzies, Underhill assumes a role which has three primary functions: co-discerner, resource person and balancing element in the life of her directee. The first of these duties contrasts with an understanding of a director as someone necessarily and overly directive. Throughout the years of their writing, Underhill consistently urged Menzies to listen to her own attractions in prayer, to respond to her natural *attrait* rather than looking for ready-made answers and systems. Such a sensitivity to the uniqueness of each person's path to God was obvious even in her earliest letters of direction. In 1908 Underhill wrote to Margaret Robinson, perhaps her earliest directee, 'The fact that I say I think I have found a path in one direction is no valid reason for you to alter your course . . . do not give up the form of prayer that comes naturally to you'.[10] The following year when Robinson had been tempted to compare her spiritual growth and progress with someone else's, Underhill reminded: 'Each spiritual life is unique and its personal quality should be above all things respected'.[11]

Although she made specific suggestions to Lucy Menzies and other inquirers, Underhill frequently qualified her advice with such provisos as, 'You must only do so if you clearly feel it is God's call for you'.[12] Never does she present a single way of approaching God or suggest that a particular method can substitute for individual ongoing discernment. She presupposed that there has first been a peaceful listening for that call. The task of the spiritual guide was to affirm that invitation rather than dictate it before the directee had perceived it.

For her the role of director was co-listener and discerner rather than the expert instructor who had ready-made answers about the path one should follow. Thus she quickly reacted when one correspondent misinterpreted a previous suggestion as having been a hope on Underhill's part to make the writer 'a thorough-going Catholic'. Underhill's response clarifies her self-understanding of her role as guide. 'I hope', she explained, 'I shall never try to make you any particular thing! My job is simply to try to help you find out what *God* wants you to be, and what will help and support your particular type of soul in His service.'[13] There was to be only one Creator, and she was not it. The director, especially Underhill as director, was never to be 'a sort of she-who-must-be-obeyed'. Only one Person deserved such obedience and surrender. This basic self-deprecation plus her basic presupposition that the director's job is secondary to the directee's personal reflection on the experience of God in his or her life, did not prevent Underhill from offering specific advice when she deemed it appropriate. She also clearly believed that acting as a resource person, drawing upon what she had learned in her own journey and in encounters with other seekers, could be a valuable service.

Thus Evelyn Underhill proposed reading materials and definite times for prayer, the latter, one surmises after reading the ongoing correspondence with Lucy Menzies, more to provide limits for such an overly conscientious personality than to prescribe absolutes. As a self-educated and recognized scholar on the spiritual life, Underhill's research provided her with the richest treasures of the Christian spiritual tradition to draw upon in her reading suggestions. Her own experiences, about which she was typically reticent, she was willing to share when she considered them helpful for her directee. Regarding her positive encouragement toward Church membership, she explained, 'I stood out against it myself for so long and have been so thoroughly convinced of my own error, that I do not want other people to waste time in the same way'.[14] About sacramental practice she confessed and advocated, 'After being myself both a non-sacramentalist and a sacramentalist, there is no doubt at all left in my own mind as to what is the simplest and most direct channel through which grace comes to the soul'.[15] If these personal revelations could be a resource for assisting another's growth, even these guarded stories could be shared.

Perhaps the most consistent and important function Underhill exercised was that of moderator for her often overly anxious charge. Without knowing anything of Menzies' personal background, a reader of Underhill's letters would perceive her directee as one prone to overexertion, ill health, and a certain Pelagian rigidity in her approach to the spiritual life. Whereas Menzies strained toward a perfectionism which tended to overly spiritualize life and stretch her health to the breaking point, Underhill constantly encouraged her toward an incarnational approach, one which presupposed a holistic understanding of how Christian spirituality should be embodied. Letter after letter addressed the issue of Menzies' poor health, always urging her to do whatever is necessary to take care of herself. 'It is physically as much as spiritually I want you quieted and normalized', Underhill exhorted, 'the body must not be driven beyond its strength.'[16] When Menzies pursued the question of adding physical penances or fasting to her Rule, Underhill discouraged forms of asceticism which would jeopardize her health. 'Fragile persons are never allowed to fast',[17] reminded this balancing guide. The more Menzies struggled to achieve her own spiritualized ideal, the more Underhill called her back to being-in-the-world.

Avoiding any suggestion of extra penances, greater effort, longer prayers, Underhill stabilized Menzies' over-intensity with psychologically and spiritually sound advice. A letter to an evidently distraught Menzies directed:

Take *special* pains now to keep up fully or develop some definite non-religious interest, e.g. your music. Work at it, consider it an obligation to do so. It is more necessary to your spiritual health; and you will very soon find that it has a steadying effect. 'Good works' won't do—it must be something you really like for its own sake. . . . If you could take a few days off and keep quite quiet it would be good, but if this is impossible at any rate go along gently, look after your body, don't saturate yourself the whole time with mystical books . . . . Hot milk and a thoroughly foolish novel are better things for you to go to bed on just now than St Teresa.[18]

Some letters reveal Menzies as tending to overdramatize experiences of both consolation and darkness, thus eliciting from Underhill an attempt to moderate her moods and reminding her that there is a psychic as well as a spiritual side to all of her experiences. In one case Underhill writes, 'It is your psychic side which has been too fully roused and upset your equilibrium. . . . It is not God but your too eagerly enjoying psyche which keeps you awake and tears you to bits with an over-exciting joy.'[19] When the emotional pendulum had finally swung in the other direction, Underhill would again try to balance Menzies' reaction with the gentle reminder: 'Quiet acceptance and commonsense are the way to get fervour back again. Repulsive programme, isn't it?'[20]

If one were to choose a word characteristic of this modulating role that Underhill played, it might well be 'gentle'. Whether it was countering a sense of scrupulous preoccupation with sin, warning against over-intensity, or tempering Menzies' moods of jubilation or desolation, Underhill, throughout the years of their relationship, constantly sprinkles her advice with gentleness: 'Keep quiet and in a state of gentle acceptance',[21] 'sink down gently into that self-abandoned peace'[22]—always the emphasis falls on a quiet relaxing of effort and strain, a growing sense of surrender and abandonment to God, a 'resting in the Lord'. '"Adherence" rather than effort'[23] becomes one of Underhill's favourite images. But such advice does not encourage a quietistic response. Always a staunch opponent of such an approach to prayer and contemplation, Underhill used fecundity as the criterion for judging the reality of a life of prayer. 'What are the fruits of the encounter?' is always a key question.

The aim of direction

Judging from the correspondence with Lucy Menzies, Underhill's immediate aim as spiritual guide appears to be sensitizing her directee to the realities of her life so that she might view these events as sacramental encounters with the living God. Her aim includes a broadening of Menzies' vision to perceive all aspects of her daily existence, not just the 'spiritual' or religious elements, as potential mediations of God's presence. Such a consciousness would ultimately lead to adoration. The focus, Underhill contended, should more and more be on God's presence and action rather than on self-scrutinizing introspection.

Everything is to be done with an awareness of the human condition and a sensitivity to the fact that life grows at its own pace and rhythm. As the correspondence chronicles Menzies' shifts from the emotionally positive experience of light and presence to the negative onslaught of darkness and a sense of absence, the reader finds Underhill urging Menzies to accept such movement as natural and necessary for growth. In response to one desperate sounding letter, Underhill's advice is typical of the balance she tried to instil in Menzies:

> But you MUST settle down and quiet yourself. Your present state if encouraged will be in the end as bad for you spiritually as physically. I know it is not easy to do. Nevertheless it will in the nature of things come about gradually and I want you to help it all you know. If you allow rapture or vehemence to have its way too much, you risk a violent reaction to dryness, whereas if you

act prudently you will keep the deep steady permanent peace, in the long run more precious and more fruitful than the dazzling light.[24]

Self-preoccupation and 'soul-scraping' are to be avoided at all costs and non–religious interests are frequently recommended as an antidote for such introspection. The final test of real spiritual life, a consistent refrain in Underhill's thought since her writing of *Mysticism*, is not so much the dissecting of one's particular stage in prayer, but rather the fruitfulness of a holy life: 'The test is not of course our understanding of this or that, but the effects produced by the bits of work we are given to do—or rather, which are done through us'.[25] The aim of her direction is always to instil a theocentric, not an introspective focus.

Underhill's qualifications as a spiritual guide

As an analysis of her writings and method confirms, Evelyn Underhill embodied a fortuitous combination of solid theological insight, a critical knowledge of psychology and natural human skills which qualified her for such a role. The last section of this article suggests reasons for Underhill's personal effectiveness as a guide.

As one who continued the quest for God throughout her lifetime, often struggling through periods of darkness or searching for certitude about the validity of that pursuit, Underhill first of all possessed an experiential knowledge of the power that one soul can have on another. She had for a long time travelled her faith pilgrimage alone, only gradually risking sharing her quest and questions with others.[26] A preoccupation with the interconnectedness of souls often coloured Underhill's thinking and writing. In letters of direction as early as 1908, she had challenged a correspondent who tended to make religion a '*tête-à-tête*' affair rather than viewing herself as part of the Communion of Saints, 'one of the household of faith, related to every other soul in that household, living and dead'.[27] This relational horizon repeatedly appears as the background in Underhill's understanding how one grows in the spiritual life.

Underhill closely associated this union of souls with a frequently expressed but never fully developed theology of redemption, that is, 'that strange power of one spirit to penetrate, illuminate, support and rescue other spirits, through which so much of the spiritual work of the world seems to be done'.[28] Consistent with an increasingly incarnational spirituality, Underhill envisioned the creative and transforming experience of redemption as manifested through the lives and concern of Christians affecting one another in contemporary situations. The situation of spiritual guidance was a significant context for such an experience. Just as God could use bodies and minds to transform and improve the physical world, so too could God use human spirits to continue the saving and creative work of redemption.[29] From her perspective, not only a director of souls, but anyone living a truly contemplative life is involved in mediatorship, 'a sort of redemptive and clarifying power working on other souls—a tiny co-operation in the work of Christ'.[30]

Reviewing the classical traditions of spiritual direction to determine characteristics typically associated with such ministry, Martin Thornton in *Spiritual direction* concludes that 'all authorities without exception top the list with *learning*'.[31] He continues, 'Knowledge comes before anything, including personal holiness, because all [people] are different and personal sanctity can be, indeed must be, ascetically narrow. Saints can inspire but they need not be good practical guides for everyone.'[32] Although such a claim may at first be disconcerting to the pietistic ear, a search of many of the great guides of the past substantiates his claim. If this be the case, Evelyn Underhill unquestionably possessed this important quality. She was recognized as a committed scholar, writer and creative explorer of the spiritual life early in her career. The poetry and novels of her younger days gave way to her growing mystical, spiritual and theological interests. In the course of her research, she walked with the giants of the past and absorbed their collective wisdom. Whether it was an introduction to a new translation of one of the mystics, an insightful essay or book on some aspect of the spiritual life, a carefully researched lecture to collegians, retreatants or clergy, or a finely analytic review of other contemporary authors, Underhill's work witnessed to an unselfish love of learning which had to be shared.

In an address to teachers presented in 1927, Underhill's encouragement reflects another of her major qualifications as spiritual director. In her clarification of the essential elements of their role as instructors of young people, Underhill gave primacy to a sense of vision. As she stated:

> the most important thing for you is your vision, your sense of that God whom your work must glorify. The richer, deeper, wider, truer your vision of Divine Reality the more real, rich and fruitful your work is going to be. You must feel the mysterious attraction of God, His loveliness and wonder, if you are ever going—in however simple a way—to impart it to others. [33]

As a spiritual teacher herself, Underhill spent a major portion of her ministry refining the initial vision that had first stimulated her to undertake her spiritual quest. That first sight of reality gradually led to a sharpened vision of the Love of God, most especially appearing in the presence of the incarnate Christ. With such an emphasis, Underhill's approach to spiritual guidance avoided the two poles about which she warned other teachers, that of dwelling in a 'spiritual dreamland remote from actual life, or sink[ing] to the merely naturalistic strangely compounded human personality which psychology invites us to accept'. [34] As she immersed herself in the lives of an increasing number of retreatants and directees, the vision of a spirituality founded on the sense of the Divine in the midst of real life intensified.

As a corrective to an ethereal spirituality, Underhill increasingly advocated an incarnational and sacramental approach to Christian holiness. The principle of incarnation provided the foundation, and sacramentalism as the 'self-imparting of the Infinite God, in humanity and for humanity', [35] was derivative of it. Both of these help explain the attractiveness of her approach for individuals who might not otherwise have considered themselves as particularly 'spiritual'. She based her sacramentalism upon the belief that grace comes 'through the medium of things—God coming into our souls by means of humblest accidents—the intermingling of spirit and sense',[36] and encouraged her listeners to share the consciousness of God-in-their-midst. A constantly recurring refrain in her talks and writing urged individuals to discover the medium of ordinary daily life as the channel of God's self-communication. There is no need to go outside normal experience to discover the already present God. With such an overriding vision in mind, one can understand the homey examples and deceptively simple style of so much of Underhill's work. As she admitted to one correspondent: 'I have been during my life (I am now approaching 60) through many phases of religious belief and I now realize—have done in fact for some time— that human beings can make little real progress on a basis of vague spirituality'.[37] This finding God in the 'sacrament of the present moment' was attractive to busy and world-involved directees. She provided the witness of one who had spent her adult years trying to live the truth she now spent her time so generously sharing, that Christianity means 'getting down to actual ordinary life as the medium of the Incarnation'.[38]

It would be the details of ordinary life rather than pietistic religiosity that Underhill would repeatedly emphasize in her letters of guidance. For a correspondent tending to do otherwise she would remind:

> I feel with you, especially just at present, that it is most necessary to keep your human, non-theological contacts and interests supple and alive. Kindly acts of service, firm discipline of your tendency to judge other people, to look at them and their views critically, etc., and all kinds of humble work in which you can forget yourself, are all things which will do most to make your soul fit to realize Christ. So do keep up all your general interests, mix with people, love them, but don't try to 'do them good' or discuss religion with them! All this will make a better preparation for your Retreat than reading religious books and thinking of your soul.[39]

Escapist spiritualizing of the ordinary human demands never failed to elicit a similar reminder to her 'family' of directees.

As previously mentioned, Underhill's approach to spiritual guidance incorporated a profound respect for the uniqueness of each individual's path to God, his or her natural *attrait*. Such an attitude further qualified her as a spiritual mentor. Hers was an inclusive approach to spiritual living, recognizing that different people were called to different paths to prayer. Although Underhill knew well the spiritual traditions and patterns of spiritual development suggested in classical writings, she never substituted them for an attentiveness to the inner urgings of the Spirit in each directee's life. For her, '*no* account of "states of prayer" reduced to a system can be really accurate, because we are not machines and each go [*sic*] within certain general limitations our own way'.[40] In this conviction Underhill never lost her initial admiration for the first hand experience of reality which she had so admired and sought to share in her research on the mystics. A second-hand experience, or a blind following in the footsteps someone else had trod, could never substitute for the personal quest. Near the end of her life, writing to her friend Maisie Spens, Underhill mused about the apparent inability of Christians to use their gifts of power seriously. Her musing was triggered by the growing grip of another world war. She reflected:

> It is because our Christianity is so impoverished, so second-hand and non-organic, that we now feel we are incapable of the transformation of life which is needed to get humanity out of its present mess.[41]

It was that sense of personal power, coming from a belief in the presence of God acting in each person's life to which Underhill had committed so much of her energizing of others.

Underhill's relational skills clearly complemented her theological foundations, thus helping to explain the attraction which members of her 'family' felt in approaching her. Throughout her life, individuals came to Underhill with various troubles and questions about faith, about life decisions, about church, most especially about a life of prayer. Underhill must have been a consummate listener, a crucial ability for anyone who would attract such devoted directees. Olive Wynon recounted one interview which illustrates the impact of this skill:

One young woman who went to see her . . . says that
she can never forget the way Evelyn *listened*. It was a
winter afternoon; gradually the daylight faded, and still
the two sat on in the light of the fire; the house was
absolutely quiet, and Evelyn listened, as this girl had
never been listened to before; there was a sense of being
utterly understood. When Evelyn spoke, at the end, her
few words were wise and quiet, and she followed the
talk with a letter of direction which was invaluable in its
wisdom and loving understanding.[42]

Her natural listening ability was refined through the years of
practice with her directees. She did not lose this ability to listen
and give clear direction even when recuperating from frequent
bouts of debilitating illness or struggling with less obvious
rounds of her own doubts, when 'not only [her] own inner
experience, but the whole spiritual scheme seem[ed] in
question'.[43] She never let her own questionings confuse the
clear direction she gave to her directees.

The encouragement Underhill offered to other teachers
relates to her own experiences of doubt and reflects perhaps
the most significant of her characteristics as spiritual guide. In
her address she reminded them:

Your vocation is a very exciting one, and sometimes
spiritual emptiness and exhaustion may be part of the
price you have to pay for fulfilling it. Hungry and
thirsty, conscious of your ignorance and poverty, you
must still feed and cherish those lambs to whom you
are sent; and out of your own need still give what you
can to other souls.[44]

Above all other characteristics, Underhill's sense that direction of souls was her real vocation would explain her efficacy
in such a role. She began such ministering reluctantly, fearing
that her own inadequacies and uncertainties disqualified her as
anyone's guide. But she never failed to respond to the many
who, not surprisingly in light of the nature of her writings,
came seeking her advice. She did not choose this path initially,
but rather, was chosen to undertake such ministry and res-

ponded wholeheartedly to the call. As Barkway has commented:

> A sense of vocation will alone supply the right motive and support for its exercise, when one's own natural energy is exhausted and when one's own natural compassion is depleted . . . [Underhill] combined a metaphysical passion for absolutes with an intense compassion for the least of human needs. She had no use for what she called the 'museum-like atmosphere of much traditional piety,' and was always anxious that Martha should not be under-rated by those who admired Mary.[45]

The evidence of her continually growing 'family' of directees, her constant response to requests as a speaker and retreat director, and the steadfastness with which she continued her work until her death: all verify the fact that Evelyn Underhill possessed such a sense of vocation.

In one of her many book reviews, she commented on the appearance of saints and teachers at various points in history:

> Saints, and those vigorous spiritual teachers and reformers who yet fall short of the serene heights of holiness, seem always to appear because they are required to fill a certain place; and against all odds— often enough against their own preferences—they somehow reach that place.[46]

Most especially in the period between the two World Wars in England, Evelyn Underhill, even if somewhat reluctantly, filled the role of 'spiritual director of her generation', affecting the lives of many of her contemporaries and of all those who would be touched and taught by her writings. As she commented in another review, 'the true masters of the spiritual life lived what they taught, and taught in order to share their discoveries'.[47]

The witness of her commitment to spiritual guidance and the effectiveness of her work with twentieth-century searchers qualifies Evelyn Underhill for the ranks of those whom she so admired and presents her as a credible model for spiritual direction today.

Notes

1 Quotation from Evelyn Underhill in a 5 December 1882 notebook entry. Cited in Cropper, Margaret: *Evelyn Underhill* (London: Longmans, Green, and Co., 1958), p. 6.

2 Cited in Barkway, Lumsden: 'Introduction' to *An anthology of the love of God*, by Evelyn Underhill (Wilton, CT: Morehouse-Barlow Co., 1976), p. 17.

3 Bodgener, Henry: 'Evelyn Underhill: a spiritual director to her generation', in *The London Quarterly and Holborn Review*, vol. 27 (June 1958).

4 At the General Convention of the Episcopal Church in Detroit, Michigan in 1988, deputies voted to make this inclusion.

5 Underhill, Evelyn: *The letters of Evelyn Underhill*, ed. Charles Williams (London: Longmans, Green and Co., 1940), p. 125.

6 For more detailed accounts of the life of Evelyn Underhill, three biographical sources are available: Cropper, *op. cit.*; Armstrong, Christopher: *Evelyn Underhill: an introduction to her life and writing* (Grand Rapids, MI: Eerdmans, 1975); and Greene, Dana: *Evelyn Underhill: artist of the infinite life* (New York: Crossroad, forthcoming).

7 The most sustained discussion of her theoretical insights regarding spiritual guidance can be found in her 1926 address to the clergy of the Liverpool Anglican diocese which was later published as *Concerning the inner life* (London: Methuen and Co., 1926).

8 Listed as 'To a friend 1923–41' in the *Letters*, these were written to Miss Lucy Menzies, a close friend and devoted disciple of Underhill.

9 Cited in Barkway, Lumsden: 'Lucy Menzies: a memoir', in *Evelyn Underhill* by Margaret Cropper, p. xvii.

10 *Letters.*, p. 73.

11 *Ibid.*, p. 107.

12 *Ibid.*, p. 317.

13 *Ibid.*, p. 189.

14 *Ibid.*, pp. 311–312.

15 *Ibid.*, p. 317.

16 *Ibid.*, p. 317.

17 *Ibid.*, p. 314.

18 *Ibid.*, p. 313.

19 *Ibid.*, p. 315.

20 *Ibid.*, p. 319.

21 *Ibid.*, p. 316.

22 *Ibid.*, p. 322.

23 *Ibid.*, p. 335.

24 *Ibid.*, p. 312.

25 *Ibid.*, p. 336.

26 Among those whom Underhill would eventually trust in this capacity, she would see none more influential than Baron Friedrich von Hügel who began as her director at a critical period in 1921. Dom John

Chapman, Bishop Walter Frere and Reverend R. H. Ward would also share her journey at differing times.

27 *Letters*, pp. 81, 83.

28 Underhill, Evelyn: 'The possibility of prayer', in *Theology*, vol. 14 (April 1927), pp. 202–203.

29 Underhill, Evelyn: 'The teacher's vocation', in *Collected Papers*, ed. Lucy Menzies (London: Longmans, Green and Co., 1946), p. 198.

30 *Letters*, p. 323.

31 Thornton, Martin: *Spiritual direction* (Cambridge, MA: Cowley Publications, 1984), p. 18.

32 *Ibid.*

33 The talk was later reprinted as 'The teacher's vocation' and was included in *Collected Papers*, pp. 182–199.

34 *Ibid.*, p. 193.

35 *Letters*, p. 193.

36 *Ibid.*, p. 155.

37 *Ibid.*, p. 239.

38 *Ibid.*, p. 259.

39 *Ibid.*, p. 188.

40 *Ibid.*, p. 328.

41 *Ibid.*, p. 296.

42 Wynon, Olive: 'Evelyn Underhill', in *Desire for God: a study of three spiritual classics* (London: Collins, Fontana Books, 1966), p. 97.

43 Letter to Baron von Hügel cited in Cropper, p. 108.

44 Underhill, 'The spiritual life of the teacher', pp. 210–211.

45 Barkway, 'Evelyn Underhill', p. 369.

46 Underhill, Evelyn: 'Types of holiness', *Spectator* (1 June 1929), p. 865.

47 Underhill, Evelyn: 'A historian of the soul', *Spectator* (22 December 1928), p. 963.

(vol. 30, no. 2, April 1990)

C. S. Lewis as Spiritual Mentor

Edward C. Sellner

Introduction

There is an emerging consensus in our contemporary society on the importance of people acting as guides to others. While developmental psychologists affirm the contribution mentors can make regarding career and professional choices, self-help groups such as Alcoholics Anonymous and Alanon speak of the value of sponsors for ongoing recovery. In the area of Christian spirituality, the need for sponsors in the conversion process and spiritual guides for ongoing transformation is once again being recognized as important if not essential to the life of faith. As a pastoral theologian, I have for some time been interested in these various forms of mentoring. I believe that they can be of significant help not only for younger people in their formative years, but for all of us throughout life as we face unexpected crises and predictable transitions. I am also convinced that the ministry of being a *spiritual* mentor or guide never was an exclusively clerical domain, and that more lay people should consider this particular form of ministry for themselves—as many already are.

In order to help people name some of the mentoring they have already experienced or done as well as to help lay people recognize their own potential as spiritual mentors, I propose in this article a model or paradigm for such ministry: the Anglican convert and Christian apologist, C. S. Lewis. More than twenty years after his death, he has become one of the most popular Christian writers in the twentieth century with an appeal that transcends ages, interests and theologies. Science fiction fans appreciate his novels; children's imaginations are touched by his *Narnia* tales; fundamentalists value his clear statements on Christianity; many adults find guidance from him regarding the meaning of suffering, the dimensions of grief and the ways of prayer. Lewis also speaks to those of us who study or teach theology because he seems to consider theology itself not only as an intellectual journey (important as that is), but also as a journey of the heart: a search for wisdom and the holy life. If we agree with Pascal's definition of a great man as someone who is not at one extremity or another, but touches both at once, we can see in Lewis's broad appeal intimations of greatness.

There is more than just his appeal as a writer, however; there are the very real accomplishments that can be found in his daily life and ministry. A professional in his own right as professor of English literature at Oxford and Cambridge Universities in England, he also acted as a lay theologian, preacher and spiritual guide. Believing that the Church means 'the whole body of practising Christians' and that it is silly, even wrong to expect the clergy to do everything,[1] Lewis demonstrated in many ways how mentoring in general and spiritual mentoring in particular can be an important part of lay ministry. This article explores three areas where he mentored others: through teaching, letter-writing and preaching. It attempts to discern what qualities and strengths he brought to these ministries, and the implications of his mentoring for people today who, whether professionally trained or not, see themselves called to mentoring relationships, especially those associated with spiritual guidance.

C. S. Lewis *as tutor*

As much as Lewis today is recognized for his extensive writings, the primary vocation out of which his writing and all his ministries flowed was that of being a teacher. For over thirty years he taught students, most of that time at Magdalen College, Oxford.

The published remarks of former students whom Lewis tutored provide insight into certain qualities which contributed to his effectiveness as a teacher, and to their own respect for and genuine love of the man. One of those students, H. M. Blamires, describes Lewis as someone who knew both how 'to nourish a pupil with encouragement and how to press criticism when it was needed without causing resentment'. Lewis did not think of himself 'as taking pupils through a course; rather he saw his pupils as having two years or so under his guidance, during which they could start on a process which would occupy the responsive ones for the rest of their lives'.[2] Derek Brewer speaks of him as an ideal tutor who was conscientious, efficient, intellectually brilliant and a man of wide culture. 'One of his most notable characteristics', Brewer says, 'was his magnanimity, his generous acceptance of variety and difference.'[3] Luke Rigby, another student who, like Brewer, had Lewis as a tutor during World War II, confirms this opinion, and then adds:

> What stands out in my memory is the warmth of the
> man. He was always welcoming and showed total
> interest and concern. The startling contrast between his
> achievement . . . and my mediocre promise did not
> open a gulf; he was a true master, the true teacher. He
> shared his appreciation and enthusiasm and thereby
> instilled confidence. . . .[4]

These are brief comments from only three of Lewis's thousands of students, but they are representative of many. When we study one of these tutoring relationships in more detail, we gain an even better understanding of Lewis as teacher and guide, and, as he himself moved toward conversion at the age of 31, of his ministry as a spiritual mentor.

One of the earliest students Lewis tutored at Oxford was Bede Griffiths, later to become a Benedictine monk and author of his own conversion story, *The golden string*. Griffiths entered Magdalen College as an undergraduate in 1925, just after Lewis became a tutor of English literature there. 'Lewis was at this time', according to Griffiths, 'no more Christian than I was.'[5] Though the younger man had no contact with Lewis during his first two years, Lewis became his tutor during Griffiths' third year. Those weekly sessions in English literature revealed to the student some of his tutor's gifts:

Lewis had the most exact and penetrating mind I had ever encountered, and his criticism of the essays which I brought to him . . . was the best education which I could have had. He had always a complete mastery of the subject, and never allowed any looseness of thought or expression. But these criticisms often led on to a general discussion, which was sometimes continued almost to midnight, and we began now to think along almost identical lines.[6]

Lewis's mentoring gradually went beyond the subject of literature for, as Griffiths attests, while their relationship 'ripened into friendship', it was through Lewis 'that my mind was gradually brought back to Christianity'. 'Both he and I came to religion by way of literature', Griffiths acknowledges, and as they read together 'we both began to discover more and more of the religious background of what we were reading.'[7]

Conversion did not happen suddenly for either of them, but involved a long process of shared questions and common readings in Chaucer, Spencer, Shakespeare, Milton, Wordsworth and Keats. While it was happening, Griffiths says, 'I was probably nearer to Lewis than anyone else'.[8] When the younger man left Oxford still searching, the two continued to correspond by mail. Like the conversion stories of others before them,[9] the turning-point for both men came in solitude when they surrendered to a Higher Power, and knelt and prayed. Though Lewis was converted first and though each man later came to identify his conversion with different ecclesial traditions, both men's stories reveal similar steps and phases: (1) years of searching, (2) a time of self-scrutiny or inventory, (3) the acknowledgment of sin, (4) surrender in solitude, and (5) an experience of God's overwhelming love for them despite their original reluctance, blindness or stubbornness.[10] What is also striking is how each depended on the other for guidance and encouragement during those years of searching—even though Lewis had originally started as the older, more experienced and more educated of the two. Lewis tells us in his autobiography that Griffiths was 'my chief-companion on this stage of the road',[11] and dedicates his book, *Surprised by joy*, to his friend. Griffiths says that 'we were simply two friends finding our way to what was believed to be the truth'.[12] The younger man also points to some of the underlying dimensions of their relationship:

> He [Lewis] always treated me as an equal in every
> respect, as I believe that he treated all his other friends.
> In going through his correspondence with me, which
> covered more than thirty years, I have been touched to
> see how unvarying was his friendship, how totally he
> accepted me, appreciating what I said, disagreeing
> when necessary, but always with complete sincerity,
> giving his time and attention to answering my letters,
> as though he had nothing else to do. . . . I think it was
> through him that I really discovered the meaning of
> friendship. . . . There are not many things in my life
> more precious to me than that friendship.[13]

C. S. Lewis as letter-writer

Lewis's continuing to correspond with Griffiths after the younger man had left Oxford was characteristic of him, for he consistently maintained relationships by mail when distance separated him from friends. As his fame grew through his books, however, the volume of mail from friends and strangers increased dramatically, and it became more difficult for him to keep up. Still, he answered the letters as soon as he could, sometimes with the help of his brother, Warren. Lewis's response to people in this way became another form of spiritual mentoring: encouraging and guiding others as they faced the questions of life and faith. Clyde Kilby, an editor of some of those letters, tells us that the main reason Lewis answered them so conscientiously was that he believed 'taking time out to advise or encourage another Christian was both a humbling of one's talents before the Lord and also as much the work of the Holy Spirit as producing a book'.[14] Another editor, James Como, describes Lewis as an 'epistolist who steadily corresponded with literally thousands of strangers seeking advice and comfort', many of whom 'attributed their religious conversions, reawakenings and even vocations to Lewis's influence'.[15] One of these was Joy Davidman, the woman Lewis married late in life. Their relationship too began with themselves as 'pen-friends', after Lewis's writings had influenced Joy's own conversion.[16]

Many of the thousands of letters Lewis wrote have been edited and published in separate volumes. Perhaps the most interesting correspondence in which Lewis acted as spiritual mentor is found in the book, *Letters to an American lady*. Here, unlike other books of his published letters, we can discern the dynamics of an ongoing relationship with one person in particular and Lewis's response as guide. These letters were written to a woman he had never met, a Roman Catholic widow, described by those who knew her as a very charming and gracious southern aristocratic woman who was a writer of articles, poems and stories. Because she wished to remain anonymous when the letters were published, she is referred to simply as Mary, 'an American lady'.[17] Lewis wrote to her from 1950 to a few months before his death 22 November 1963, and even though some of the letters are brief due to the pressure of other responsibilities, Lewis's concern for the woman is evident. His letters to her reveal how spiritual mentoring, while it definitely includes discussion of the spiritual life, often goes beyond so-called 'religious' topics and 'God-talk'.

In those letters, Lewis discussed everything with her—from the price of books to his love for his homeland, Ireland, and his numerous visits there: 'All the mountains look like mountains in a story, and there are wooded valleys, and golden sands, and the smell of peat from every cottage'.[18] However, when she is faced with an unnamed 'terrible affliction', Lewis is not afraid to offer serious advice: 'The great thing, as you have obviously seen, (both as regards pain and financial worries) is to live from day to day and hour to hour not adding the past or future to the present'. In another letter, he suggests that she avoid taking other people's inventories: 'Try not to think—much less speak of *their* sins. One's own are a more profitable theme!' Concerning the paradox of ministry, he tells her that 'very often I expect, the service He really demands is that of *not* being (apparently) used, or not in the way we expect, or not in a way we can perceive'. For the most part, any advice he gives is presented in the context of his own life: 'What most often interrupts my own prayers is not great distractions but tiny ones—things one will have to do or avoid in the course of the next hour'.[19]

This is perhaps the most common characteristic of Lewis's guidance: a willingness to share his sacred journey in all its joy and sorrow with her. Describing his life and others' as 'a wandering to find home', he tells her of his marriage in 1956 to Joy Davidman, and how 'no one can mark the exact moment at which friendship becomes love'. He speaks of the adoption of Joy's two sons as his own, and the adjustment that produced: 'My brother and I have been coping with them for their Christmas holidays. Nice boys, but gruelling work for two old bachelors! I'm dead tired now.' When his wife dies of cancer four years later, he acknowledges his sense of overwhelming loss and speaks of his own insights into the dimensions of grief: 'It isn't a state, but a process. It keeps on changing—like a winding road with quite a new landscape at each bend.' As his life draws to a close, Lewis enunciates a principle underlying all mentoring: 'we are members of one another whether we choose to recognize the fact or not'.[20] He also talks about an experience of personal conversion and reconciliation with a long-time (and long-dead) enemy:

> Do you know, only a few weeks ago I realized that I at last *had* forgiven the cruel schoolmaster who so darkened my childhood. I'd been trying to do it for years; and like you, each time I thought I'd done it, I found, after a week or so it all had to be attempted over again. But this time I feel sure it is the real thing. And (like learning to swim or to ride a bicycle) the moment it does happen it seems so easy and you wonder why on earth you didn't do it years ago.[21]

His last letters to the American lady allude to his own death and confirm his belief in resurrection. He tells her that 'it will be fun when we at last meet', and, in farewell: 'I am quite comfortable but very easily tired. . . . So you must expect my letters to be very few and very short. More a wave of the hand than a letter.'[22]

Sheldon Vanauken, author of *A severe mercy*, summarizes what many experienced through Lewis's letter-writing. For him, Lewis was 'a strong, genial, stimulating, loving presence in my life. . . . above all, a friend'.[23] One other observation can be made. As much as Lewis's writing to people had a positive effect on their lives, he too learned, even to the point of incorporating that style of composition into two highly readable and successful books which took the form of letters: *The Screwtape letters*, and *Letters to Malcolm: chiefly on prayer*. The latter, published posthumously, discusses, as Lewis did with the American lady, the dimensions of prayer, including its many distractions.[24]

C. S. Lewis as preacher

Not a great deal is written about Lewis as a lay preacher, especially when we consider the amount of space his biographers give to other aspects of his career. When we turn to some of Lewis's published remarks as well as the recollections of friends, however, we discover how extensively he was involved in this form of spiritual mentoring.[25] Not only did he preach at various Oxford and University of London chapels throughout his career, he also served during World War II on the Staff of the Chaplains' Department of the Royal Air Force. This was at the time he was giving his ecumenical 'Broadcast Talks' for the BBC explaining what he called 'plain Christianity'.[26] Such involvement—in addition to his other professional responsibilities—might surprise us and even Lewis himself. As a friend of his recalled, 'Lewis often said that if anyone had told him in his atheist days that he would someday step into a pulpit and preach he would have considered that man raving mad'.[27]

Those who heard Lewis preach relate how much they experienced his sermons as a form of *personal* spiritual guidance despite their being part of large, crowded congregations or a vast radio audience. A colleague of Lewis's at Oxford, Father Gervase Mathew, tells us that no matter what the occasion, Lewis always 'forged a personal link with those

who heard him'.[28] Erik Routley, a student at Oxford during
the war years, suggests that so many people felt that linkage
because of Lewis's personal attentiveness and serious concentration on his listeners when he spoke. According to Routley,
this was Lewis's 'great secret' and it explains why so many
people had 'precious memories' of him.[29] Routley was present
on two occasions when Lewis preached in Oxford's Church of
St Mary the Virgin. Lewis's first sermon there, in the place
where such notables as John Wesley and John Henry Newman
also had preached, was delivered in the fall of 1939. That Lewis
as a layman had been asked to preach at St Mary's was
evidently a public recognition of his varied talents in other
areas, since Walter Hooper, his biographer, says that 'perhaps
the greatest accolade given Lewis' was this invitation.[30] As
Routley remembers the occasion:

> It was odd enough in those days to have a preacher
> there who wasn't a clergyman of the Church of
> England, and I thought I would go along. The service
> was held at 8.00 p.m. on Sunday, and I suppose I
> arrived about ten minutes before eight. There was
> hardly a seat to be had.[31]

The young man's initial curiosity was rewarded, for he heard
Lewis preach one of the great sermons of his career, 'Learning
in war-time'.

'We are members of one body', Lewis told his congregation, 'but differentiated members, each with his own vocation.' Whatever our vocations might be, rooted as they are
in our upbringing, talents, choices and circumstances beyond
our control, all find their value in one principle: 'The work of
Beethoven, and the work of a charwoman, become spiritual
on precisely the same condition, that of being offered to God,
of being done humbly "as to the Lord"'. Discerning our
vocation also includes, Lewis said, leaving the future in God's
hands:

> Never, in peace and war, commit your virtue or your
> happiness to the future. Happy work is best done by the
> man who takes his long-term plans somewhat lightly
> and works from moment to moment 'as to the Lord'.[32]

Routley returned to the University Church in June 1941, to hear Lewis preach the sermon entitled 'The weight of glory', described by two of his biographers as 'perhaps the most sublime piece of prose' ever to come from Lewis's pen.[33] Again, Routley tells us, 'the place was packed solid before the service began', and yet, the manner in which Lewis 'used words as precision tools, the effortless rhythm of sentences, the scholarship made friendly, the sternness made beautiful— these things all made it impossible for the listener to notice the passing of time'.[34] What especially touched his listeners was the power of Lewis's convictions, evident in the passage which is the origin of the sermon's title:

> It may be possible for each to think too much of his own potential glory hereafter; it is hardly possible for him to think too often or too deeply about that of his neighbor. The load, or weight, or burden of my neighbor's glory should be laid daily on my back, a load so heavy that only humility can carry it. . . . There are no *ordinary* people. You have never talked to a mere mortal . . . [I]t is immortals whom we joke with, work with, marry, snub, and exploit.[35]

Routley left the church after the service, deeply moved by what he called Lewis's poetry in the service of the gospel.

Stuart Babbage, a chaplain in the British Royal Air Force, gives us another account of Lewis's preaching, this time to a congregation not composed of young university students. In *C. S. Lewis: speaker and teacher*, Babbage describes 'one unforgettable night' when Lewis spoke to a select congregation of servicemen. As he tells the story, Lewis had been warned earlier that the officers and airmen to whom he would preach that evening would possibly face some form of ostracism from their more sceptical comrades for their participation in the religious service. Lewis had said then to Babbage that 'it might be helpful if I told them something of what it costs me to be a Christian'.

That evening, with the Air Force chapel just as uncomfortably crowded as any Oxford church, Lewis evidently remembered his earlier conversation. As Babbage recalls the scene:

151

Lewis stood in the aisle, a dishevelled and dumpy figure in a baggy suit. Having invoked the Name of the Father, the Son, and the Holy Spirit, he announced his text: 'If any man will come after me, let him deny himself, and take up his cross, and follow me'.

So skilful in his use of metaphor and story, Lewis then went on to describe in vivid imagery the torture and brutal death of Jesus. He did not stop there, however, but brought the experience of Jesus into dialogue with his own:

> Lewis told us what it had cost him, as an Oxford don, to be a Christian. . . . His liberal and rational friends, he explained, did not object to his intellectual interest in Christianity; . . . but to insist on seriously practising it—that was going too far. He did not mind being accused of religious mania, that familiar gibe of the natural man; what he was unprepared for was the intense hostility and animosity of his professional colleagues.

Lewis related these hurtful memories, Babbage tells us, because of his concern for those who were listening to him. He also reminded them by way of concluding that any form of ostracism they might face was not so unusual or unexpected if each of them recalled the original gospel story of a man who experienced new life in spite of suffering and even death. The simplicity of Lewis's message and the personal witness he gave profoundly affected his listeners, 'for this was powerful preaching, born of intense and personally felt emotion'.[36]

According to Babbage, a number of factors obviously contributed to Lewis's effectiveness as a preacher: his ability as a story-teller; his speaking clearly and directly in 'patterns of ordinary conversation'; his bringing into dialogue (as a pastoral theologian would) contemporary experience and Christian tradition. Most important, Babbage posits, was Lewis's instinctive appreciation of empathy and self-identification. He knew how 'to disarm his hearers by placing himself on the same level as those to whom he spoke'. This was not just clever deception or mere posturing: 'Lewis was emphatic that he was neither a professional theologian nor a clergyman. He was, he insisted, a "mere Christian"', struggling like the rest of his listeners to understand and make sense of life and the Christian heritage. Lewis's 'itinerant ministry', travelling the length and breadth of England during wartime instead of staying safe within Oxford's hallowed halls, revealed to Babbage Lewis's vast charity and that he had a 'pastor's heart'.[37]

The foundation of Lewis's mentoring

Clearly, Lewis was a very effective spiritual mentor, a layman of many gifts and qualities, all of which he brought to his ministry. Some of those qualities have already been named: his personal warmth and hospitality, his sense of humour and magnanimity, his willingness to share the wisdom gained from personal experience and reflection upon it. In retrospect, perhaps Lewis's greatest quality, the one which connects all the others, was his care: a deep and abiding concern that Austin Farrer, a colleague and friend of Lewis, described as Lewis's 'taking of the world into his heart'.[38] This capacity for loving was manifest in his compassion and profound respect toward others. It was also evident in his genuine humility: that joyful acceptance of himself as a 'mere Christian' who desired nothing more than to 'compare notes' with others rather than 'presuming to instruct'.[39] Most of all, when we consider all of Lewis's mentoring, this care was manifest in what his brother Warren called Lewis's 'remarkable talent for friendship'.[40] As our research shows, many people considered Lewis beyond his degrees and scholarly achievements (even in spite of them) as, quite simply, a friend: someone who cared deeply about them, treated them as equals, loved them as they were. Judging from his many friendships as well as his numerous writings on that theme, it is no wonder that he tells us in *Surprised by joy* how 'friendship has been by far the chief source of my happiness'.[41] As a manifestation of his care, it was also the foundation of his mentoring.

A story told by Clifford Morris expresses not only how Lewis's friendship and care were often linked in people's minds, but also how Lewis believed friendship itself, like prayer, is based upon trust and speaking the truth to one another:

> I remember that I once wanted to speak to him [Lewis] about something that was in the nature of a very personal and delicate matter, and he must have sensed my diffidence. I shall never forget . . . how he turned to me, how he smiled at me, and how he then said with tremendous affection, 'My dear Morris, *friends* can say *anything* to one another, and be quite sure that no confidence will be broken'. His written words—so deservedly popular—and his spoken words to private individuals—so remembered and cherished—were freely given, but not without care.[42]

As Morris's story reveals and Lewis's other relationships confirm, Lewis as spiritual mentor encouraged and invited people, through his care, to speak from the heart—to speak openly and honestly about themselves in ways that often led to greater depth in the relationship as well as, in many cases, to conversion, 'a change of heart'. John Henry Newman equated friendship with 'heart speaking to heart',[43] and in the history of Christian spirituality, it is one of the most ancient and valued practices. The desert fathers and mothers believed that this *exagoreusis*, opening one's heart, leads to *hesychia*, inner peace of heart, and John Cassian, writing in the fifth century, speaks of its healing power: 'The foul serpent from the dark underground cavern must be released; otherwise it will rot'.[44] Carl Jung, writing in the twentieth century, would agree with Cassian on the need for self-revelation, but he also was convinced that any guidance which leads to healing or transformation depends not only on honest communication between people, but on the wisdom and care of the guide: 'The practice of this art lies in the heart; if your heart is false, the physician within you will be false'.[45]

Now we begin to see why Farrer referred to Lewis's friendship and care in terms of the heart. The qualities Lewis brought to his ministry, especially his care, had a transforming effect on people, helping many to discern a direction in their lives as well as the presence of a caring God who is with us as friend and companion on our journeys. Such charisms used for community service have often been associated in the past with the power of ordination. The chaplain Babbage, for example, quoted earlier, compared Lewis's care to his having a pastor's heart. What Lewis's ministry teaches us, however, is that one does not have to be 'officially' ordained to manifest a care called 'pastoral' nor that only the ordained have the power to effect dramatic change. As Chad Walsh writes in *Light on C. S. Lewis* when discussing one form of Lewis's mentoring: 'Though no bishop ever laid hands upon his head, he was a genuine pastoral counsellor via the postal system to many fellow pilgrims who perhaps never sat in the study of an ordained minister'.[46] In some mysterious way, all Lewis's forms of spiritual mentoring transcended the distinctions between those who are or are not ordained, revealing that there is no greater ministry than that advocated by Jesus: 'I call you friends . . . love one another as I have loved you' (John 15: 12–17).

Implications for our mentoring

What are some of the implications of Lewis's mentoring for our own ministries? What are some lessons he as spiritual mentor can teach us, a people of a different age and members of a seemingly more complex society and Church? Presupposing that each of us will draw his or her own conclusions, let me initially delineate some here.

First, Lewis can help us recognize the importance of friendship, *our* friendship, as the foundation of any mentoring we do. We may not have all Lewis's talents and qualities, but all of us, made in God's image, have the capacity to reach out with care, to offer others our friendship when it is appropriate to do so. The inter-relationship between friendship and mentoring is affirmed not only by Lewis's ministry, but by such people as the Yale psychologist, Daniel Levinson, in his work, *The seasons of a man's life*, and by such groups as Alcoholics Anonymous.[47] Even Thomas Merton, echoing the words of Lewis to Morris, describes the spiritual director as primarily a friend with whom we can say 'what we really mean in the depths of our souls, not what we think we are expected to say'.[48] We can see in this unity of opinion that just as there are no 'ordinary people', fundamentally there really is no ordinary mentoring if it is done with respect, compassion and care.

Second, as Lewis's mentoring reveals, it is often difficult to distinguish spiritual mentoring from other forms. While the spiritual mentor's relationship may be characterized by more depth and focused more on the 'spiritual' dimensions of life, such as conversion, vocation and the quality of our relationships with neighbour and God, it is often closely intertwined with other forms of mentoring like those of being a teacher, sponsor or counsellor. As Lewis's relationship with Bede Griffiths shows, spiritual mentoring *in practice* sometimes only occurs because other forms of mentoring have, in fact, preceded it. Perhaps the real difference between spiritual mentoring and other forms is related more to the Christian beliefs and vision the spiritual mentor brings to the relationship than to any difference in specific functions. Certainly, if we agree with Lewis that 'there is no essential quarrel between the spiritual life and the human activities as such',[49] we can see that to exclude any of the ordinary activities of 'mere Christianity' is to deny the fundamental goodness of creation, the unity of our humanity-divinity, and the sacredness of our journeys through time.

Third, Lewis's ministry teaches us that our spiritual mentoring can take many forms. It need not be limited to only one-to-one relationships, but can include large groups inside or outside of liturgical settings. What is important in spiritual mentoring is not whether we are ordained, but that we are convinced of the value of mentoring and that, through our pastoral care, we are able to forge a link with others and speak a language of the heart.

Fourth, Lewis's mentoring reminds us that any linkage between ourselves and others depends on the willingness *and courage* to share our lives and stories—not as people with all the answers, but as those who are searching too for wisdom in the midst of multiple responsibilities and uncertainties. Lewis's sermon to the Norfolk airmen bears this out: honestly sharing our struggles and dreams brings us closer to one another, not farther apart. As Lewis said so often, 'we are members of one another', and the sharing of our stories confirms how much we have in common.

Fifth, although we are not necessarily as talented as Lewis, we all have the ability and responsibility to identify and develop the qualities we do have. We can do this in the same way Lewis did: by taking time to reflect on our experiences and the questions which they raise. This reflection is not only theology in its most basic sense as 'faith seeking understanding', but also a form of prayer which can become a daily practice and discipline. Through our contemplation, we might develop an ever-deepening gratitude and wonder for all those who have loved us first—long before we had awakened to a Higher Power of Love. We might begin to see what they have contributed, and what we, in turn, can contribute to other lives. Such reflection, what Lewis described as 'going down into the cellar',[50] might even help us begin to accept and celebrate both our strengths and limitations, in their totality, as resources for our ministry.

Sixth, Lewis's many significant relationships consistently demonstrate how all mentoring, especially spiritual mentoring, is a form of empowerment which helps others discern their vocations, acknowledge their gifts, and begin to give shape to their dreams. As Lewis's and Griffiths' relationship also reveals, there is a paradox present in such empowering. Helping others discern their call and encouraging them to risk changes can affect the mentor as much as the person being mentored. In a very real way, mentoring contributes to each person's process of ongoing conversion and discernment of vocational response. This mutuality in mentoring, so often experienced by those who call themselves friends, affirms the most fundamental belief of all Christians: it is not Christianity in the abstract that saves, but Christianity in the flesh.

Finally, Lewis teaches us that genuine mentoring transcends space and time. An encounter with a mentor is not wholly dependent on physical meetings, but on the deepest level of communication: the communion of souls. This communion of souls is clearly demonstrated in all Lewis's mentoring relationships, most especially with the American lady. In retrospect, we can see how—though they never met—in a very real sense they had.

Conclusion

The ancient Irish had a word for someone who acts as a friendly mentor to another human being. The word is *anamchara*, Gaelic for 'soul friend', someone who joyfully embraces our life, questions, and suffering as an extension of his or her own. The Irish also believed that anyone without a soul friend was 'like a body without a head' or like 'the water of a limey well, not good to drink nor good for wishing'.[51] C. S. Lewis stands in that tradition. For many of us, when we read his books or the stories about him, we encounter a friend who opens windows on our souls revealing *our* belief in the ministry of all the baptized, our search for a united Church which values the gifts of everyone, *our* need for friendships and genuine community.

To propose Lewis as a model of spiritual mentoring is in no way to deny his human limitations. As various friends of his admit, Lewis could be stubborn when he thought he was right as well as intolerant of certain aspects of modern life which we might consider essential to an informed citizenry. (He refused, for example, to listen to a radio or read a daily newspaper, stating that if anything were important enough someone would tell him.) His views on women and the headship of families—at least until he met and married Joy Davidman—would be considered by many today as archaic, if not outright sexist. Still, as we have seen, his gifts far surpassed his limitations, and even some of those limitations can be seen, like our own, as the reverse side of certain strengths. Whether or not we agree with all of Lewis's opinions (and we would be unthinking cultists if we did), many of us, like the Cambridge scientist who met him for the first time, perceive him as 'a very good man, to whom goodness did not come easily'.[52] In that recognition, we are given hope in our own struggle to live holy lives.

Anyone who considers Lewis a soul friend and visits his beloved Oxford experiences his presence in certain places: Magdalen College where he tutored and wrote so many letters, the Church of St Mary the Virgin where he preached, the Eastgate Hotel where he first met Joy Davidman, the Eagle and Child pub where he and the Inklings met each week.

While the words of Shakespeare, 'Men must endure their going hence', imprinted so starkly on Lewis's tomb in the country churchyard, remind us of the reality of death and of our own mortality, those other places and Lewis's own words remind us of a greater reality: how our friendships survive death itself. As he wrote in his last book:

> Then the new earth and sky, the same yet not the same as these, will live in us as we have risen in Christ. And once again, after who knows what aeons of the silence and the dark, the birds will sing and the waters flow, and the lights and shadows move across the hills, and the faces of our friends laugh upon us with amazed recognition.[53]

Notes

1 See Lewis, C. S.: *Mere Christianity* (New York: Macmillan, 1952), p. 65.

2 H. M. Blamires, quoted in Lewis, Warren (ed.): *Letters of C. S. Lewis* (New York: Harcourt, Brace, Jovanovich, 1966), p. 17.

3 See Brewer, Derek: 'The tutor; a portrait,' pp. 42–48, in Como, James T. (ed.): *C. S. Lewis at the breakfast table* (New York: Macmillan, 1979).

4 See Rigby, Luke, OSB: 'A solid man', pp. 38–40 in Como, *C. S. Lewis at the breakfast table*.

5 Griffiths, Bede: *The golden string* (Springfield, IL: Templegate, 1954), p. 32.

6 *Ibid.*, p. 48.

7 See *idem*, 'The adventure of faith', pp. 11–15 in Como, *C. S. Lewis at the breakfast table*.

8 *Ibid.*, p. 11.

9 Both St Augustine and Thomas Merton, for example, discuss in their autobiographies how, after years of searching and struggling with questions, each experienced the culmination of his conversion process in solitude. See Augustine, *The confessions*, Book VIII, chapter 12, and Merton's *The seven storey mountain* (New York: Harcourt, Brace, Jovanovich, 1948), pp. 215 ff.

10 See Lewis, C. S.: *Surprised by joy* (New York: Harcourt, Brace & World, 1955), pp. 226–229 and see Griffiths, *The golden string*, pp. 102–108.

11 Lewis, *Surprised by joy*, p. 234.

12 Griffiths, 'The adventure of faith', p. 16.

13 *Ibid.*, pp. 19, 24.

14 Kilby, Clyde S. (ed.): *C. S. Lewis: Letters to an American lady* (Grand Rapids, MI: Eerdmans, 1967), p. 7.

15 See Como, *C. S. Lewis at the breakfast table*, pp. xxi–xxv.

16 See Kilby, Clyde and Lamp Mead, Marjorie (eds): *Brothers and friends* (San Francisco: Harper & Row, 1982), p. 244 and Dorsett, Lyle: *And God came in* (New York: Macmillan, 1983), pp. 69 ff.

17 For a description of the American lady and Lewis's relationship to her, see Kilby, Clyde (ed.): *Letters to an American lady*, pp. 8–9.

18 *Ibid.*, pp. 12, 30–32, 43.

19 *Ibid.*, pp. 67, 93, 70–71 respectively.

20 *Ibid.*, pp. 81, 63, 89, 109.

21 *Ibid.*, p. 117.

22 *Ibid.*, pp. 116 and 121.

23 Vanauken, Sheldon: *A severe mercy* (New York: Bantam Books, 1979), p. 229.

24 See Lewis, *Letters to Malcolm: chiefly on prayer* (New York: Harcourt, Brace, Jovanovich, 1963), especially pp. 23, 90–91.

25 See, for example, the preface in Lewis, C. S., *The weight of glory and other addresses* (New York: Macmillan, 1949) where Lewis speaks of 'the too numerous addresses I was induced to give during the late war and the years that immediately followed it'; also Hooper, Walter (ed.): *They stand together* (New York: Macmillan, 1979), p. 491, where Lewis, in a letter to his friend, Arthur Greeves, discusses spending his vacation lecturing and preaching to the Royal Air Force.

26 Lewis, C. S.: *Broadcast talks* (London: Geoffrey Bles, 1942), p. 5.

27 Green, Roger Lancelyn and Hooper, Walter: *C. S. Lewis: a biography* (New York: Harcourt, Brace, Jovanovich, 1974), p. 184.

28 Mathew, Gervase: 'Orator', p. 96 in Como, *C. S. Lewis at the breakfast table*.

29 Routley, Erik: 'A prophet', p. 36 in Como, *C. S. Lewis at the breakfast table*.

30 Hooper, Walter: *Through joy and beyond* (New York: Macmillan, 1972), p. 97.

31 See Routley, 'A prophet', pp. 33–34.

32 See Lewis, *The weight of glory and other addresses*, pp. 43–54.

33 Green and Hooper, *C. S. Lewis: a biography*, p. 203.

34 Routley, 'A prophet', p. 34.

35 See Lewis, *The weight of glory and other addresses*, pp. 1–15.

36 See Babbage, Stuart Barton: 'To the Royal Air Force', pp. 99–101 in Keefe, Carolyn (ed.): *C. S. Lewis: speaker and teacher* (Grand Rapids, MI: Zondervan Publishing Co., 1971).

37 *Ibid.*, pp. 94–97.

38 Farrer, Austin: 'In his image', p. 242, in Como, *C. S. Lewis at the breakfast table*.

39 Lewis, C. S.: *Reflections on the psalms* (New York: Harcourt, Brace, Jovanovich, 1958), p. 2.

40 Lewis, Warren, ed., *Letters of C. S. Lewis*, p. 13.

41 Lewis, C. S.: *Surprised by joy*, p. 33.

42 Morris, Clifford: 'A Christian gentleman', p. 198, in Como, *C. S. Lewis at the breakfast table*.

43 Newman's personal motto was '*cor ad cor loquitur*'. See Martin, Brian: *John Henry Newman: his life and work* (New York: Oxford University Press, 1982; London: Geoffrey Chapman Mowbray, 1989/Mahwah, NJ: Paulist Press, 1990), p. 141.

44 See Corcoran, Sr Donald: 'Spiritual guidance', pp. 448–451 in *Christian spirituality; origins to the twelfth century*, ed. Bernard McGinn and John Meyendorff (New York: Crossroad, 1985).

45 See Jung, Carl: *The Spirit in man, art, and literature* (Princeton: Princeton University Press, 1966).

46 See Walsh, Chad: 'Impact on America', p. 116 in Giff, Jocelyn (ed.): *Light on C. S. Lewis* (London: Geoffrey Bles Ltd, 1965).

47 See Levinson, Daniel: *The seasons of a man's life* (New York: Alfred Knopf, 1978), p. 97, where he describes mentoring as simply friendship with someone a little more experienced who acts as a guide. Regarding the A.A. sponsor see Alcoholics Anonymous, *Questions and answers on sponsorship* (New York: A.A., 1976) and my *Guidance on our journeys* (Center City, MN: Hazelden Publications, 1984).

48 See Merton, Thomas: *Spiritual direction and meditation* (Collegeville, MN: Liturgical Press, 1960), pp. 40, 29.

49 See Lewis, C. S.: *The weight of glory and other addresses*, pp. 47–48.

50 See Rigby, 'A solid man', pp. 65–66.

51 *Book of Leinster*, 283b, lines 26ff., my translation.

52 See Brewer, 'The tutor: a portrait', p. 64.

53 Lewis, C. S.: *Letters to Malcolm: chiefly on prayer*, p. 124.

(vol. 27, no. 4, October 1987)

PART II

Spiritual Direction and Other Faiths

The *Guru* in Hinduism

Michael Barnes SJ

Not by reasoning is this sacred doctrine to be attained;
Taught by another it is well understood.
Katha Upanishad 2.9.

Nowadays spiritual directors are out and the *guru* is in—a wise
preceptor who solves all problems with a mystic saying or
some mildly incomprehensible *koan*. The deeper appreciation
we now have for Indian spirituality is clearly to be welcomed.
Even when it takes the form of a sort of craze for oriental
exotica there are immense benefits to be gained from an
acquaintance with another religious tradition and from the
dialogue-in-practice which it occasions. But the *guru* in Hinduism is both more and less than a spiritual director and our
homely caricature (which, no doubt, no-one takes seriously)
does have the unfortunate side-effect of trivializing the richness of the real Hindu tradition. Certainly the *guru* is a spiritual
guide. But that does not say a great deal for Hinduism is all
about *sādhana*, a word which connotes the purposive quest of a
particular goal and might almost be translated as the search for
one's literal 'spiritual direction'; the *guru* is but one means to
this general and all-embracing end.

More importantly, the *guru* is what in India is often called a
jñāni or 'realized soul'. He is the one who knows, who has
experienced the presence of God within. And only the one
who has attained such a contemplative knowledge of God can
communicate it to others. To speak of the *guru*, therefore, is to
take up a theme which is profoundly Indian and which only
really makes sense against its properly Indian background.

What is it that he knows? And how is that knowledge to be passed on? The object of this article is to answer such questions by finding the right setting, by considering what sort of a tradition the *guru* comes from, and by suggesting an appropriately Indian understanding of his role.

To find our Indian setting let us begin in the holy city of Varanasi or Benares. Here every devout Hindu wishes to die, to be cremated at the burning *ghat* and have his ashes returned to the sacred river Ganges and thence, he hopes, to immortality with the gods. Varanasi is a centre of pilgrimage. Every morning, as the sun rises over the river, devotees swarm down to the bathing-places to perform their ritual ablutions. The endless tinkling bells and cymbals, the singing of *bhajans*, the recitation of prayers, and, perhaps more than anything else, the cheerfully chaotic city itself with its narrow winding back-streets where one's progress is quite likely to be halted by a somnolent but quite immovable cow, all tell of a religion of great power and colour but precious little organization. The mistake is probably to regard Hinduism as one religion. It is really a whole complex of beliefs and practices, some complementary, some contradictory, which defy reduction to easy dogmas and formulae. To pick out one or two as 'key' is to risk distortion. Nevertheless, a certain ill-defined structure does make itself felt. It is probably best illustrated by the image of the mighty river Ganges itself.

For obvious reasons rivers are regarded as sacred and no river is more sacred than the Ganges. The water which flows from the Himalayas brings life and a source of purification. More importantly it represents the whole cycle of creation which emanates from the home of the gods, Mount Meru, the centre of the universe, and includes the whole continuum of creation, from the gods themselves to the crops which grow along the riverbanks, and the thousands of tiny creatures who depend ultimately on the life-giving waters for their very existence. The act of piety which casts the ashes of the dead into the river simply completes the cycle. Creation returns to the source from which it comes. The river flows on to become one with the vastness of the ocean from whence it will return eventually as rain upon the cosmic mountain and the whole cycle begins again. This is the cycle of *Samsāra*, literally what-flows-together, a word which denotes the endless round of births, deaths and rebirths, and which we have come to call the transmigration of souls. Two other ideas make up the basic structure of Indian religion, whether at Varanasi or elsewhere: the first is the concept of *Karma*, literally work, which refers to the positive or negative value of one's actions as the determining factor of the nature of one's next life; the other is *Moksha*, the state of absolute release, however conceived, from the whole painful cycle of rebirth.

This decidedly unwieldy complex of ideas did not emerge as the logical outcome of an original revelation or teaching. Hinduism can be traced back to the *Vedas*, perhaps as far as 1500 BC, but formative influences were at work long before that, and perhaps the most significant creative period in the religion comes with the *Upanishads*, the earliest of which are to be dated around 700 BC. Here we find references to groups of ascetics who have renounced their normal worldly ties and are wandering around the country seeking for the way to achieve *Moksha* and existing by begging in the villages. Where these people come from and how they are to be distinguished from the distinctly heterodox Buddhist and Jain communities who flourished at approximately the same time, is still a matter of scholarly dispute. One point, however, is clear: the religion we call Hinduism is the result of a long-established tension between the traditional religion of society characterized by devotion and ritual, keeping in tune with *Samsāra*, the whole cycle of creation, and the more radical asceticism of the renouncer with its concern for personal experience and assurance that one has achieved true *Moksha*. Both these types of religion are present in modern Varanasi. In large temples and the most basic of wayside shrines people make their offerings and recite prayers, a witness to the extraordinary faith which characterizes the holy city. But alongside the ordinary devotees and pilgrims are the spiritual élite, the holy men, usually clad in saffron robes, often dusty and dirty and looking more than slightly disreputable, and just occasionally showing by their peaceful and serene expressions that they have come close to the *Moksha* they seek.

Just how many are charlatans it is difficult to say. The influx of Western seekers-after-truth on the various well-travelled hippie trails means that there is an adequate supply of gullible customers. But India itself has always been fascinated by the exotic and mysterious. Stories abound of the marvellous feats and esoteric powers enjoyed by all sorts of weird and wonderful characters. In the *Rig Veda*, for instance, we hear of the long-haired ascetic who drinks hallucinatory drugs and 'rides with the rush of the wind'.[1] The ancient epics and *Purānas* are full of the exploits of spiritual virtuosi who find the way to *Moksha* the hard way—by self-inflicted torture, for instance, standing for years on one leg or with one arm held up in the air. Nor are these legends just fanciful stories, as pictures in contemporary magazines indicate. In every temple compound is to be found a gaggle of homeless mendicants, clanking their tins and begging for alms—another hurdle to be negotiated by the intrepid tourist, but, for the devout Hindu, figures of great holiness and sources of religious merit. What began as a rejection of the tradition, born of a dissatisfaction with the ritual of the *Veda*, has now become a respected part of the mainstream and institutionalized under the title of *Sannyāsa*. A true *sannyāsi* has abandoned all ties with the world and wanders homeless, begging his food and eating only enough to sustain his life in a relentless search for Ultimate Truth.

Yet the *sannyāsi* is not a parasite upon society. If anything, the reverse is the truth—at least religiously. For the holy man is a sacrament of the Divine—not just a reminder of religious values in a world given over to the pursuit of gain and self-interest, but a real contact with the God who is 'so hard to see'. Merely to set eyes on a holy man, still more to enter into his presence and hold converse with him, is in some sense a communion with God. The relationship of the pupil with his *guru* is one aspect of this vision of the Divine present in and through the human. The primary religious act is not to seek advice or direction but to receive *darshan*—a word which literally means observation or sight, but connotes the act of entering into the presence of the *guru* in order to benefit from the Divine Power which, as it were, radiates from him. In the first place the *guru* is simply a teacher. The earliest *guru*s were brahmins whose task was to preserve the traditional lore of the *Vedas* by passing it on to the privileged higher castes. Young boys went through a stage of life called *Brahmacarya* when they gave themselves over totally to the direction of their teacher. According to the ancient texts they should revere him even more than their parents, for whereas parents give physical life, it is in the power of the *guru* to bring about a second, a spiritual birth. But the word *guru* means weighty or authoritative, and that gives some indication of his true function. The real *guru* has personal authority, not something inherited or the possession of a privileged caste, but a clear indication that this man has himself experienced the Divine. He knows. He has entered the presence of God.

The *guru* is more than a teacher or personal mentor. He is also a philosopher and a sort of spiritual artist, conjuring new ideas and themes out of the richness of Vedic religion. As the sage who knows, the teacher of the one who seeks to learn, he is the guide to our understanding of the *Upanishads*, those complex mystical writings which are the philosophical heart of so much of Indian religion. The word *Upanishad* means something like sitting-down-near. The texts themselves are often couched in the form of a dialogue between the *guru* and the disciple whom he initiates into the true meaning of the ancient Vedic sacrifice. And the teaching is often esoteric, a private revelation. Thus when the young man, Artabhāga, comes to the great sage Yājñavalkya and asks what happens to a person after death, he gets the reply, 'Artabhāga, my dear, take my hand. We two only will know of this. This is not for us two to speak of in public.' The author of the text comments: 'The two went away and deliberated. What they said was *karma* [action]. What they praised was *karma*. Verily, one becomes good by good action, bad by bad action.'[2]

This is not book learning. Such teaching is to be assimilated through the heart. The external ritual must be interiorized; the gods are to be found through introspection and meditation. Ultimately, teach the sages, *Brahman*, the impersonal Holy Power which pervades the universe, is to be integrated with *Ātman*, that spiritual power which is the 'spark of the Divine', the individual's own deepest self. In a celebrated dialogue Uddālaka tries to explain to his pupil, Śvetaketu:

'Place this salt in the water. In the morning come unto me.'

Then he did so.

Then he said to him: 'That salt you placed in the water last evening—please bring it hither'.

Then he grasped for it but did not find it, as it was completely dissolved.

'Please take a sip of it from this end', he said. 'How is it?'

'Salt.'

'Take a sip from the middle', said he. 'How is it?'

'Salt.'

'Take a sip from that end', said he. 'How is it?'

'Salt.'

'Set it aside. Then come unto me.'

He did so, saying, 'It is always the same'.

Then he said to him: 'Verily, indeed, my dear, you do not perceive.

Being here. Verily indeed, it is here.

That which is the finest essence—this whole world has that as its soul. That is Reality. That is *Ātman* [Soul]. That art thou, Śvetaketu.'[3]

The *guru* is the one who has already experienced this identity in his own life, whose past *karma* has been neutralized through a mystical gnosis, and who has therefore achieved *Moksha*, true liberation of the Spirit which is, as it were, imprisoned in his mortal body. The teaching of the *Upanishads* is often notoriously obscure, but then knowledge has to be thoroughly assimilated; it cannot simply be taken on trust. The *guru's* experience must become that of his pupil. We search the texts in vain for the secret of 'how it is done'. Everything depends not on technique but on the living tradition which is passed on only through a personal and very intimate relationship. For the disciple the *guru* is the means of direct access to God.

The understanding of *Moksha* varies. For some schools— and this is particularly true of the *Upanishads*—it is just a monistic merging of the self back into the One from which it came, as the drop of water is reunited with the ocean. But there are also theistic schools where the *summum bonum* is the vision of a personal God. All depends on the relationship of loving devotion or *bhakti* which is established with him. In this type of religion the most celebrated *guru* is undoubtedly the Krishna of the *Bhagavad Gītā* who appears as the charioteer of the young warrior Arjuna but is really an incarnation of the great god Vishnu. The dialogue of the *Gītā* begins with a careful imparting of information, gradually builds up the level of trust between teacher and disciple and climaxes with the most incredible theophany in which Krishna reveals himself in all his glory to his adoring pupil. Having assumed his human form once again, Krishna addresses Arjuna:

> Right hard to see is this my form which you have seen: this is the form the gods themselves forever crave to see. Not by the *vedas* or grim-ascetic-practice, not by the giving of alms or sacrifice can I be seen in such a form as you did see Me; but by worship-of-love addressed to Me, none other, Arjuna, can I be known and seen in such a form and as I really am. So can my lovers enter into Me. Do works for Me, make Me your highest goal, be loyal-in-love to Me, cut off all other attachments, have no hatred for any other being at all: for all who do thus shall come to Me.[4]

Krishna is in fact the *guru* par excellence—the complete and undivided focus of attention. Arjuna is told simply to surrender his entire will and all his actions to Krishna. More than a teacher, Krishna has become the centre of all adoration.

The position that Krishna holds in the *Bhagavad Gītā*, combining the qualities of the all-knowing sage with the compassion of the Divine, goes some way to explaining the high position which the *guru* holds in contemporary Hinduism. Most modern Hindus follow the way of *Bhakti*, that is to say are devotees of one of the two great gods, Vishnu or Siva, or of one of their many incarnations or local forms. In addition devotion is also accorded to the various forms of the goddess and to any number of lesser gods and spirits. Such religion is often highly emotional and charged with a deep and moving faith; great emphasis is placed on the value of personal experience. For the most part, the holy man or *sannyāsi*, whether he is a *guru* who initiates disciples into the secrets of the sect, or just one of the eccentric crew of hangers-on muttering *mantras* at the temple gate, is a remote and mysterious figure. But without him Hinduism would lose much of its creative energy. At one level the *guru* is just a teacher—of anything, from dancing or singing to the esoteric secrets of religion. But there are also leaders of sects, maintaining age-old traditions, heads of *maths* or monasteries, and men whose claim to fame is simply their very obvious holiness and wisdom. But even such broad definitions fail to fit the complexity of Hinduism. In general a *guru* is anyone or indeed anything (in Sikhism, for instance, the *guru* is the book of sacred scriptures, the *Guru Granth Sahib*) through which one attains enlightenment or *Moksha*. The *guru* is the means, a focus in which the Divine has become so intensely localized that for the devotee he or it *is* the Divine.

While it is difficult to be precise, the career of the *guru* tends to follow a fairly typical pattern. As a young man he leaves home, preferring the wandering life of *Sannyāsa* to the more conventional way of marriage. He moves from one holy place to another, perhaps encountering various teachers on the way, until finally he meets the *guru* with whom he can establish an immediate and lasting rapport. The disciple remains with the *guru* in his *ashram* or hermitage, committing himself to him and promising to obey him in everything. Eventually he will receive initiation or *dīkshā* from his teacher. He is given a special *mantra*, perhaps a verse from scripture or a sacred syllable, which is believed to have an inherent power for enlightenment concentrated within it. The *mantra* is kept secret; it is the personal gift of the *guru* and is appropriate for the age, temperament and spiritual progress of the disciple. In some way it sums up the teaching of the *guru*. The disciple makes it the centre of his devotion, repeating it over and over again. The *mantra* is the key to *Moksha*—the direct communication of *guru* to disciple. Once he has grasped the full import of his master's instruction and achieved great spiritual progress, the disciple, while still maintaining his loyalty to the *guru*, may leave the *ashram* or found his own elsewhere. His reputation for holiness will eventually bring him his own disciples in turn. Or he may succeed his old master when he dies, thus continuing the tradition of initiation handed down from one generation of *guru*s to another.

Strictly speaking a holy man only becomes a *guru* when he

has a disciple. In the first place he is the one who has obtained *Moksha* and is therefore able to guide others by his own experience. But the communication of that experience is not a purely intellectual exercise. More often than not it takes place in silence as *guru* and disciple meditate together, and the pupil learns to feed off the deep spiritual riches which radiate from the master. Abhishiktananda, the Benedictine priest Henri Le Saux, who led the life of a traditional Indian *sannyāsi* for almost twenty-five years and who came under the influence of one of the most remarkable of contemporary *guru*s, Ramana Maharshi, the sage of Tiruvannamalai in south India, tries to explain:

> If the *guru* keeps silence, there is between him and his disciple a communion and communication on a level much deeper than that of normal consciousness. If the *guru* chooses to speak, his teaching, behind and beneath the words he uses, reaches and opens up in the disciple the very same depth from which it has arisen in the soul of the *guru*. Such is the only means of communicating spiritual truth.[5]

What is required on the part of the disciple is nothing less than total openness and complete surrender to his *guru*. At which point the Christian may well object that such obedience to a human *guru* must be incompatible with discipleship of Christ. For if Jesus says 'You must not allow yourselves to be called Rabbi, since you have only one Master' (Matthew 23:8), then none other than Jesus should be called *guru* either. And in the gospels Jesus does appear precisely as a *guru*: he calls himself teacher but he is also the Way, the Truth and the Life and the Light of the world. Above all he is the Word of God who makes known the Father's glory to humankind. Certainly a Christian will find some difficulty over the degree of veneration given to the *guru* and the seeming ease with which Hindus multiply incarnations of the Divine. The uniqueness of Christ can be easily compromised.

Yet may we not also be missing an important insight? The risen Christ, the Christian's *guru*, speaks through silence in the same way as the ideal human *guru* speaks to his disciple. Our Western caricature misses the vital point: the *guru* teaches not by what he does, or even by what he says, but by what he is.

The true *guru* does not entice or manipulate. He is but a holy presence, a still silence at the heart of a religion which is restlessly seeking the Divine. Most Hindus practise a religion which is based on the temple and the tiny shrines along the roads and in the corners of their houses. Few have ever sought out the *guru* in the silence of far off *ashrams*. But everyone knows that the holy men are there, that the sacred knowledge is being taught and lived—by a very few, perhaps, but by enough to give life and inspiration to the religion of millions of devotees. That there are men in whom the mystical merging of the soul into the One has actually been experienced is a fact, not just an ideal. Unfortunately, of course, the exaggerated respect shown to some of the more notorious Western exports shows Hinduism in a very poor light; all too easily *gurus* can be treated as super-psychiatrists, the objects of a vapid personality cult. Sometimes they deserve no better. But away from the packaged joss-sticks, the instant *Nirvāna* and the benign images of bearded mystics the real tradition is rather different.

In a religion which looks towards the return of all things to their source in the Divine, the *guru* is no longer an individual, still less a personality. He has died completely to this world. Only the One remains. How much of this essentially monistic vision is compatible with Christianity raises many a tricky theological issue which are not to be solved in a handful of pithy sentences. Suffice it to say in conclusion that the relationship of *guru* and disciple is not to be equated with the Western idea of spiritual direction. The disciple may seek advice and the *guru* may give it. But unless both are at the same time actively seeking that deeper relationship with God which transcends all human language, no amount of talk will lead to enlightenment. Ultimately the *guru* teaches through example: that in love and humility a silence can be created in which the voice of God may be heard.

Notes

[1] *Rig Veda*, X, 136.

[2] *Brihadāranyaka Upanishad*, 3.2.13. Translated from *The thirteen principal Upanishads* by R. E. Hume (London, 1931).

[3] *Chāndogya Upanishad*, 6.13.1 (*ibid.*).

[4] *Bhagavad Gītā*, 11, 52–55. Translated from R. C. Zaehner's edition with commentary (London, 1969).

[5] Abhishiktananda, *Saccidananda, a Christian approach to Advaitic experience* (Delhi, 1974), pp. 27–28.

(vol. 24, no. 2, April 1984)

Masters and Mastery in Zen

Michael Barnes SJ

Zen masters, though occasionally to be found on the mystic fringes of an Iris Murdoch novel or wandering absent-mindedly through the pages of one of the Sunday supplements, are necessarily rather obscure—not to say obscurantist—characters. Like all religious virtuosi they are single-minded and ascetic, yet curiously manage somehow to combine profundity with humanity, wisdom with humour. They are hardly cosy characters, objects of admiration rather than affection and, to followers of a more comfortable and consoling religion, perhaps even something of a threat. It is not difficult to understand why this should be so. Their religion seems magnificently straightforward, thin on dogma and admirably free of aggressive argumentation. Yet, for all its superficial attractiveness, Zen is a lonely way and not for the faint-hearted. Perhaps to the average Westerner this parti-cular form of Buddhism seems to reflect too much the Chinese or Japanese character—remote and rather forbidding. Perhaps, too, the familiarity we often find in other religious traditions is obscured by the distinctly uncomfortable silence which hangs haughtily over so much of the religion of the Far East. But to anyone who is prepared to remain still long enough to note his or her discomfort Zen offers more than an object-lesson to stoicism. The Christian will find plenty that is familiar and much that is challenging. This little sketch of Zen and the *roshi* or master may not remove the obscurity: it might at least explain the context and ease our suspicion.

The aim of Buddhism, according to a modern collection of chants, is 'to dispel the clouds of ignorance and to make shine the sun of enlightenment'.[1] To become a master means coming to terms with one fact of experience which has become a sort of fundamental principle in all forms of Buddhism: we never actually perceive anything as it really is. All our experiencing, our understanding, even our recognition of objects or persons is conditioned by memories of the past or fears, hopes and anxieties for the future. Not a very profound observation, perhaps; more a statement of the obvious. But immediately it gives the lie to the popular caricature of the Zen master as the other-worldly mystic rapt in contemplation of the eternal *Nirvāna*, the Totally Other, Utterly Transcendent or whatever. Zen concentrates on *this* world, on a correct view of the present in which the distorting effects of our petty ego have been eradicated and the full reality—the beauty *and* the pain—of our world are accepted and contemplated with complete peace and equanimity. The first Noble Truth taught by the Buddha speaks of suffering at the heart of all human experience. But the real sickness, once properly diagnosed, is seen to lie not in the world 'out there' but in the nature of the human subject who brings suffering upon himself by refusing to accept that world as it really is. As one recent writer puts it, 'the desire for becoming other than what present experience gives'.[2]

In the whole massively complex vocabulary of the various canons perhaps the single most typically Buddhist word is not one of the four Noble Truths nor one of the elements which makes up the Noble Eightfold Path, but the simple adjective which describes each element: the word 'right'. The Buddha does not just insist on striving or mindfulness or concentration but on *right* striving, *right* mindfulness, *right* concentration. But what makes a practice 'right'? That it leads to the goal—enlightenment. The Buddha saw himself essentially as a practical teacher or physician who could diagnose the ills of the world and prescribe a cure for those who wanted it. All forms of Buddhism—and this is especially true of Zen which prides itself on maintaining the essential purity of the original meditative tradition—teach a solution to or salvation from the present human condition. But in the first place—and in the last place too—one must *see* correctly. Only the right diagnosis will lead to the right cure; only the one who sees and accepts the present conditioned world of *Samsāra* and rebirth will gain an insight into the unconditioned: what is usually referred to as *Nirvāna*. In fact so essentially linked have these two become that in the more broadly-based and expansive *Mahāyāna* tradition they are identified. This is the ultimate Buddhist paradox: the one who lives completely in touch with *this* world of *Samsāra* is the most perfectly enlightened and in touch with the Ultimate.

Zen pushes this *Mahāyāna* notion to its extreme and thus tries to combine an absolutist concern for correct metaphysical analysis with a typically pragmatic Buddhist humanism. There are no secrets, no esoteric doctrines, no mysterious initiation rites. Zen is essentially practical and direct. But, if this is the orthodox Zen opinion of itself, the immediate impression one picks up is of philosophical perversity, hiding nihilism behind a façade of profundity. Horrific and rather unsubtle stories about the practice of the early patriarchs abound. Bodhidharma, for instance, the legendary founder of Zen, who brought the tradition from India to China, is supposed to have practised 'wall-gazing' for nine years until his legs dropped off. One of Bodhidharma's pupils, on being refused admission as a disciple, cut off one of his arms just to show the master how serious he was. Such stories may be dismissed as fanciful but, even today, Zen training, which involves long hours of silent sitting and various forms of physical beating and mental gymnastics, seems outrageously self-indulgent, not to say masochistic. Do not the enigmatic *koans* and the endlessly baffling stories about how such-and-such a master reached enlightenment serve only to confuse rather than clarify? Is not the average Western sceptic justified in regarding Zen as a typical example of human religiosity: at best a frustrating search for some sort of 'religious' experience, at worst a vain attempt to manipulate the divine?

We forget one thing. Zen is not the sort of pre-packaged spiritual technology which comes with its own built-in guarantee of satisfaction. Zen cannot be learnt from a book; no religious tradition can be understood merely by reading the words on a page. Buddhism, as much as any religion, depends on the living tradition, on the practice of the saints and their countless disciples. As an aside we may note that, throughout the history of Buddhism, whenever the *Sangha*, the community of Buddhist monks, dies out, the authentic practice is soon lost. The demise of Buddhism in its native India is only the most obvious example. Yet one of the most significant characteristics which Buddhism takes from its Indian roots has never been lost: the central position of the holy man, the enlightened one who has the power to instruct and inspire, in short to be another Buddha. The *Mahāyānist* ideal is the compassionate *Bodhisattva*, the 'being-for-enlightenment' who puts off his own ultimate *Nirvāna* in order to lead others to theirs. In the ancient *Theravāda* tradition too we find the Way of Deliverance, described in many sermons, as beginning when the householder 'hears the words of a *Tathāgata*' (one who has 'fared so') and resolves to 'go forth from home to the homeless life'.[3] Right view, the first step on the Noble Eightfold Path, begins with an attitude of trust in the teacher. In the Tantric tradition of Tibet the monk often takes a fourth refuge; in addition to the Buddha, the Dharma or Buddha's teaching and the *Sangha*, he seeks refuge in his teacher or *guru*, the embodiment of the Buddhist ideal. And in Zen, perhaps more than in other Buddhist schools, the way to enlightenment depends on the relationship established between teacher and pupil. The *roshi*, like all *bodhisattvas*, seeks not just his own enlightenment but the enlightenment of others too; his very *raison d'être* is to instruct, to be the medium whereby the Buddha's teaching continues.

In addition to all the many spiritual techniques which are shared with *Mahāyānists* and *Theravādins* alike, Zen emphasizes the formal interview in which spiritual progress can periodically be established. So much of Zen literature is based on the verbal sparring between master and pupil and only makes sense if it is seen as the record of a particular relationship and not as general rules of instruction. The aim is simple: to help the pupil see correctly, to accept everything that present experience gives. The obstacles, however, are formidable. The classical formula gives three: greed, hatred and delusion. They cannot be separated, the one growing from the others and enmeshing the individual in a net of his own making. Exacting periods of self-discipline and constant attention are required before the moment of liberating insight occurs. Much of Zen practice—the careful instruction on posture, the measured breathing, the deepening awareness of every aspect of experience—aim to overcome the three defilements which inhibit the growth of another triad, the three trainings: morality, concentration and wisdom. But enlightenment does not come through personal discipline alone. The story is told of the monk in a hurry who eagerly enquired of his teacher how long it would take for him to be enlightened. 'Perhaps ten years', said the teacher. 'But if I tried very hard?' asked the pupil. 'Then it would probably take you twenty', came the reply. Effort is not enough and can be positively unhelpful in developing true wisdom.

The function of the teacher—apart from elementary advice and direction—is to provide the liberating insight, to discern when the moment has arrived quite literally to shake the pupil out of his everyday awareness and to induce that indescribable experience called *Nirvāna* or *Satori*. The interview between master and pupil is hardly akin to Western notions of spiritual direction. The meeting is described by one author as having the 'sudden death quality of a duel'.[4] Each pupil has only a few seconds with the master, when his turn comes, after waiting some time in the queue, he is already keyed-up; he knows exactly what he wants to say, but he never knows what to expect. The master wastes no time in assessing the pupil's progress and problems. Sometimes he provides advice; sometimes he deliberately provokes or shocks—even to the extent of boxing his pupil's ears or (an old favourite) twisting his nose. The purpose, however, is not to punish. The point is, rather, that the spiritual crisis sometimes only comes through a physical one; the pupil is knocked out of his spiritual rut. Not that the shock has to be physical. Many of the best stories make the 'provocation' a statement of the obvious or the deliberately paradoxical. Dumoulin quotes an example:

> A monk once asked Chao-chou, 'Master, I am still a novice. Show me the way!' Chao-chou said, 'Have you finished your breakfast?' 'I have', replied the monk. 'Then go wash your bowl!' Thereupon the monk was enlightened.[5]

The master's role then, is primarily to act as a catalyst, to trigger an appropriate response from the pupil. To that end he must have established a real human relationship with the pupil. Zen stories are not, therefore, funds of universal wisdom but intended for particular individuals. What *is* universal is the respect with which all pupils regard the master, as an enlightened one. His charism is not, in the first place, the skill of the director but the sympathetic wisdom of one who has 'gone before'. The atmosphere of the interview may be highly charged, but not because the pupil is nervous or the teacher overbearing. Rather the former realizes he is in the presence of a wise man who speaks only of what he knows. Each word counts; no doubt the mood of constant expectation combined with a few terse phrases can be enough to provoke the insight into the nature of reality which is the aim of Zen. The early text attributed to Bodhidarma sums up:

> A special tradition outside the scriptures;
> No dependence on words and letters;
> Direct pointing at the soul of man;
> Seeing into one's own nature, and the attainment of Buddhahood.[6]

Members of the Zen school trace their own origins right back beyond Bodhidharma to the Buddha himself. One day while preaching to the assembled *Sangha* the Buddha held up a golden lotus flower. None in the assembly understood except the great elder, Mahākāsyapa, who looked at the master and smiled. The Buddha said: 'I have the True Dharma Eye, marvellous mind of *Nirvāna*. This now I transmit to you, Mahākāsyapa.' The great Theravādin scholar, the Venerable Walpola Rahula, has to admit that this episode is 'of doubtful origin' and points out that the whole notion of truth being handed down through a sort of hierarchy is 'absolutely repugnant to the spirit of Buddha's teaching'.[7] Nevertheless, the story illustrates one of the key elements of the ethos of Zen: the passing on of the 'seal of the Buddha-mind' from master to pupil.[8] Where does this particular ethos come from? Zen comes from the Chinese *Ch'an*, meaning meditation, and it owes its peculiar quality as much to the native Chinese Taoist religion as to its ancient Indian roots. The Taoist sage, like the Indian *sannyāsi*, retires to the forests and mountains in search of contemplative peace, but he is much more a sign of contradiction than his Indian counterpart. He seems almost deliberately opposed to the stolid conservatism and conventionality of Confucianism. He represents the spontaneous side of the Chinese character, that which keeps intuitively in touch with the everyday world of birth and death, growth and decay. Whereas the Indian *sannyāsi* is a refugee from the world, responding to the universal call to seek *Moksha*, release or other-worldly value, the Chinese sage lives very consciously in harmony with this world and the everyday rhythms of nature.

We must be careful, however, not to overstate the case. The two are not opposed; they complement each other. And it is this fundamental complementarity of inner vision which allowed Buddhism to grow so fruitfully on Chinese soil. The celebrated distinction between gradual and sudden enlightenment which some Chinese commentators put down to a fundamental difference in temperament—the Indians, with their inclination to scientific analysis, preferring the former and the Chinese, with their deeply ingrained intuitive sense, given to the latter—is found in all forms of Buddhism; it says more about the complex nature of the enlightenment experience than it does about the Chinese contribution to Buddhist culture. Zen does have its own—admittedly pretty undefinable—quality, but it is one which has fundamentally enhanced rather than changed the basic Buddhist spirit: to see and accept the true nature of reality.

How then are we to describe the special character of Zen? The name of the school takes us back to the Sanskrit *Dhyāna*, meditation, and we would not go far wrong in assuming from this that Zen is remarkable not for any special doctrine so much as for practice. But the first thing that must strike the student of Zen is the influence exercised by so many of the ancient patriarchs and masters. They all seem quite eccentric, given to extravagant gestures and crazy expressions. They are iconoclastic too: on one particularly cold night T'ien-jan took down the wooden Buddha-image from the wall of the temple and made a fire out of it. After all, it was no more than a piece of wood. And Hui-neng, the legendary sixth patriarch and founder of the southern school of Ch'an which emphasizes sudden enlightenment, is supposed to have torn up the *sūtras* in order to show that enlightenment does not consist in learning words but in having experience.

The actions of such men remind us more of the Jewish prophets than of Indian mystics. There is more than a little of the prophet in Ma-tsu, one of the successors of Hui-neng and influential in the founding of the powerful Lin-chi sect. He used paradox, rudeness of manner and plain brutality to induce enlightenment, on one occasion grabbing and twisting the nose of a disciple until the poor man cried out with pain. The disciple—of course—attained instant enlightenment. For Ma-tsu constant sitting in meditation was not enough. He recalled the occasion when his own master questioned him rather roughly:

> 'Why are you sitting in meditation?' 'In order to
> become a Buddha', replied the aggrieved disciple. The
> master took up a tile and started polishing it. 'What are
> you doing?' asked Ma-tsu. 'Polishing this stone to make
> a mirror', replied the master. 'But how can you make a
> mirror out of a tile?' asked Ma-tsu. 'How can you make
> a Buddha by sitting in meditation?' came the reply.

What 'more' is required? The endless—seemingly ludicrous— stories about enlightenment being attained by breaking a leg, losing a finger, or being beaten over the head are meant to underline the fact that all methods and means are in the last resort only intended to help one see correctly. To use the Buddha's favourite illustration: the raft which is used to cross over the stream must be left behind when it has served its purpose. 'What is the Buddha?' a monk asked Yun-men. 'A dried-up shit-stick', came the reply. The Buddha is everything. To be enlightened is to see the Buddha-nature in all things. It is simply a matter of Right View.

In Japan there are two major branches of Zen—Rinzai, the successor of the Chinese southern or Lin-chi school, and Soto which reaches back to the ninth century Ts'ao-tung sect in China. The greatest soto master is acknowledged to be Dogen (1200–1253) who learnt his Zen in China where he first sought an answer to the problem of innate and acquired *Nirvāna*: if all things contain a Buddha-nature, then why did the Buddhas and the Bodhisattvas arouse the longing for enlightenment and engage in ascetic practices? The monastery where Dogen finally solved his problem was notable for its extreme ascetism. Dogen learnt to sit in meditation for long hours and it is largely through his influence that *zazen* or sitting-meditation is accepted as the central practice of all Zen, representing the age-old traditions of the Buddha and the patriarchs.

An account of Zen training and techniques of meditation by a modern master, Katsuki Sekida, bears witness to the continuing influence of Dogen's teaching and to the claim of Zen to present no esoteric teaching but simple practical methods for reaching enlightenment.[9] Soto attaches great importance to right surroundings, to posture, to regular breathing and to mindfulness. Various ways of sitting are recommended, the ideal being the lotus-posture which produces the perfect solid base on which the body naturally squats upright. But other postures are possible. It is important to be comfortable, with the weight firmly anchored so that the breath can sink naturally into the belly area, the *tanden*, the source of all vitality and power. Correct posture helps correct breathing, allowing the vital energy of the body to flow unhindered—to find, as it were, its natural level. In *zazen* one does not force the breathing into a special pattern: the body finds its own equilibrium. In this Zen differs from Yoga. In the latter consciousness is deliberately conformed to—and therefore formed by—the pattern of breathing. In Zen, as taught by Dogen, the meditator must allow the breath to regulate itself so that one becomes conscious of the movement and of the unity of mind and body. In Dogen's own words, 'Free yourself from all attachments . . . Bring to an end all desires, all concepts and judgments. Do not think about how to become a Buddha.'[10] Enlightenment is, of course, a special experience and must be prepared for with great patience, but it is not different *in kind* from every moment spent in the peaceful practice of *zazen*. Why desire anything for the future when everything is to be found in the present moment? All things already contain the Buddha-nature. If only—Dogen would say—we could recognize the fact and rest content.

Unlike the calm and contemplative Dogen, Hakuin (1685–1768), the great representative of the rinzai school, appears as an ecstatic for whom enlightenment is a regular—and deeply emotional—experience. A sudden rapture can seize him, whether in meditation or walking or standing still, whether in the temple or out in the country. Nevertheless he agrees with Dogen that only long hours in painstaking formal meditation will lead to enlightenment. For Hakuin meditation means especially the practice of the *koan*—a puzzling, paradoxical or even nonsensical statement which challenges and tries the limits of the problem-solving intellect. *Koan* means literally 'public notice' or 'public announcement'. The technique is said to go back to the earliest days but is associated with some of the great names of the Lin-chi sect in China. Collections of the most famous *koans*, based on the anecdotal utterances of great masters, are presented to the pupil not to try his patience but, as Dumoulin puts it, as 'one great mockery of all the rules of logic'.[11] The pupil tries to solve the problem intellectually. He fails of course. Somehow the rigid straitjacket in which the mind is encased which forces the pupil to perceive and think in one particular way has got to be broken. Built up gradually is a certain doubt about the normal mode of perception and with it an inevitable psychic tension. Sooner or later something must snap—and then true enlightenment can begin.

The process is often explained by analogy with archery. There comes the crucial moment when the archer must give way to the enormous tension he is fighting to control. At that point he lets go and the arrow is allowed to shoot itself. The art of Japanese *sumi-e* painting and calligraphy (and Hakuin was nothing if not a great artist) depends on the painter overcoming his natural desire to control and direct the brush. Katsuki Sekida speaks of his own experience of entering a state of absorption or *samādhi* in which the picture seemed to paint itself; he was quite unaware of any process of thinking *about* the picture. The brush strokes follow automatically from the regular rhythm induced by controlled breathing.

But—to return to Hakuin and the *koan*—such a strange method of meditation only begins to make sense when we understand that what is being developed is not an intellectual 'answer' but a moment of intuition which goes quite beyond discourse or words. Perhaps the most famous of all Hakuin's *koans* is the sound of one hand clapping. If what we have said above is correct, there is no right or wrong answer. Hakuin once gave it to one of his female disciples:

> 'What is the sound of one hand?' he asked her. 'Much better than hearing the sound of Hakuin's hand is to clap both hands—then we can do business!' she shot back. Hakuin replied: 'If you can really do business by clapping both hands, you don't need to hear the sound of one hand'.[12]

The one hand *koan* was the product of Hakuin's old age. He believed that, more than any other problem, it had the power to awaken doubt and, with the tension that great doubt induced, provoke great enlightenment. However we may seek to explain the process psychologically, it seems clear that the moment of release after a period of intense confinement or pressure brings with it a tremendous stimulus and a moment of great exaltation. But it is probably a mistake to see the *koan* technique as a practice limited to times of meditation. It represents not so much 'a problem' but the paradox of life itself—which one must live with patience and which can only be resolved in the stillness of inner recollection. That much must be an experience of all religions. Tempting as it is, however, to speculate about Christian parallels, let us end rather with some words of the great master himself:

> A man went astray and arrived at a spot which had never been trodden by the foot of man. Before him there yawned a bottomless chasm. His feet stood on the slippery moss of a rock and no secure foothold appeared around him. He could step neither forward nor backward. Only death awaited him. The vine which he grasped with his left hand and the tendril which he held with his right hand could offer him little help. His life hung as by a single thread. Were he to release both hands at once, his dry bones would come to nought.
>
> Thus it is with the zen disciple. By pursuing a single *koan* he comes to a point where his mind is as if dead and his will as if extinguished. This state is like a wide void over a deep chasm and no hold remains for hand or foot. All thoughts vanish and in his bosom burns hot

anxiety. But then suddenly it occurs that with the *koan* both body and mind break. This is the instant when the hands are released over the abyss. In this sudden upsurge it is as if one drinks water and knows for oneself heat and cold. Great joy wells up. This is called rebirth [in the Pure Land]. This is termed seeing into one's nature. Everything depends on pushing forward and not doubting that with the help of this concentration one will eventually penetrate to the ground of one's nature.[13]

Notes

[1] *Daily Sutras for chanting and recitation* (London: Zen Society), p. 43.

[2] Carrithers, Michael: *The Buddha* (OUP, 1983), p. 64.

[3] Sāmaññaphala Sutta, DN 1, 62 ff. (PTS ed.).

[4] Robinson, Richard H. and Johnson, Willard L.: *The Buddhist religion* (Belmont, CA: Wadsworth, 3rd ed. 1983), p. 179.

[5] Dumoulin, Heinrich: *A history of Zen Buddhism* (Faber, 1963), p. 37.

[6] Quoted in Dumoulin, *op. cit.*, p. 67.

[7] Rahula, Walpola: *Zen and the taming of the bull* (Gordon Fraser, 1978), p. 19.

[8] Dumoulin, *op. cit.*, p. 68.

[9] Sekida, Katsuki: *Zen training, methods and philosophy* (New York: Weatherhill, 1975). Perhaps more accessible is Kennett, Jiyu: *Selling water by the river* (Allen and Unwin, 1973), a manual of Zen training which provides a fascinating insight into the religious practices of Zen.

[10] Quoted in Dumoulin, *op. cit.*, pp. 163–164.

[11] Dumoulin, *op. cit.*, p. 130.

[12] Quoted in Stevens, John: 'Zen and the common man', in *The middle way*, vol. 60, 1 (May 1985), p. 33.

[13] Quoted in Dumoulin, *op. cit.*, p. 259.

(vol. 26, no. 3, July 1986)

Spiritual Guidance in Islam: I
A case study: Sharafuddin Maneri

Paul Jackson sj

Divine guidance

The notion of guidance is firmly established in Islam at its most fundamental level, that of God's guidance of his people. This is done through divine revelation granted to the various prophets to enable them to guide the people along the path to God. The original Islamic notion was very simple: there is only one religion (*dīn*)[1] which consists in acknowledging and worshipping the one true God. Unfortunately human beings were continually falling into the sin of placing somebody or something on the same level as God (*shirk*). The popular expression of this root sin was polytheism with its consequent idol-worship. God was thus moved to send prophets down the ages to call people back to the one true religion, that of belief in one God. This was Muhammad's pristine under-standing, for he saw himself as a prophet sent by God to call his own people, the Arabs, from idolatry to the worship of the one true God, Allah. For him the various monotheistic reli-gions were merely different forms of the one true religion. Only later on in Medina, when the Jews refused to acknow-ledge his prophetic mission, did he begin to think of Islam as a distinct religion. Thus it is the prophet Muhammad (d. 632) who channels divine revelation to the Arabs through the Quran, the very word of God.

Another fundamental pivot on which the whole notion of guidance rests is found in the following Quranic verse: 'Your Lord brought forth descendants from the loins of Adam's children, and made them testify against themselves. He said: "Am I not your Lord?" They replied: "We bear witness that you are". This he did, lest you should say on the day of resurrection: "We had no knowledge of that"' (Q7:172). This covenant is given the visual form of God's summoning, as it were, every single human being before him for an instant in order to establish in clear terms the relationship of his lordship over each one of them. This is the common interpretation, but it needs to be pointed out that it is not a domineering type of lordship which is meant but one where the Lord looks after, cherishes, nourishes and educates those who are dependent upon him. It is a literary expression of the ontological dependence inherent in the creator–creature relationship and forms, as it were, the metaphysical backdrop for the entire spiritual life of the Sufis, the mystic saints of Islam.

Prophetic guidance

Although God's revelation, as found in its final form in the Quran, gives the general framework of the needed guidance, and even provides some detailed injunctions, a pious Muslim will have to look elsewhere to find the answers to a whole host of practical difficulties that arise in everyday living. Thus occurred the gradual development of Islamic law (shari'at) which one Muslim author has described as 'the way or road in the religion of Muhammad, which God has established for the guidance of his people, both for the worship of God and for the duties of life'.[2] The word itself originally refers to the beaten track leading to a well or spring—an image which lends itself to poetic development. Suffice it to say that one follows the beaten track along with everybody else: one does not try to find a new path for oneself. In addition to the divine guidance contained in the Quran the other great source is that provided by the example (sunna) of the Prophet himself and as found recorded in the Traditions (hadīth). These two sources were elaborated by the early jurists who made use of analogical reasoning and general consensus. Thus was born Islamic jurisprudence (fiqh).[3] Because of the comparative simplicity of Islamic belief, the great minds were more interested in answering the question, 'What is God's will for me in this particular situation?' than to grapple with theological problems such as exercised the great Christian thinkers down the centuries, who had the mysteries of the incarnation and redemption to contend with, not to mention that of the Trinity.

Community guidance

Because of geographical and other consequent difficulties, different schools (*maḍhab*) grew up in different centres. Even today orthodox Sunni Muslims—who form the vast majority—belong to one or other of the four great schools. There is no such thing as a uniform law for all Muslims. Interestingly enough, the root meaning of *maḍhab* is a road entered upon, from which the notion of a school emerges. We notice once again the central idea of going along a given road together with others and not seeking to blaze a new trail for oneself. The pious Muslim in India, for example, when confronted with a particularly knotty problem which the local officials do not seem to know how to handle, will write to the Dar ul-Ulum in Deoband for an official answer—known as a *fatwā*—from a highly trained specialist, a *muftī*. This decision will be given according to the Hanafite school, the one commonly followed in India.

Compensating somewhat for the lack of due regard for individualistic behaviour is the purpose behind the whole emphasis on law, namely the heartfelt desire to do the will of God. No matter what action a person may perform the most important aspect that has to be considered is whether it conforms to the divine will or not. For example, if you ask an ordinary Indian Muslim why he is observing the annual month-long fast, the most common answer is simply because it is God's will!

The Sufis

As Islam spread in the early centuries, here and there individuals were drawn to a more personal response to the divine mystery. We read about Hasan of Basra (d. 728), Malik Dinar

(d. 748) and Rabi'a, the outstanding woman Sufi (d. 801). By the tenth century we find that Sufi Orders (*ṭarīqat*) have developed around famous Sufis, such as Junaid of Baghdad (d. 910). Later on the more popular term was *silsila* (a chain) because, by this time, great emphasis was placed on being able to trace one's spiritual initiation back to Ali (d. 661), Muhammad's first cousin and son-in-law to whom—it was commonly believed—Muhammad had entrusted special esoteric knowledge and spiritual power. This was one example of Shi'a influence in the development of Sufism. The word *ṭarīqat* was still used to indicate a specific group. The word itself means road, way or path. Sufis were often called 'The people of the way' while the more common term—Sufi—comes from the early practice of wearing wool (*ṣūf*) in imitation of Christian ascetics.

In so far as Sufis sought a more personal and intimate union with God there was tension with the jurists who were concerned with observable actions. One class of Sufis—those without the law (*bē 'shar'*)—did not help matters, for they considered themselves to be beyond the law. The most famous Sufis, however, adhered strictly to the law—those with the law (*bā 'shar'*)—and were indeed most scrupulous in its observance.

As mentioned, the outstanding Sufis attracted disciples and thus the institution of personalized guidance developed in Islam. This aspect was especially prominent in India, probably being reinforced by the Hindu tradition of the master–disciple (*guru–chēlā*) relationship. With this general background, let us look at a renowned Indian Sufi spiritual guide, Sheikh Sharafuddin Maneri.

The life of Sharafuddin Maneri

Before delving deeply into what Sharafuddin Maneri has to offer in the line of spiritual guidance it will be helpful to draw a brief life-sketch of the man.[4] He was born in Maner, about 25 kilometres west of Patna, the capital of Bihar state in present-day India, around 1290 CE. Both his father, Yahya, and his mother, Bibi Razia, belonged to families which were steeped in the Sufi tradition. Thus young Ahmad—as he was called—grew up in a God-centred milieu from his very birth. He had three brothers and at least one sister, but his was the specially graced nature which responded to the inspiring example of his pious parents. He did his early schooling in Maner but, when he reached his teens, a famous scholar, Maulana Abu Tau'ama, called in to Maner on his way from Delhi to Sonargaon, the old capital of East Bengal, situated on the outskirts of Dhaka, the present capital of Bangladesh. Young Ahmad was eager to seize the opportunity to pursue his studies under such an eminent scholar, while Abu Tau'ama saw what a promising student he was and readily acceded to his request—made with his father's permission—to accompany him to Sonargaon, arriving there in the year 1304.

He was a diligent and capable student and threw himself whole-heartedly into his studies. Years of such unrelieved intellectual activity eventually put a severe strain on his health and we are told that he fell ill. The physicians of the locality recommended intercourse, so he took a slave-girl by whom he had a son, Zakiuddin. This probably occurred when he was close to thirty years of age. The arrangement was quite in accordance with Islamic law and Zakiuddin had the full rights of a legitimate son. When Ahmad left Sonargaon in 1323 he took his young son with him to Maner. Sharafuddin[5] himself says absolutely nothing about the boy's mother, and no ancient manuscript mentions her name. Sharafuddin could have exercised his right to marry if and when he wished, but he chose not to do so and lived a celibate life from the time he left Sonargaon until his death on 2 January 1381.

The highly educated thirty-three-year-old Sharafuddin could not settle down in Maner, yet it was not a thirst for knowledge that impelled him to go to Delhi, as he felt a confident satisfaction in his intellectual attainments. What was stirring within him was a desire to give himself completely to God, to seek him alone, and he felt the need for guidance. Sheikh Nizamuddin Auliya was the most renowned Sufi Sheikh at that time so Sharafuddin set out to meet him, in the spring of 1324, having entrusted his son wholly into the care of his own mother, Bibi Razia. The meeting proved to be disappointing. Nizamuddin recognized his worth but he was an old man with death just around the corner (d. April 1325), and Sharafuddin felt no attraction to become his disciple. He then set off to meet another famous Sufi of Panipat, Bu Qalandar, also near death (d. September 1324). He was impressed by his high spiritual attainments but noticed that he was not capable of offering guidance. Disappointed, he returned to Delhi and was on the point of leaving when his brother persuaded him to meet a lesser known Sufi, Sheikh Najibuddin Firdausi (d. 1332), who lived quite close to the Qutb Minar. It was this meeting which changed his life and enabled him to become a great spiritual guide himself, for he was instantly attracted to Najibuddin and entrusted himself to his care and guidance. He remained with him until his death eight years later, having experienced for himself what it meant to be lovingly guided.

With the death of his guide he no longer wished to remain in Delhi and set out to return to Maner but, on the way, he turned aside into the jungle of Bihia in order to be alone with the Alone. After a year or so he ended up in a cave in Rajgir, a hilly locality south of Patna, noted for its religious association with the Buddha, Mahavir, and countless Hindu, Buddhist and Jain ascetics. His cave was near a small spring and the spot is still a place of pilgrimage today. It is known as 'Makhdum Kund', for Sharafuddin became known as 'Makhdum-i Jahan' (the teacher of the world). Today he is referred to by the local people as 'Makhdum Sahib'. He managed only a modicum of privacy in his cave because some of Nizamuddin Auliya's disciples came to him for guidance, while the ordinary people came to get him to intercede with the local Muslim administrator by having him write petitions on their behalf. Because Nizamuddin's disciples were coming all the way from Bihar town, eighteen kilometres away, to consult him, he decided it would be easier for them if he were to go to Bihar each Friday for the congregational prayer and people could consult him there. Gradually his sojourn there was extended to Saturday, Sunday and even longer as the crowds grew. Finally he was simply forced to remain there permanently. This took place by 1336. He spent the rest of his life there until his death in 1381. He was buried next to his mother in a spot not far from his residence. People still come daily to his tomb to seek his intercession and, on his feast-day—the day he died, known as 'urs (marriage) because on that day he experienced the heavenly nuptials—huge crowds of people come. The word *Sharif* has been added to the name Bihar to indicate that the town has been honoured by his presence.

Sharafuddin the guide

The first thing we notice about Sharafuddin as a spiritual guide is the fact that he never sought to guide anybody. He was earnestly seeking intimate union with God in his cave in Rajgir when people came to him for guidance. Sheikh Bukhari, his first permanent disciple, went to him first when he was in Rajgir. His practice of going to Bihar each Friday was not in order to get more disciples—that was an unforeseen but not unexpected development—but simply to make things easier for those who were already coming to consult him. It was one of countless expressions of his exquisite sense of courtesy.

Sharafuddin himself took no initiative to construct any buildings which would formalize and institutionalize his standing as a Sheikh, a spiritual guide. His first humble dwelling was prepared for him by the chief Chishti disciple who had been visiting him in Rajgir. When the reigning Sultan, Muhammad bin Tughluq (1325–1351) heard that he had emerged from solitude he sent him a Bulgharian carpet and ordered the governor of Bihar to construct a large *khānqāh* (hospice) for him and his disciples to live in, and directed that certain revenues should be utilized for its upkeep. All of this embarrassed Sharafuddin. He was loath to accept either the carpet or the hospice, but had to acquiesce when the governor reminded him what would probably happen to him if the Sultan's order was not executed! One cannot help but contrast his behaviour with that of some others who are eager to set themselves up as guides and to collect funds for an imposing establishment.

Literary productions

Sharafuddin left a number of Persian works behind him, in addition to several records (*malfūz*) made of his discourses.

Was there a subtle desire for fame at work here? One has only to examine the genesis of each of his literary productions in order to scotch such an interpretation. His first book is actually a collection of letters written to Qazi Shamsuddin who, on account of his administrative duties, was unable to come for personal guidance. Sharafuddin began to correspond with him. His secretary, Zain Badr Arabi, realized the value of the letters and asked permission to make a collection of them. Sharafuddin continued writing but made sure that he covered all the topics needed for anyone who wished to follow the Sufi path. Thus was produced the collection known as *The hundred letters*.[6] Similarly his other writings originated in others' needs, not his own.

Personal guidance

Three of Sharafuddin's hundred letters—numbers 5, 6 and 7—deal specifically with the topic of guidance, but the whole collection constitutes a manual for guidance. For Sharafuddin, the desire for personalized guidance, over and above what is available for all, is a grace from God. It is a genuine call from God himself. A person cannot decide to travel the Sufi way in a sincere, whole-hearted fashion, unless he or she is called by God, for 'the seed is such that it requires nothing except the divine grace in order to fall into the soil of one's heart' (p. 25).[7] He also speaks of those who 'place their feet on the path of seeking due to the irresistible attraction of the divine favour' (p. 32). Without this inner attraction, no guide can 'make an unruly novice into an earnest seeker' (p. 36).

Granted the presence of such an attraction, a novice, 'after undergoing genuine repentance, should seek a spiritual guide. He should be perfect, well versed in the vicissitudes of the way, and firmly established in his high state. In short, he should be a man who has experienced both the horror of God's majesty and the delight of his beauty' (p. 25).

For the Sufis, the central image of the spiritual life is that of a path or way (*rāh*) leading to God. Playing upon this image, Sharafuddin underscores the need for guidance:

Remember, too, that an ordinary road is infested with thieves and robbers, so that one cannot travel along it without an escort. As for the mystic way, the world, one's ego, devils, men and jinn all infest this way, thus making it impossible to travel along it without an experienced, holy man as one's escort. Remember, further, that there are many slippery places where it is easy to fall. And one can be plagued with misfortune and dangers from behind. Many philosophers and worldly-minded people, as well as others lacking faith, piety or any semblance of morality, have become followers of their own base desires. They have gone without a perfect sheikh or leader who has reached his goal on this way, and have instead trusted in their own intellectual powers. They entered the wilderness where they fell and perished, losing even their faith. (p. 26)

Anyone who enters upon the Sufi way should not be surprised if difficulties occur: quite the contrary!

In the course of his pilgrimage he should expect to be assailed by spiritual crises. Also, various types of mystical experiences might occur: some might be satanic; others might be produced by his own ego; still others could come from the merciful one himself. This is entirely new to the novice and he cannot discern the source of these spiritual experiences. He needs the assistance of one well versed in discerning these various spirits. (p. 27)

As the pilgrim passes through various spiritual stages (*maqām*) he might reach one 'when his soul is stripped bare of its outer garment and a ray of the divine light will illumine it'. At this stage anything is possible—even the power to perform miracles and to achieve such a sense of union with God as to become proud of this fact. Unless he is guided by a sheikh at such a time 'there would be great fear that he might lose his faith and fall into the wilderness of imagining himself as God incarnate or as one identical with God' (p. 27).

Sharafuddin is very much aware of the heady wine of both spiritual bliss and spiritual acclaim. It is not that he refers to them only once or twice and then gives a couple of illustrative anecdotes. Rather, his *Letters* and recorded discourses make it abundantly clear that he had drunk deeply of these twin cups but had not been inebriated by them. This treatment of both topics occurs in many different situations and displays both a surety of touch and an uncompromising attitude towards anything less than God. Having passed through these temptations himself he is able to guide others with a quiet certainty born of personal conviction.

The common period of training for a novice is three years, each devoted to a particular aim: 'One year's service on behalf of other people; one year devoted to God; and another year spent in watching over one's own heart' (p. 29). One feature of this period might well be a forty-day retreat (*chilla*) for, speaking of repentance as 'a radical shift in one's basic nature', Sharafuddin says that 'whoever commands a novice to undergo a forty-day retreat commands it for the sake of this change, in order that his very nature might be transformed' (p. 23). What was merely 'conventional faith' becomes 'real faith'. Letter 96 is devoted to the topic of such a retreat. In it he insists on the need for the 'protection of an experienced spiritual guide'; 'a properly constituted foundation'; 'fidelity to the requisite conditions of sincerity during the retreat itself'; and having a right intention, that is, 'in order that their faith might rest more secure; that they might be enabled therein to discern the various states of their souls; and, finally, in order that they might be able to perform all their actions sincerely for the sake of God Almighty'. Near the tomb of Sharafuddin's guide, Najibuddin, is a very ancient one-room structure which is obviously a prayer-cell. A modern scrawled notice had *chilla-gāh* (that is a place to perform the forty-day retreat, as well as other personal devotions). It seems that Sharafuddin made his retreat there, under the guidance of Najibuddin, and learned from personal experience about the fruits of such a retreat.

A simple question facing the would-be novice was: 'Where will a novice find a sheikh? . . . By what means can he recognize him as being *the* man?' (p. 31). His answer is simple, even simplistic, yet it too is the fruit of personal experience: 'Each one of those who seek God has been allotted all that is necessary for him' (p. 32). God will provide. This is an answer born of faith, not of human reasoning, and there are countless seekers who would endorse it.

While due place is given to guidance by means of personal instructions, much more emphasis is placed on the fruits of an intimate association with one's guide, who is one's *pīr-i suḥbaṭ* (guide by association). This makes sense, for nowadays we are much more aware of the way our basic attitudes were communicated to us. As the adage puts it, 'values are caught, not taught'. This is why openness of heart is so needed and Sharafuddin can write: 'When a righteous novice perceives, in his own heart, the beauty of a sheikh, he becomes enamoured of the beauty of his saintliness, draws peace and contentment from him, and begins his search' (p. 32). We see in this teaching an echo of his relationship with his own guide, Najibuddin. He knew what it was to love his own guide and become completely open to his influence!

While Sharafuddin knows the value of guidance through books and letters when a person is not able to come for face-to-face guidance—as his *Letters* to Qazi Shamsuddin amply illustrate—nevertheless he would not approve of a novice who turned to books as a substitute for a guide when one was available. He has strong words on the topic: 'If a novice wants to learn all about these states from books, he becomes exactly like someone who associates with the dead—and he too becomes dead at heart' (p. 36)! This is because the greatest enemy to be overcome is that of human pride, and humble submission to another is the most effective tool for the task. 'The novice should follow the wishes of the sheikh, not his own! In this respect it has been said: "Discipleship is the abandonment of all one's own desires"' (p. 32).

Sharafuddin has five letters (81–85) devoted explicitly to the struggle with one's carnal or animal soul, also known as the lower soul. It is one's *nafs*, the source of all unruly behaviour, from the grossly inhuman to the most subtle expressions of human pride. Naturally, during the unrelenting struggle against one's unruly soul one needs 'the grace and favour of Almighty God, and the shade of the riches of a compassionate spiritual master' (p. 333). He teaches clearly that temptation 'has to take its origin from a man's inner desire'. It is only when such sinful desires have 'begun to appear that Satan pounces on them, drawing them out into the full light of a person's heart'. Thus 'Satan depends on the reality of the lower soul and the inordinate desire of the servant' (p. 336). This is a very fine distinction for a Muslim spiritual guide of medieval Bihar!

Conclusion

Sharafuddin himself was an inspiration to countless disciples while his words, though primarily devoted to guidance, have also served to communicate both inspiration and encouragement to countless readers down the centuries. The Muslims of Bihar are understandably grateful to God for having sent such an outstanding spiritual guide into their midst.

Notes

[1] The word *dīn* means religion or 'the faith' as in the title 'Defender of the Faith' found on British coins. It, as well as all other words quoted, is in the singular number.

[2] Hughes, T.: *Dictionary of Islam*, p. 285.

[3] The classic work is Macdonald, D.: *Development of Muslim theology, jurisprudence and constitutional theory*, pp. 65–117.

[4] For a detailed exposition see Jackson, Paul: *The way of a Sufi: Sharafuddin Maneri* (Delhi: TAD, 1986).

[5] The word 'Sharafuddin' is actually a title meaning 'The honour of the Faith'. It gradually replaced his given name, Ahmad. By the time he had become a renowned Sufi nobody would have dreamt of addressing him as 'Ahmad'.

[6] *Sharafuddin Maneri: The hundred letters*, trans. Paul Jackson (New York: Paulist Press and London: SPCK, 1980) in the series 'The Classics of Western Spirituality'.

[7] The page numbers refer to the work just quoted.

(vol. 27, no. 2, April 1987)

Spiritual Guidance in Islam: II

John Renard SJ

In an earlier look at the Islamic tradition, Paul Jackson sketched out the development of the theory and practice of spiritual guidance. Against that backdrop he then treated at somewhat greater length the life and works of Sharafuddin Maneri, one of the major figures in the history of South Asian Islamic spirituality.

To provide a slightly different perspective on this vast subject, I propose to give a brief survey of some of the principal kinds of *sources* of the tradition and of prominent *themes* in Islamic spiritual guidance, and then take a closer look at a contemporary of Maneri's from the opposite (western) end of the medieval Islamic world. Ibn 'Abbad of Ronda also lived in the fourteenth century (1330–1390) and wrote important letters of spiritual direction. But unlike Maneri, Ibn 'Abbad was born in Spain and lived most of his life in Morocco, wrote his letters in Arabic rather than in Persian, and belonged to a religious order whose 'charism' contributed towards the development of a kind of 'lay spirituality'.

Sources

Across the length and breadth of Maneri and Ibn 'Abbad's world, Muslim spiritual writers developed the tradition of spiritual guidance through a variety of literary forms. Many variations on the theme occur in such indirect types of spiritual counsel as one finds in the sapiential anecdotes of Persian storytellers and mystical poets, or in occasional exegetical works where a text prompts the interpreter to expound on some technical term of particular significance in Islamic spirituality. It will suit our purpose here to mention only four types of literature: manuals, conversations of the shaykhs, treatises on proper conduct and letters of spiritual direction.

From around the tenth century, compendia or manuals on the major themes and requirements of the Sufi Path (the mystical dimension of Islam, understood in a general way) began to appear. These often lengthy treatises functioned partly as biographical dictionaries, many including explicitly a 'Who's Who Among Sufis' segment, and partly as lexica of the technical terminology and theory requisite for an adequate understanding of the Path. Some also included sections specifically devoted to advising the novice or 'seeker' as to conduct expected of him in relation to the spiritual guide (the shaykh). [1]

A second literary genre developed from collections of discourses and *obiter dicta* of the more famous and revered guides. Such sayings recorded by disciples (a type known as *malfuz*, to which Paul Jackson referred in his discussion of Maneri), had in most instances the added authority of directives or advice from one's own shaykh or a major figure in one's own religious order. In any case, the form intentionally preserved the exemplary reflections of some shaykhs for the emulation of seekers, although the content rarely followed the organizational structure of a formal treatise. [2]

Combining the more direct authority of a particular guide's instructions to a specific group of seekers along with the order of topics found in the treatise or manual form, spiritual writers developed a third genre. Books of *Adab* contain the shaykh's directives on a variety of matters of external behaviour, such as garb, conversation, eating, travelling and companionship. Even though these generally small documents emphasize especially the seeker's outward deportment, they do so in the belief that the outer and the inner condition are inseparable: behaviour both expresses one's attitude and helps to mould and transform one interiorly by subtly modifying one's inner disposition. [3]

Still more direct and more personal, correspondence from a shaykh to a particular seeker constitutes the last important form of spiritual guidance. In their letters the guides address, of course, the more predictable 'generic' issues, such as the use of various traditional methods of prayer, spiritual reading, fasting and pilgrimage. Beyond that, however, this more personal vehicle for guidance affords us a glimpse into numerous individual matters of conscience and religious experience. Topics range from scruples over the acceptance of stipends for instructing children in the faith, to confusion over the absence of sensible consolation while reciting scripture, to the perennial question of how to find a suitable spiritual director.[4]

Themes in Islamic spiritual guidance

Muslim spiritual writers regard the need of a spiritual guide as of paramount importance, analogous to humanity's need of a prophet to reveal God's word. Even Moses had to apprentice to his father-in-law (Shu'ayb, a prophet in Islamic tradition) as preparation for encountering God. The ordinary wayfarer faces far too many perils on the path to hazard the journey alone. On the other hand, one cannot simply designate one's own shaykh; God grants guidance as a gift.

Qualifications of the guide form a second theme. Virtually every document on spiritual guidance mentions these in greater or lesser detail. Najm ad-Din Daya Razi (d. 1256) wrote one of the more extensive treatises on the subject. His *Path of God's bondsmen*, based in part on similar work by earlier writers, lists the following attributes of the authentic guide: servitude to God alone, reception of truth directly from God, privileged access to God's mercy, a heart purified of all non-divine forms of knowledge, rebirth into knowledge of the essence of God's presence. Other attributes that follow are correct belief, intelligence, liberality, courage, chastity, lofty aspiration, compassion, forbearance, forgiveness, sweet temper, selflessness, contentment with one's lot, dignity, tranquillity, steadfastness and a presence worthy of reverence.[5]

Razi's subsequent chapter outlines the third theme, that of the behaviour (*adab*) required of the seeker or novice. In order to fan the spark God 'strikes from flint' within the individual, the seeker must willingly submit to the tutelage of the guide. Razi enumerates twenty essential qualities: repentance, renunciation, abandonment of family ties, proper belief, fear of God, patience, struggle against the lower self (the 'greater struggle' [jihad] as compared to struggle against external foes), courage, readiness to sacrifice, chivalrousness, sincerity, knowledge, active searching, willingness to suffer reproach without giving occasion for it, intelligence, even disposition, submission to the shaykh 'as a corpse in the hands of the corpse washer', and utter abandonment to God. Of course, Razi does not expect such lofty accomplishment of a beginner; only an awareness that the path makes severe demands.[6]

Given a guide and a seeker capable of high aspiration, the relationship of spiritual guidance may advance to the task of assessing the seeker's inner needs and naming God's manner of dealing with this unique individual. One might characterize the essence of the relationship in terms of one overarching concern and four subordinate themes, and still stop just short of unhelpful entanglement in the wonderfully complex and centuries-old unfolding of Islamic spiritual anthropology. Above all the seeker must appreciate humanity's absolute need of God and God's absolute willingness to fill that need by providing all necessities for the journey. However, not all 'provisions' available will prove equally beneficial for a given individual; some the seeker must learn to reject so as to move on.

Within that context, the analysis of the interior life turns upon a discernment of four aspects of the inner 'provisions' that present themselves. The shaykh helps the seeker through a heightened awareness of the immediate source, duration, content and affective tone of the more critical provisions that take the form of 'movements of soul'.

A 'negative psychic force'[7] implanted at creation renders the process exceedingly difficult: the lower self of each person threatens constantly to roil the waters for its own selfish ends and to ensure that it need not stir from its bed of torpor. Though Muslim writers differ as to the precise enumeration of the sources of crucial interior movements, the lower self (nafs) figures prominently in all their analyses. Nafs can generate its own movements. Other immediate sources authors list variously as God, Satan, a good angel, reason, certitude, the spirit, the 'world' and so forth.[8]

Taking note of a given movement's duration allows the guide to specify more minutely the experience's valence. Some types occur only momentarily and in rapid succession. Others perdure and, once fended off if necessary, continue to badger the seeker and cause inner turmoil and anxiety. Still others, of a more welcome sort, remain but make their presence felt very subtly, like an ant crawling across a black stone in the dead of night.

In the case of those movements from God that occur briefly and in succession, authorities on the subject express various opinions as to whether one ought to attend to the first or to the second suggestion, or whether both are of equal cogency since both come ultimately from God. Finally, a movement's duration can serve to indicate its source. For example, divinely given thoughts stay but momentarily so that one must pay keen attention. Satanic whisperings assault, withdraw and renew the attack. Notions originating in the lower self tend to linger, while the lower self rationalizes and procrastinates, until some desire finds satisfaction.

Content varies considerably, of course, among the several types of inner movement. Satanic 'whisperings' generally propose to the lower self some sort of congenial ease or comfort, for the lower self naturally loathes effort (its nemesis is the 'greater struggle'). Immediately from the lower self come desires for a host of physical satisfactions, honour, fame, wealth, revenge and the like. Divine intimations invariably announce themselves as such by their obvious congruence with the revealed Law, and by the recipient's fierce resistance to them. Some types of suggestion can carry a message either laudable or censurable in content. In those cases, one must judge the movement's value by the other criteria.

Some levels of religious experience seem closely related to the individual's effort and striving and appear to perdure, so that one could characterize them as 'plateaux'. Muslim authors have named these 'stations'. Many inner experiences, however, will not yield to purely discursive analysis, nor do they come and go merely because the subject wills it so. Muslim writers' interest in the affective tone of such experiences evolved into detailed inventories of other experiences at once more emotionally charged and fleeting, and appearing to have their origin in God rather than in human effort. These they have called 'states'. They include, for example, experiences of desire, longing, contentment and non-discursive intimate knowledge.

Whereas the 'stations' (*magamat*, pl. of *magam*) typically trace the itinerary of one who labours through the 'purgative' way of *mujahada* (striving), the 'states' (*ahwal*, pl. of *hal*) form a map of the journey through the 'illuminative' way of *mukashafa* (contemplative vision). Ideally, the distinction serves to facilitate analysis; one must not take it too literally as a clear divide between effort and grace.

With some background on the sources and themes central to the Islamic tradition of spiritual guidance as a whole, one might more readily assess the role of one classic practitioner of the art.

Ibn ʿAbbad of Ronda as spiritual guide

Born in the south Iberian hill town of Ronda, about sixty miles from Gibraltar, Ibn ʿAbbad migrated as a boy of seven to Morocco, there to spend his life. The Marinid Dynasty ruled his world, more tentatively perhaps than the average citizen would have liked. Social, economic and political conditions of his day did not fill Ibn ʿAbbad with confidence in the present or hope for the future; but the need for religious reform he regarded as of the highest priority, for upon the renewal of faith all else rested. So long as in a solitary heart a single grain of faith remained, all was not lost.

To the nurturing of that faith in individual persons Ibn ʿAbbad devoted considerable time and effort. His fifty-four extant letters constitute only a portion of his total written work. With some 'commentary' of a slightly more technical nature from his other writings, one can summarize the major concerns of this spiritual guide.

Central issues in the spiritual life

In the individual person, the death of faith goes hand in hand with egocentrism or presumptuousness. On a larger scale, that same pretentiousness results in the fragmentation of society and undermines religious community. As a subtle form of idolatry ('hidden *shirk*', 'setting up a partner with God') egocentricity takes countless forms: false humility, fear of death, acts of piety for the sake of display and a thousand other ways of clinging to one's own deeds as a source of ultimate security. The seeker must strive to counteract the tendency to egocentricity through the attitudes of 'servant-hood' or 'worshipfulness', and gratitude, which in turn arise from an awareness of one's radical insufficiency and neediness.

Authentic self-knowledge alone can keep the seeker free from the anguish of scruples and the delusion of false asceticism. Excessive austerity or undue grief over one's failures merely masks otherwise naked egocentricity. Genuine asceticism poses the never-ending challenge of discerning how God reveals himself to the seeker at this very moment, regardless of how strongly the seeker feels he 'ought' to break out and move to some other spiritual state. God works here and now, and attentiveness to that presence requires a lifetime of discipline.

Ibn 'Abbad counsels his directees to regard the 'greater struggle' of the purgative way as the other side of the coin from the 'contemplative vision' of the illuminative way. Between masochism and hedonism the path winds. Debilitating anxiety, self-doubt, ennui, fear of abandonment and the like signal the victory of egocentrism as surely as does the un-bridled search for pleasure. The greater struggle means never surrendering oneself to either stasis, while contemplative vision allows the individual to perceive God's utter transcendence and incomparable majesty in the very midst of personal and cosmic poverty and neediness. Contemplative vision both presupposes and reinforces the greater struggle's challenge to the aspirant to become a 'child of this moment'.

The role of the spiritual guide

Ibn 'Abbad expresses considerable concern over how the seeker can find guidance for the journey. During his time the emphasis in the study of religious law seems to have shifted from personal contact with an acknowledged authority to the study of secondary works. Apparently under the influence of that trend, the use of classic writings in Sufism seems similarly to have taken precedence over individual guidance. One could claim as spiritual master (or as licence-granting authority in religious law) any author whose works he had read. Ibn 'Abbad himself considers as his 'masters of initiation' in the Sufi Path the authors of the classic works through which he first became acquainted with the Path. Even when he was a disciple of the stern master Ibn 'Ashir, he maintained his independence.

On the whole, Ibn 'Abbad's approach to the role of the spiritual guide strikes one as quite balanced. He examines thoroughly in one of his Letters (Letter XVI in *Letters on the Sufi Path*) the question of whether a seeker absolutely needs a living guide. He concludes that one does not simply attach oneself to the right shaykh. God alone can provide the gift of a truly sagacious director. God decides whether and when the seeker will find personal guidance. One ought therefore neither expend too much effort searching, nor simply despair of ever finding a guide, but merely be prepared for the gift should it be granted.

God ultimately guides the heart with his light. In other words, direction occurs from within the individual seeker. Ibn 'Abbad acknowledges the already ancient tradition that God guides individuals generally in either of two ways. Some God leads along a predominantly active, purgative way. Through long periods of discipline and discursive meditation, God leads the 'wayfarer' (*salik*) upward, from the effects of the divine action in the world, to an awareness of God's names, to the contemplation of the divine attributes and finally to the divine essence. Others God guides along a predominantly passive or illuminative path. The 'attracted' or 'drawn' seeker (*majdhub*) advances as though whisked along from an experience of God's essence to an awareness of all creatures as existing 'in God'. In other words, the first type sees God in creation; the second, creation in God.

From the psychological point of view, guidance involves helping a seeker to discern the variety of guises under which the lower self, the 'world' and the Devil present themselves. A healthy individual knows the arduousness of self-mastery. Theologically speaking, guidance aims at gratitude to God and acknowledgement of one's poverty. Through gratitude of the heart, one acknowledges God as source of all goods. Through gratitude of the tongue, one sings God's praises. Through gratitude of all the senses, one engages in good works and thus brings a communitarian dimension to one's spiritual life.

Ibn ʿAbbad inherited a highly sophisticated spiritual anthropology, including an ample lexicon of finely nuanced concepts keyed to the subtleties of personal religious experience. In addition to the range of 'stations' and 'states' mentioned earlier, Ibn ʿAbbad pays special attention to the experiences of 'contraction' and 'expansion' (*gabd* and *bast*), terms that one could also translate loosely as 'desolation' and 'consolation'. Following the lead of his spiritual ancestor Ibn ʿAta Allah, Ibn ʿAbbad believes that expansion can be more dangerous than contraction, for the former might encourage the novice to think he has brought this pleasant state upon himself. A seeker could forget that God effects all such conditions.

Contraction and expansion appear rather as qualities that broadly characterize a variety of experiences than as experiences in themselves, although one could conceivably be aware of contraction or expansion without further qualification. Hope and expansion, fear and contraction often occur as pairs. In any case, the spiritual guide strives to teach the seeker, first, awareness of the inner succession of stations and states, and second, how to interpret them as indicators of how God has chosen to work in the seeker at a given moment.

About the nature of the relationship between shaykh and aspirant, Ibn ʿAbbad has several important things to say. The shaykh must treat the seeker like a son; the seeker, in turn, must practise docility, concealing nothing. Avoiding authoritarianism at all cost, the guide works to understand what the disciple has said before rendering an opinion. Ibn ʿAbbad knew of two types of shaykh. Seekers who needed basic character formation and schooling in the requirements of the revealed Law and the Sufi Path would do better with an 'instructing' shaykh. One could even enlist the services of several such guides simultaneously.

An 'educating' shaykh, on the other hand, taught by example and personal association rather than by more conventional pedagogical methods. This latter type of guide would teach a seeker already thus tutored in the basics of the tradition his personal and private invocation (*dhikr*, a mantra-like word or phrase intended to address a particular disciple's unique needs), lead him through the retreat of forty days (*chilla*), regulate his daily order (sleeping, eating, times of silence and so forth), and prescribe specific disciplinary activities. A seeker could associate with only one educating shaykh at a time. In Ibn 'Abbad's estimation, a seeker could make more rapid progress under a shaykh whom God has 'drawn' than under a 'wayfarer'.

Ibn 'Abbad's letters indicate that subject matter for spiritual direction could include virtually anything in the seeker's experience that he perceived as relating in any way with his relationship with God. Significant material thus encompassed experiences of success or failure, clarity or bewilderment, grief or elation, hope or fear, love or hate. If a correspondent expressed a powerful desire to move out of his present state, Ibn 'Abbad encouraged him to stay with it until he appreciated how that state, however distasteful, could speak a word from the Lord. The seeker needs, in short, to learn to trust his experience, and fend off the temptation to worry that he 'should' be experiencing something else.

Personal growth is perhaps the most important criterion for judging the success of the relationship of director to directee. Among the various touchstones Ibn 'Abbad used to assess growth, he regarded the broad categories of 'proper demeanour' (*husn al-adab*) and 'thinking well' of God (*husn az-zann*) as the crucial indices. Here one inevitably manifested the fruits or lack of the fundamental value of gratitude (which functioned for Ibn 'Abbad much the way love does in Christian thought), and the total approach to life that he calls 'contemplative vision'. The clearer that vision, the greater the gratitude and the smaller the danger of egocentricity. Ultimately, spiritual maturity appears in the ability to 'think well of God', that is, always allowing the Creator the benefit of the doubt and refusing to wallow in the conviction that one has God down to a predictable pattern.

Finally, Ibn 'Abbad exhibited pre-eminently the spiritual guide's virtue *sine qua non*: reticence about his qualifications as a spiritual guide. He did not consider himself an authority on matters spiritual or relating to religious law. Neither did he protest too much; only enough to leave the modern reader convinced that Ibn 'Abbad must have been an excellent spiritual guide.

Notes

[1] Good translations of this type are: Razi, Najm ad-Din Daya: *The path of God's bondsmen*, trans. Hamid Algar (New York: Caravan, 1982); Hujwiri: *The Kashf al-Mahjub*, trans. R. A. Nicholson (London: Luzac, 1976).

[2] See for example, A. J. Arberry's translation of *Discourses of Rumi* (New York: Samuel Weiser, 1972), and Paul Jackson's translation of Maneri's discourses, *Khwan-i Pur Ni'mat: a table laden with good things* (Delhi: Idarah-i Adabiyat-i Delli, 1986).

[3] See for example Ibn al-'Arabi's 'Instructions to a postulant', trans. A. Jeffrey in his edition of primary source translations, *A reader on Islam* (The Hague: Mouton, 1962); M. Milson's translation of Abu Najib Suhrawardi's *Kitab Adab al-Muridin*, entitled in English *A Sufi rule for novices* (Cambridge, MA: Harvard, 1975); and G. Boewering's translation of Ansari's short treatise, along with a brief survey of the genre, in 'The *Adab* literature of classical Sufism: Ansari's code of conduct', in Metcalf, Barbara (ed.): *Moral conduct and authority: the place of Adab in South Asian Islam* (Berkeley: University of California Press, 1984), pp. 62–87.

[4] See Paul Jackson's translation of Maneri's *The hundred letters* (New York: Paulist Press, 1980); A. H. Abdel Kader (trans.), *The life, personality and writings of al-Junayd* (London: Luzac, 1976); Shaykh al-'Arabi Darqawi, *Letters of a Sufi master*, trans. Titus Burckhardt (London: Perennial Books, 1969); and Ibn 'Abbad of Ronda's *Letters on the Sufi Path*, a translation of sixteen letters, with an extensive introduction on themes and setting of Ibn 'Abbad's spirituality, by John Renard (Mahwah, NJ: Paulist Press, 1986).

[5] Razi, *op. cit.*, pp. 243–254.

[6] *Ibid.*, pp. 255–267.

[7] Boewering, G.: *The mystical vision of existence in classical Islam* (Berlin: deGruyter, 1980), p. 253.

[8] For excellent analysis of these and related issues see Awn, Peter: *Satan's tragedy and redemption: Iblis in Sufi psychology* (Leiden: Brill, 1983), esp. pp. 64 ff.

(vol. 28, no. 1, January 1988)

Biographical Notes

LAVINIA BYRNE IBVM works at the Institute of Spirituality, Heythrop College, London, where she co-edits *The Way* and has experience in training spiritual directors. She has written *Women before God* (SPCK/Twenty-Third Publications, 1988), and *Sharing the Vision* (SPCK/Cowley Press, 1989).

BENEDICTA WARD SLG is a member of the Anglican contemplative community of the Sisters of the Love of God. She holds a doctorate from the University of Oxford, and is an historian. Her publications include *Prayers and meditations of St Anselm, Sayings of the Desert Fathers, Wisdom of the Desert Fathers,* and an introduction to *Lives of the Desert Fathers.* Her latest books are *Miracles and the medieval mind* and *The Venerable Bede.*

JEAN LECLERCQ OSB is a monk of the Abbey of Clervaux in Luxembourg. He studied theology and history in Rome and Paris and also holds honorary doctorates from Milan, Louvain and Western Michigan universities. He was until recently a professor at the Gregorian University, Rome. A leading expert on St Bernard and on Western monastic history and spirituality, his publications include *The love of learning and the desire for God* as well as contributions to collections of studies and many scholarly articles.

DIARMUID O'LAOGHAIRE SJ lectures in the Milltown Institute of Philosophy and Theology in Dublin, and elsewhere, and writes in English and Irish on the Irish spiritual tradition. He has published a collection of traditional Irish prayers.

GORDON MURSELL is an Anglican priest. He is chaplain and tutor in spirituality at Salisbury and Wells Theological College, England. His thesis on monastic spirituality was published as *The theology of the Carthusian life* at Salzburg University in 1988. His latest book, on prayer as protest, is entitled *Out of the deep* (Darton, Longman & Todd, 1989).

DAVID LONSDALE SJ is a lecturer and tutor in spirituality at Heythrop College, London University. He was co-editor, with Jill

Robson, of *Can spirituality be taught?* (British Council of Churches, 1987) and author of *Eyes to see, ears to hear: an introduction to Ignatian spirituality* (Darton, Longman & Todd, 1990).

MICHAEL BRUNDELL OCARM is a member of the Australian Province of the Carmelites, and is a graduate of Monash University, the Melbourne College of Divinity and the Gregorian University in Rome. He is based in Melbourne, where he lectures in systematic theology at the Yarra Theological Union and is director of the Carmelite Institute of Spirituality.

JOSEPH CHALMERS OCARM has a licentiate in spirituality from the Gregorian University and specializes in Carmelite spirituality. He is vocations co-ordinator for the Carmelites in the UK.

JANE TILLIER is an ordinand of the Church of England and is studying theology at Ripon College, Cuddesdon. She has a PhD in Spanish from the University of Cambridge and worked as pastoral assistant to the dean at Jesus College, Cambridge for four years.

PHILIP SHELDRAKE SJ teaches spirituality at Heythrop College, University of London, and is co-editor of *The Way*. He also conducts retreats and workshops and is the author of *Images of holiness* (Darton, Longman & Todd, 1987).

ANNE M. MINTON holds a PhD in intellectual history from New York University with a specialization in the religious thought of France and England in the seventeenth century. She has been a faculty member and administrator in schools of theology for nine years and is presently an academic administrator at Bunker Hill Community in Boston. She is an Episcopal lay woman active in parish and diocesan education programmes.

JOY M. MILOS CSJ teaches Christian spirituality at Gonzaga University, in Spokane, Washington. In addition she is the director of the CREDO Program there, a sabbatical year for people in ministry. She received her doctorate in spirituality from the Catholic University of America.

EDWARD SELLNER is associate professor of Pastoral Theology and Spirituality at the College of St Catherine, St Paul, Minnesota. He received his PhD from the University of Notre Dame in 1981. 1986–88 Chairperson of the National Association for Lay Ministry (NALM), he has contributed numerous articles on spirituality and lay ministry to journals in the United States, Ireland, England and

Germany, and is the author of *Mentoring: the ministry of spiritual kinship* (Ave Maria Press, 1990).

MICHAEL BARNES SJ studied theology at Heythrop College, London, and oriental languages and religion at Oxford. Ordained in 1976, he now teaches religious studies at Heythrop College and is the author of *Religions in conversation: Christian identity and religious pluralism* (SPCK, 1989).

PAUL JACKSON SJ was born in Brisbane, Australia, in 1937. He entered the Society of Jesus and went to Hazaribagh, India. He began special studies in 1972 in Delhi (MA in history and Diploma in Urdu); Shiraz (Persian) and Patna (doctorate on Sharafuddin Maneri). He continues his research in Patna.

JOHN RENARD SJ received his doctorate in Islamic Studies from Harvard University in 1978. Since then he has taught at St Louis University. He recently published a book on Islamic spiritual direction: *Letters on the Sufi Path* by Ibn ʿAbbad of Ronda (Paulist Press, 1986). He contributed articles on Islamic prayer in the January and April 1980 issues of *The Way*.